IMAGES
of America

TOTTENVILLE

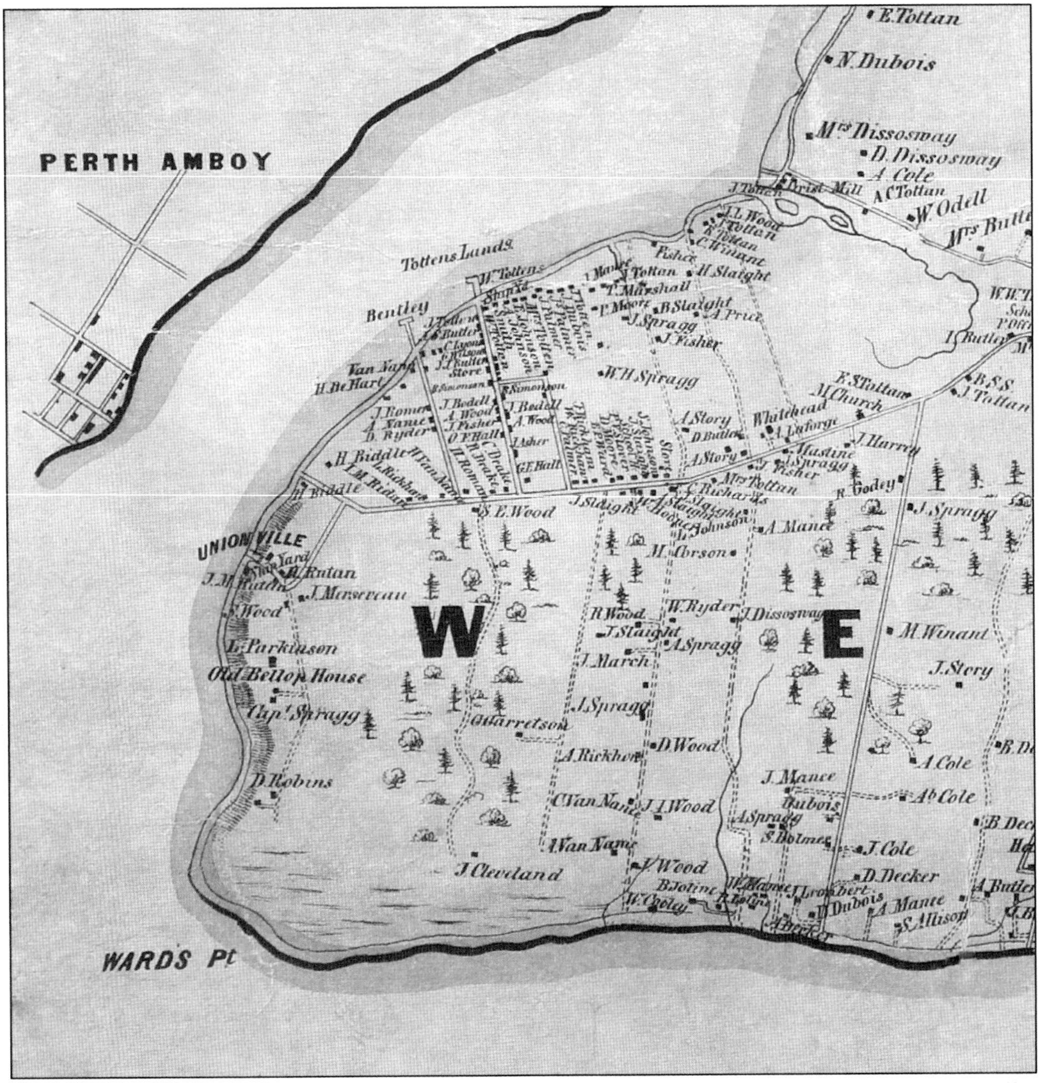

This 1850 Dripps Map detail shows the southernmost area of Staten Island, known as Tottenville. It tells the story of Tottenville during its earliest peak development period. Amboy Road, running east to west, is the major roadway in and out of Tottenville and is fairly well developed with houses and a place of worship. The most built up thoroughfare is Main Street, which ends at Tottens Landing on the map. The railroad had not yet come to Tottenville. (Courtesy of the Tottenville Historical Society.)

ON THE COVER: Since the 19th century, Tottenville's waterfront has been the community's most important asset for both business and pleasure. In this 1955 photograph, a potato sack race for children of all ages is enjoyed by members of the Tottenville Yacht Club. (Courtesy of the Leyes family; photograph by Donald Leyes.)

IMAGES
of America

TOTTENVILLE

Tottenville Historical Society

ARCADIA
PUBLISHING

ISBN 978-0-7385-7406-6

Published by Arcadia Publishing
Charleston, South Carolina

Printed in the United States of America

Library of Congress Control Number: 2010932479

For all general information, please contact Arcadia Publishing:
Telephone 843-853-2070
Fax 843-853-0044
E-mail sales@arcadiapublishing.com
For customer service and orders:
Toll-Free 1-888-313-2665

Visit us on the Internet at www.arcadiapublishing.com

Dedicated to Tottenville's new residents so they may appreciate our past, to the current residents who continue to honor and preserve our history, and to those former residents who never really left.

Contents

ACKNOWLEDGMENTS

Since the Tottenville Historical Society was founded in 2003, it has received an abundance of support from many organizations and individuals who have helped the society to flourish in many ways. We are especially grateful to those individuals who have contributed photographs, documents, and artifacts to the permanent collection of the society. Many images from their donated collections appear throughout this book and are identified accordingly. In addition, we wish to thank our members and friends who have submitted reminiscences and folk histories that are so important in writing the history of our community.

We also thank everyone who generously offered an entire family collection for us to review, especially Ted Wallen for access to photographs from the John Bieser Estate, one of the largest and earliest collections we have seen. Special thanks, too, to Beauvais-Hudson Post No. 126, American Legion, and the Wilkie-Farina family for the opportunity to view their vast collections. These privately owned images, along with the society's collections, afforded a very personal pictorial overview of the history of the community.

Special thanks to Linda Cutler Hauck, Tina Kaasmann-Dunn, and Diane Schaming, trustees of the society, who spent many hours over several months gathering and organizing photographs and information and researching, writing, and reviewing captions. Also, thanks to the Hungarian Reformed Church of Charleston for providing ample work space during the entire writing process.

Dennis Sheheen of High Rock Graphics scanned more than 200 photographs, and Merlino's Photo Studio developed many rare and fragile negatives; both were accomplished with great care, and we thank them for their professionalism and consideration.

Unless otherwise noted, images are from the permanent collection of the Tottenville Historical Society.

INTRODUCTION

Tottenville, Staten Island, New York, is the last community in southern New York before crossing the Arthur Kill waterway to New Jersey. It is the final stop on the Staten Island Railroad and one of the last areas of Staten Island to be developed after the opening of the Verrazano-Narrows Bridge in 1964. The history of Tottenville dates back well before the 1600s, when the Dutch and other Europeans arrived on Staten Island, and for centuries that history has been tied to the area's waterfront.

Attracted by an abundance of fish and oysters in the bay, the Lenape, or Lenni Lenape, also known as the Delaware Indians, settled in a string of communities along the western shores of Staten Island, including the elevated shoreline of Tottenville. The waterways were also used for transportation.

In the 17th century, Christopher Billopp, the first European to settle in Tottenville, built a stone house overlooking Raritan Bay and later (around 1709) a ferry dock at the end of Amboy Road. Formerly called King's Highway, Amboy Road is one of the oldest chartered roads on Staten Island. By the mid-1700s, the Amboy Road ferry had become an important link for travelers between New York and Philadelphia.

By the mid-19th century, Tottenville was a bustling community. Although agriculture had been the main sector of the economy, the planting and harvesting of oysters in the surrounding waters created a new industry that sparked the greatest period of commercial and residential development. Oystermen and those involved in maritime trade, shipbuilding, and ship repair established themselves in Tottenville and became wealthy. The oyster industry continued to flourish until the early 20th century. Eventually, overharvesting, disease, and pollution had a profound effect on the oyster beds, and by 1916, they were closed.

Around 1900, new industries for business and pleasure had emerged along the waterfront. The Atlantic Terra Cotta Works, established in 1897 on a large parcel of land on Ellis Street, would become one of the world's largest manufacturers of architectural terra-cotta. Its proximity to the Arthur Kill waterway was crucial for receiving and shipping materials and products. The Woolworth Building in Manhattan is entirely clad with terra-cotta from Atlantic.

With the extension of the Staten Island Railroad to Tottenville and connecting ferry service to Perth Amboy, New Jersey, for pedestrians and vehicles, the area quickly became a transportation hub. Several hotels at the foot of Main Street catered to transient travelers and bicyclists. Tottenville had also become a tourist destination for day visitors and summer vacationers from the city (Manhattan) and New Jersey. Bay Cliff Park at the foot of Amboy Road had a hotel and lake and could be reached by public transportation or boat. It offered picnic grounds, an amusement area, bathing, and a large platform for dancing. In 1902, Sea Breeze Amusement Park, which occupied the site known as Ward's Point, was developed by the Middlesex and Somerset Traction Company, bringing visitors by steamboat from South Amboy and New Brunswick, New Jersey. An early map reveals the existence of a hotel, dancing pavilion, merry-go-round, and bathhouses.

Raritan Bay Park, along the Raritan Bay waterfront, began as a summer tent colony in the early 1900s and grew to become a resort area with summer cottages, a hotel, and a long pier for fishing along with boating and swimming. By 1911, these summer residents, mostly from Manhattan and New Jersey, had organized a season-ending carnival parade and gala. The event expanded in later years to become a three-day celebration that included swimming and boating competitions and prizes for best decorated cottages, parade vehicles, and floats. This summer resort was greatly affected by World War I, and, following the war, many cottages were converted to year-round residences and sold.

Local residents today still reminisce about the good times along the waterfront. Family picnics and parties on the beach, skimming stones, jumping over waves, collecting shells, dances at the pavilion, boating, fishing, crabbing, and even teasing horseshoe crabs are memories that we will cherish forever. Tottenville has seen many changes, but its waterfront has been a consistent source of enjoyment for more than 100 years.

We hope this book will give the reader a sense of life in Tottenville in the past, and we close with words written by Dr. Mary E. Meade, first principal of the newly constructed Tottenville High School, to the graduating class of 1938: "You have lived in a school and community that believes in tradition. When you meet the great outside world you will encounter many who look down on things of the past and consider only the present, for this conflict between tradition and transition is engaging the world today. The experience of the ages shows that some of our present day arguments were settled hundreds of years ago. We should . . . hold fast to what is valuable in the past and use it to help solve your everyday problems."

One

Along the Waterfront

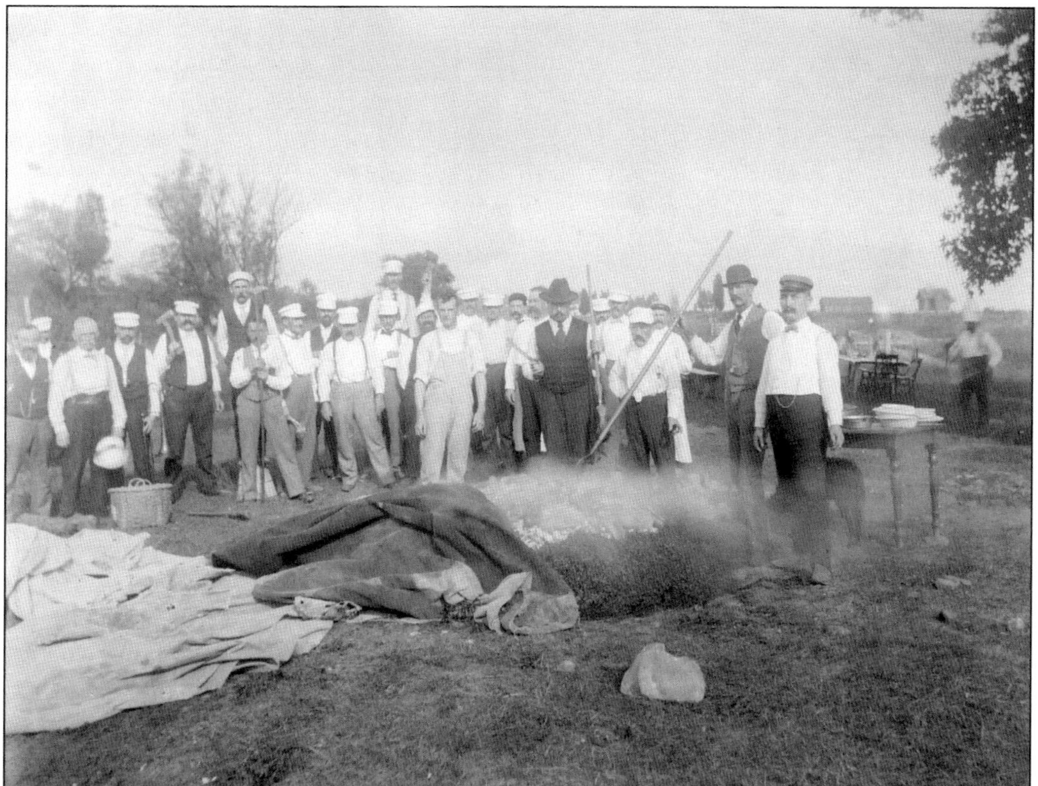

This rare 1915 photograph shows a seafood feast being prepared near the shore. Clams from Raritan Bay are cooking on the ground with a covering of seaweed to steam them. Dr. Alexander Kopetchny, a summer resident of Page Avenue, is one of the men in the group. Raritan Bay was known for abundant, high-quality shellfish, and the harvesting of clams and oysters became a lucrative industry that made the fortunes of many Tottenville families.

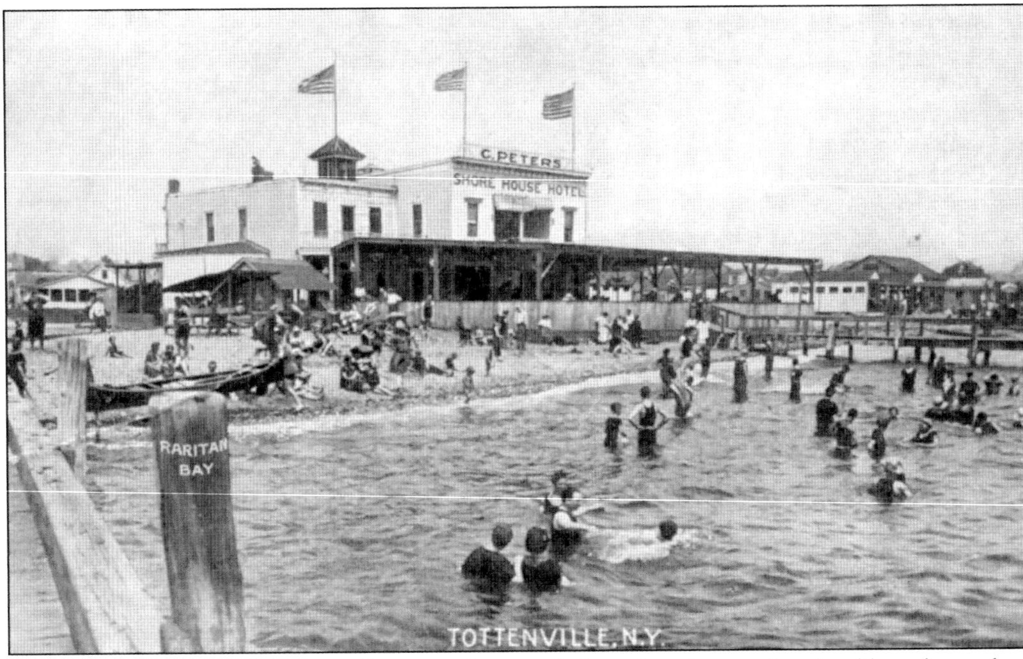

The waters surrounding Tottenville not only provided an abundance of seafood but also a place to have great summer fun. The Shore House Hotel, seen in this 1910 postcard, was one of many establishments that were located on the waterfront. The hotel offered boating, bathing, and fishing, and of course seafood dinners were a specialty.

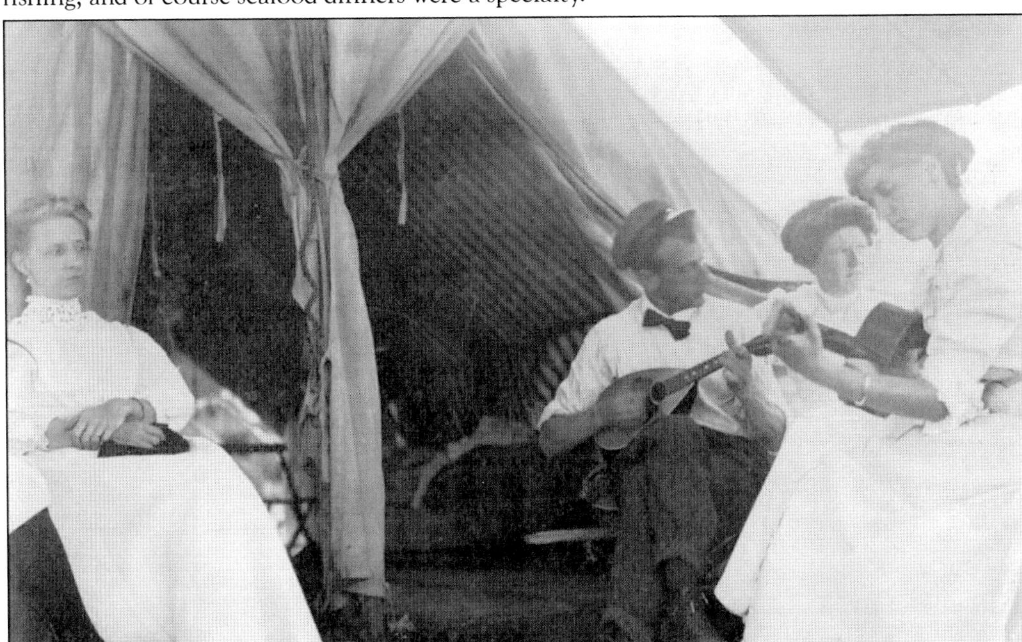

Raritan Bay Park was a summer colony along the waterfront near the foot of Yetman Avenue. The earliest seasonal residences were simple tent structures with a wooden platform floor. Later more substantial cottage homes were built. The musical Siebert family from Manhattan is pictured here in 1909 in their tent home on Rockaway Street. (Courtesy of the Audrey Snyder Collection.)

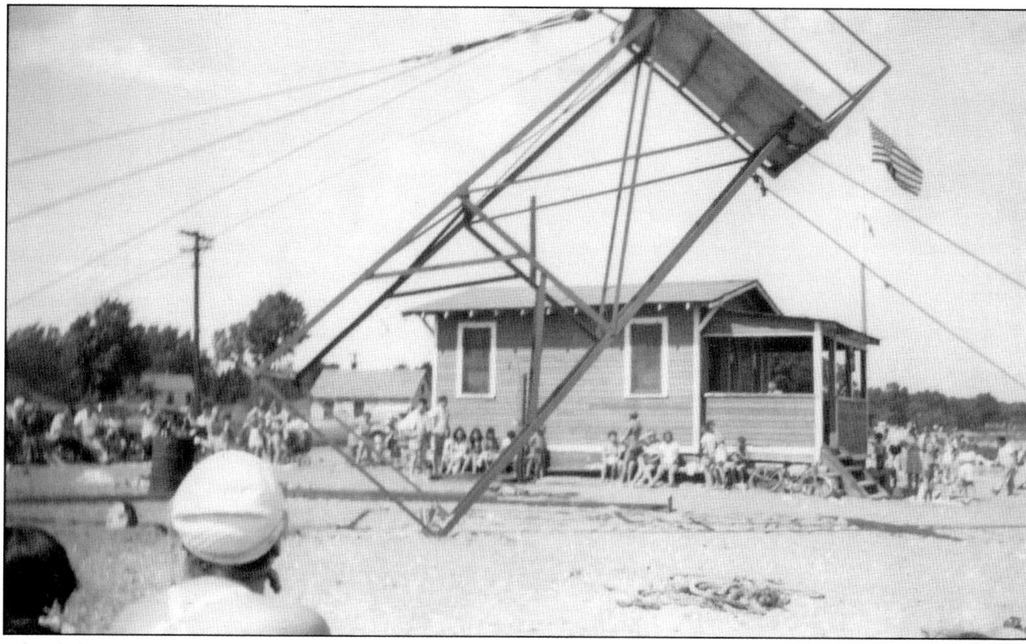

The lifeguard tower is hoisted into the water, heralding the start of the 1941 summer season at Tottenville Beach, located at the foot of Yetman Avenue. (Courtesy of the Margaret Wilson Collection.)

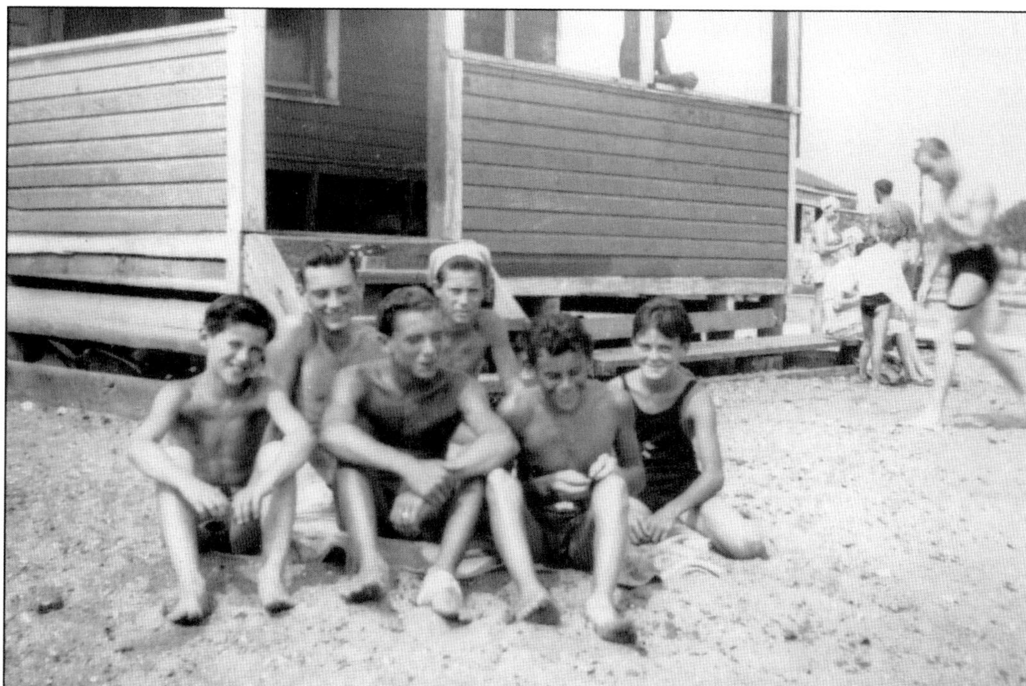

A group of junior lifeguards smiles for the camera in front of the U.S. Volunteer Life Saving Corps lifeguard shack at Tottenville Beach in 1941. Included this photograph are, from left to right, (first row) ? Buchanan, Jackie Schaaff, Donny Gough, and Walter Schaaff; (second row) Dick Schermerhorn and ? Buchanan. (Courtesy of Jane Schaaff Cole Collection.)

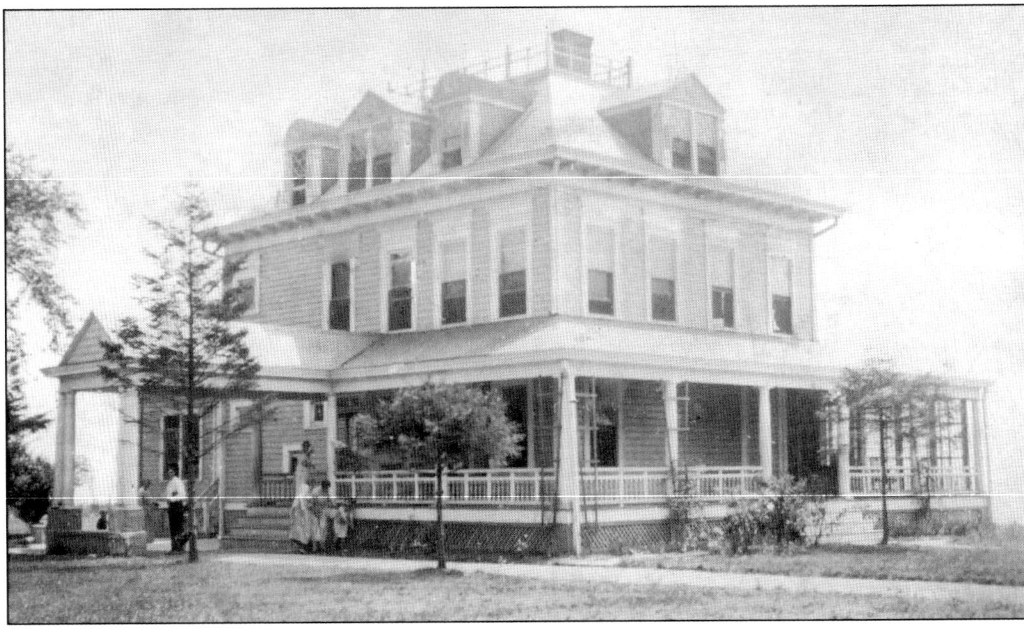

At the beginning of the 20th century, several large summer residences were built on Raritan Bay by wealthy Manhattanites. Here they could find relief from the hot city, and their families could enjoy all the benefits of waterfront property. This structure, located on Joline Avenue, was the residence of Henry Hachemeister, a former New York State assemblyman. By 1910, the house had been sold to the Volunteers of America, a national charitable organization. (Courtesy of Donna Albert.)

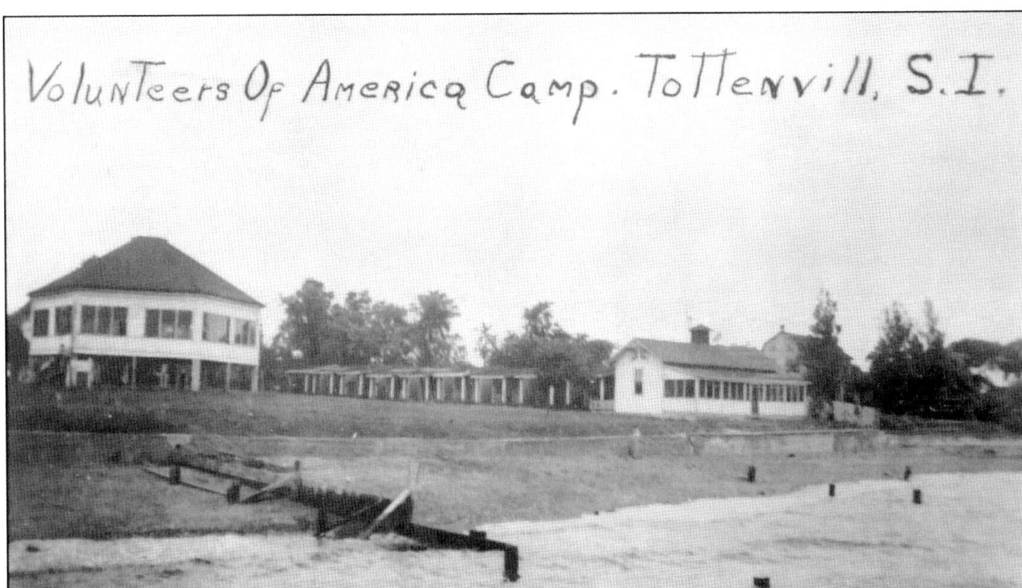

Pictured in this 1944 postcard is the Volunteers of America camp. The multisided building on the left was used both outdoors as a bandstand and indoors as a roller-skating rink.

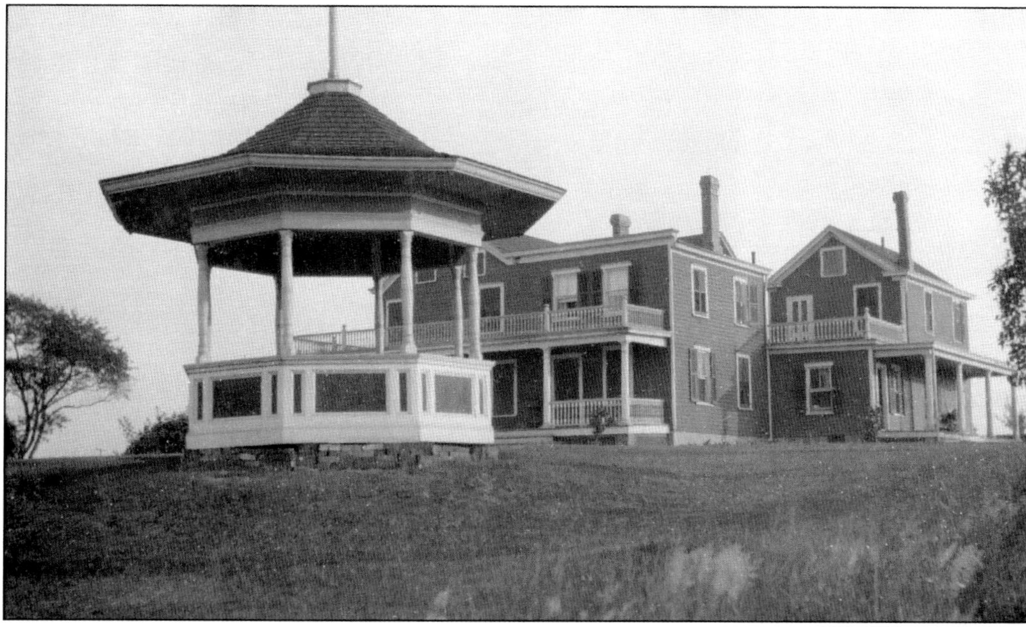

Another large estate at the foot of Loretto Street was owned by the Bishop family, as seen in this *c.* 1920 image. The property boasted not just one but two impressive matching gazebos facing the water. (Courtesy of the John Bieser Estate.)

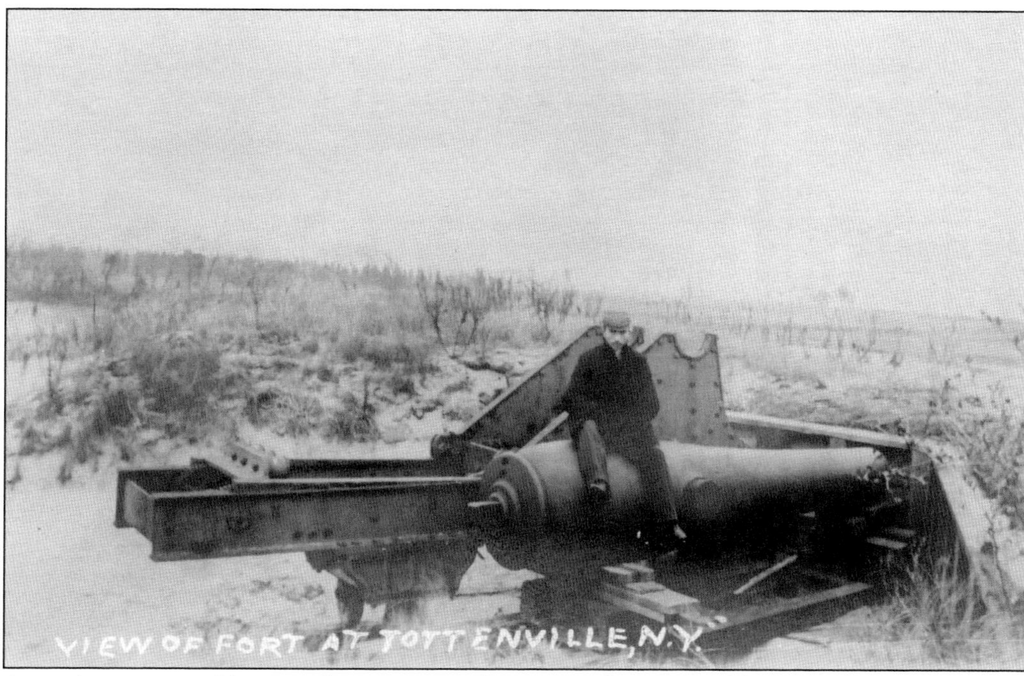

According to an oral history, the cannon in this postcard was one of three mounted guns located at Ward's Point on Raritan Bay. The guns were part of Fort Lucas, and it has been stated that some remains of the artillery could still be seen in the 1940s.

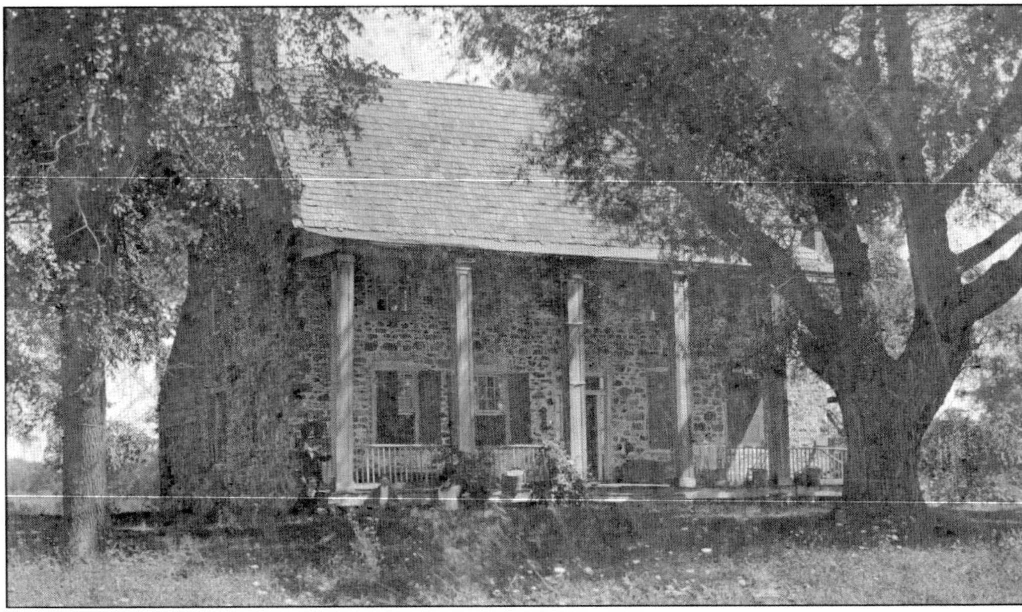

By 1920, the Billopp House, built around 1680 by Christopher Billopp, a British naval officer, had fallen into great disrepair. In 1926, a group of historians, educators, politicians, and local groups and individuals worked together to preserve and restore the home. In recognition of the historic peace conference that took place there in 1776, the name was changed to the Conference House. The two-story portico seen in this *c.* 1900 photograph was not original to the house and was removed prior to restoration. The restored house was opened to the public in 1937. (Courtesy of the Linda Cevasco Collection.)

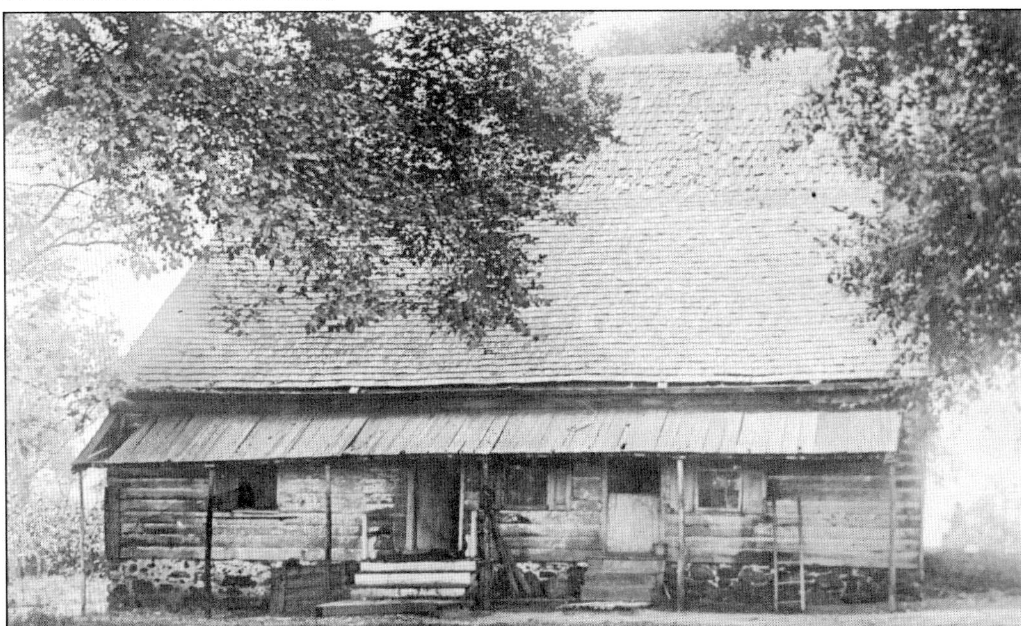

A rear view of the house shows two entrances to the caretaker's quarters in this 1900 photograph; the residence is on the left and the kitchen is on the right. It is believed this two-story addition was built in the 18th century. (Courtesy of the Linda Cevasco Collection.)

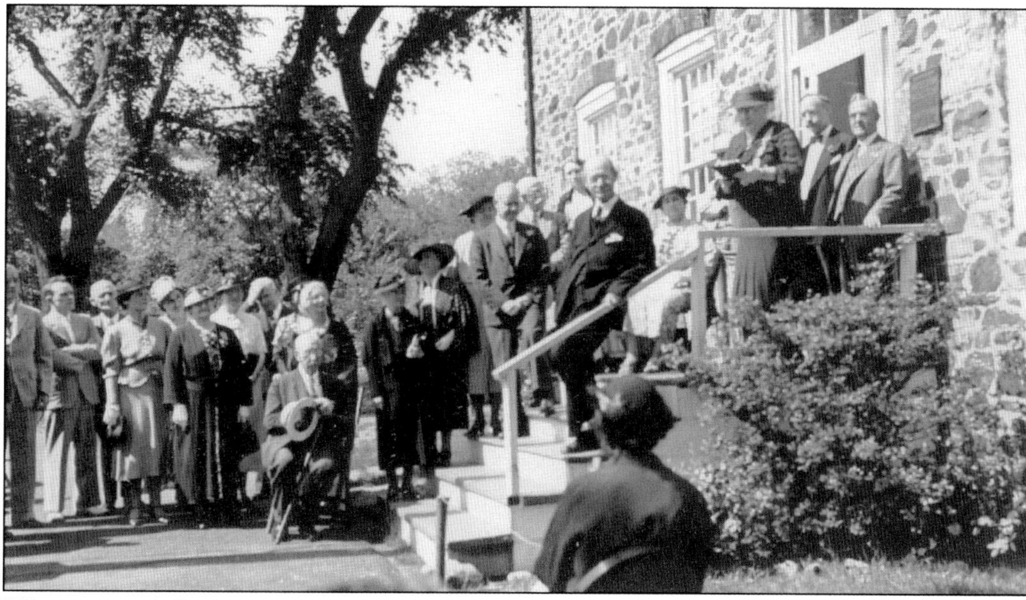

What a grand day it was on May 22, 1937. The 12-year process of restoring the Conference House "as funds became available" was completed. The day was cause for celebration, and one of the project's biggest supporters, William T. Davis, is seen descending the steps in this vintage photograph. Davis, a well-known and loved Staten Island historian, had written a book on the history of the house and was involved in its resurgence from day one. Many island dignitaries attended the opening, including Loring McMillen (second from left), who would soon burst upon the scene as one of the saviors of another island landmark, Historic Richmond Town. Two of the island's most influential and important preservationists are together in this historic picture. (Courtesy of Tina Kaasmann-Dunn.)

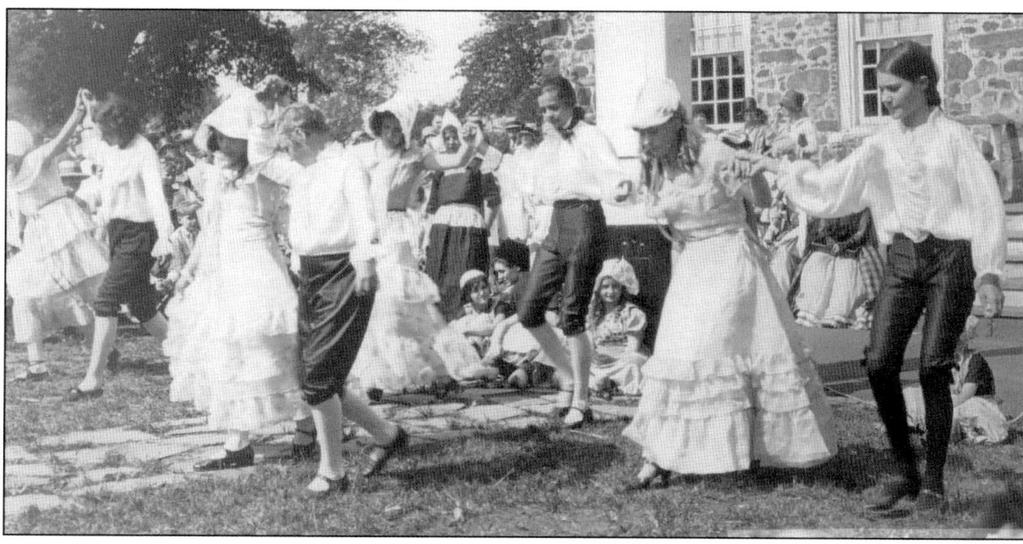

Percy Sperr, a noted Staten Island photographer, took this charming photograph during a pageant held at the Conference House in 1930. Although the structure was not yet fully restored, events were held on its lawn to show that progress was being made and to generate much-needed funds. The young people shown here are participating in colonial dancing complete with period costumes. (Courtesy of Tina Kaasmann-Dunn.)

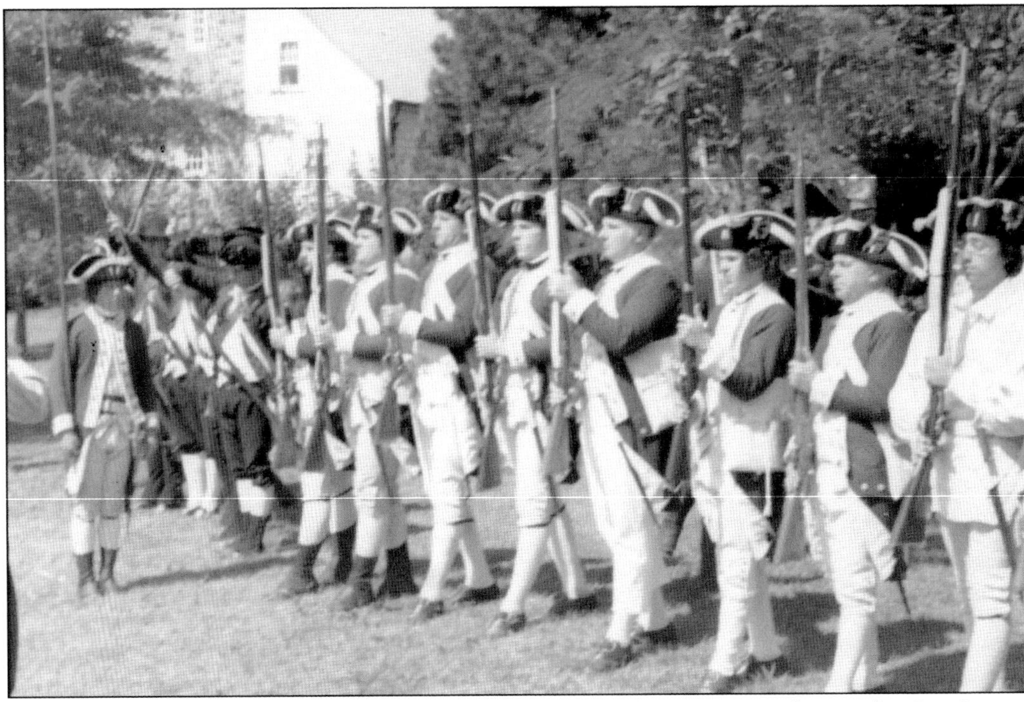

In this 1974 photograph, British troops stand at attention for inspection during the Conference House annual reenactment of the 1776 Peace Conference. (Courtesy of the Goonan family.)

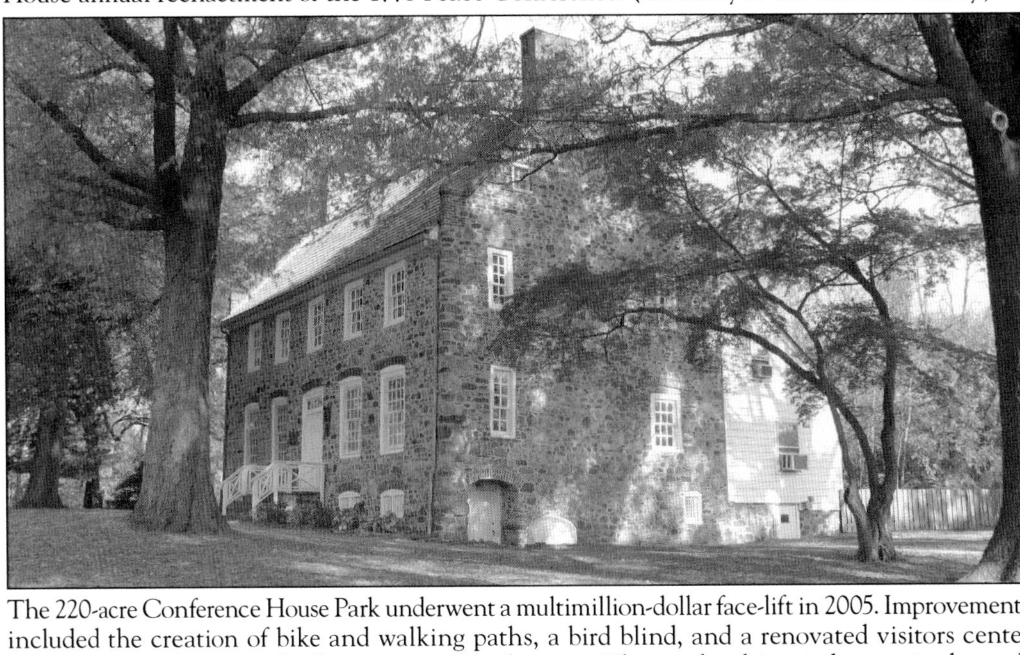

The 220-acre Conference House Park underwent a multimillion-dollar face-lift in 2005. Improvements included the creation of bike and walking paths, a bird blind, and a renovated visitors center complete with display and office space and bathrooms. Three other historic houses in the park are slowly being restored and will be open for tourists at a future date. The Conference House itself, shown in this recent photograph, remains in near-pristine condition due in large part to the commendable stewardship of the Conference House Association, which has maintained and cared for it since 1926. (Courtesy of Dennis Sheheen.)

A 400-pound iron Revolutionary War cannon, a gift from the Cutting family of Rossville to the Conference House Association in 1933, mysteriously disappeared from its stone pedestal in 1972. Staten Island was under British rule during the American Revolution. This historic cannon had been used to repel an attack by the American general John Sullivan from Carteret, New Jersey, in 1777. The cannon's whereabouts remain unknown today.

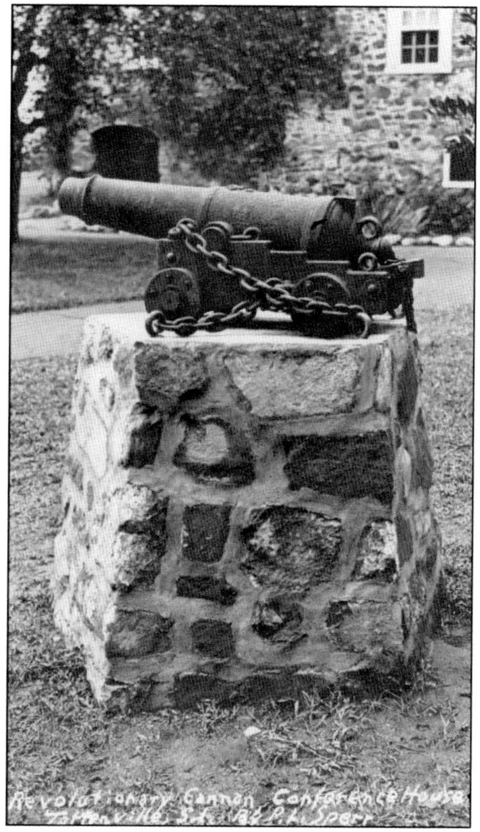

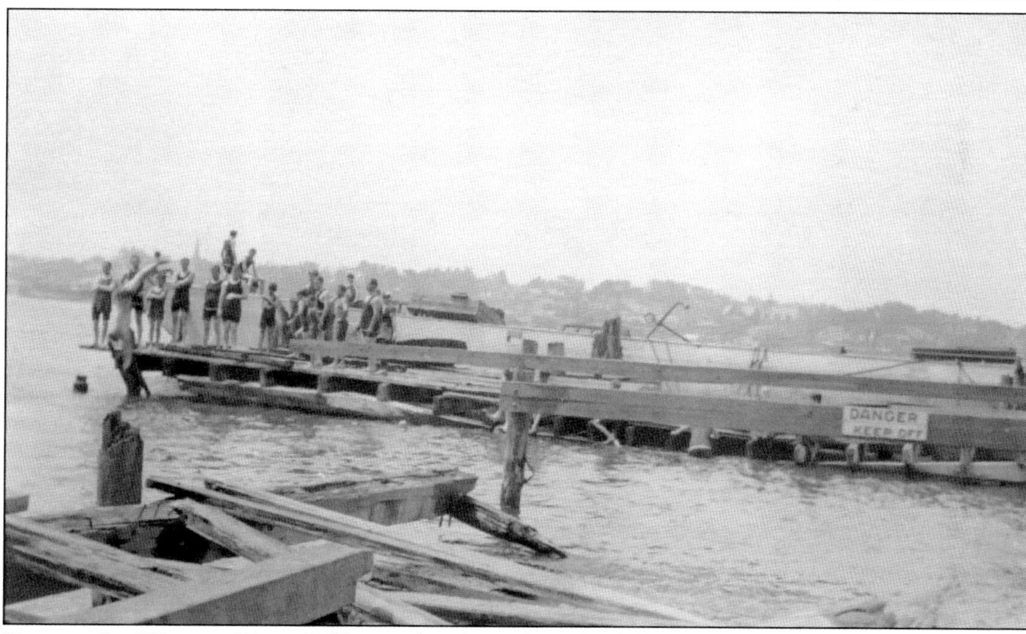

Despite the "Danger Keep Off" sign, local youths take full advantage of a summer day in the 1920s at Brown's Beach along the Arthur Kill. Perth Amboy, New Jersey, can be seen in the background. (Courtesy of the John Bieser Estate.)

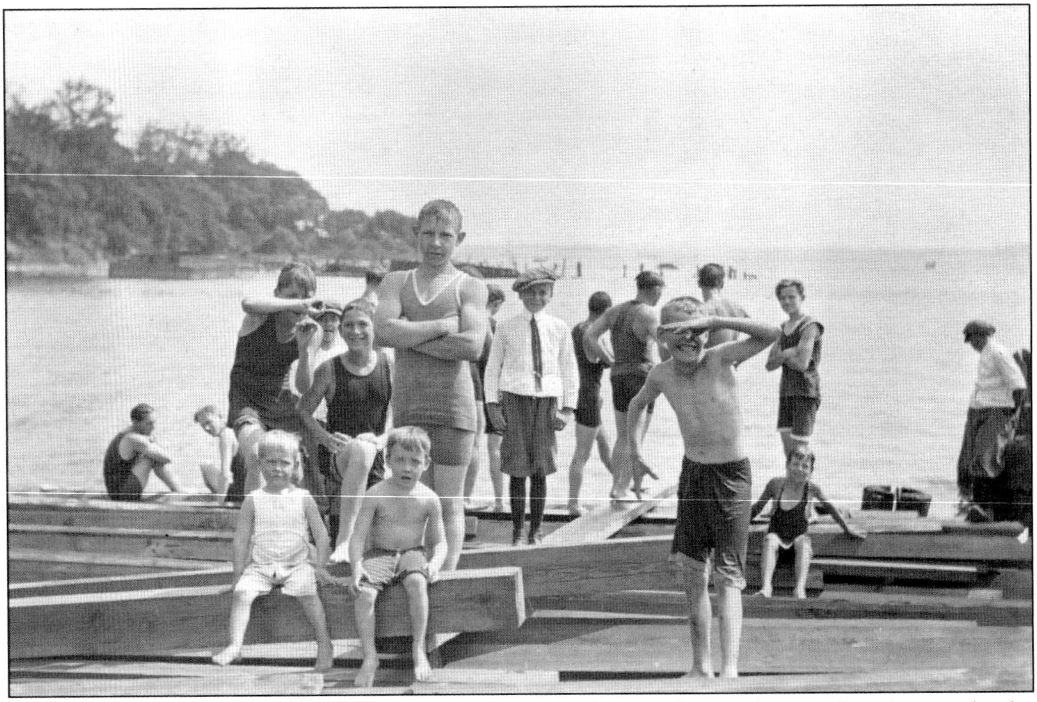

The waterfront along the Arthur Kill, referred to as the Inside Beach, was the place to be for summer fun in the early 1920s. This group of young people enjoys having a picture taken on large ship timbers at Brown's Beach, located at the foot of Amboy Road. Ace Grey is identified as the young boy with his hand over his eyes on the right. (Courtesy of the John Bieser Estate.)

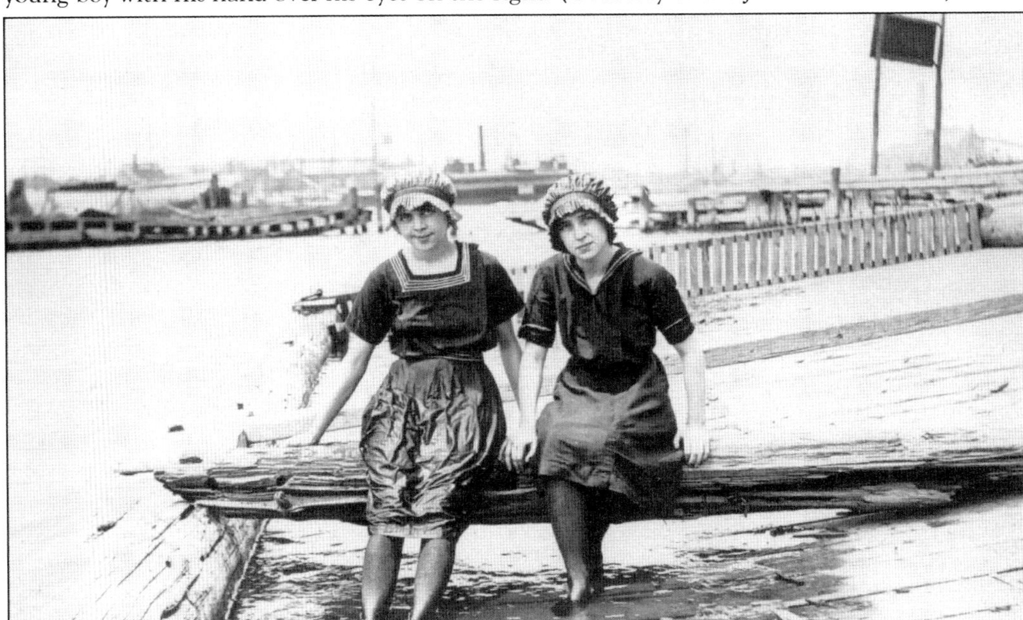

Lillian Covell (left) and her unidentified friend pose in the very latest beach fashion at Brown's Beach in this *c.* 1918 photograph. (Courtesy of the John Bieser Estate.)

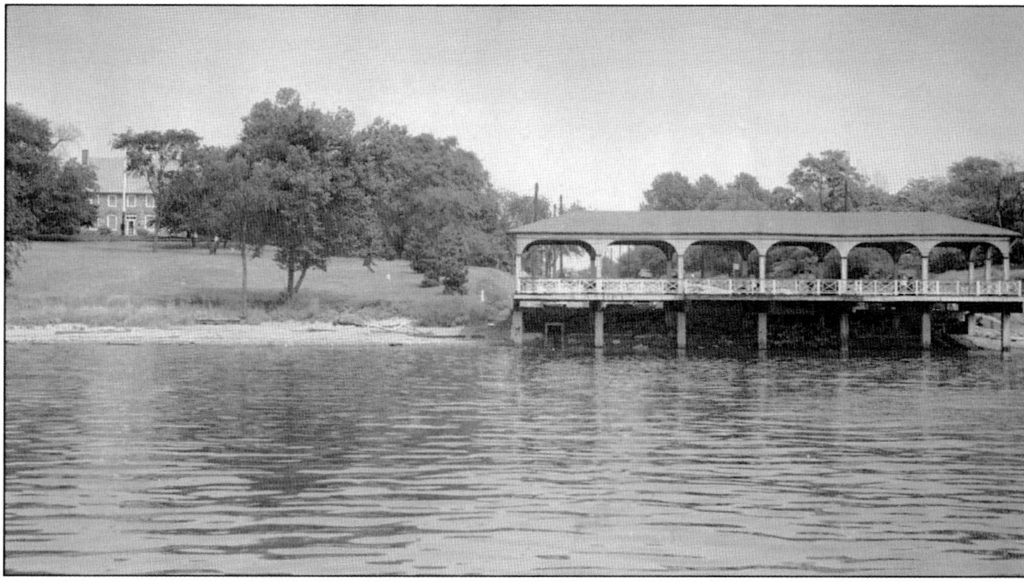

The Almer G. Russell Recreation Pavilion was erected in 1934 in honor of a Tottenville resident killed in action in France during World War I. The pavilion at the end of Hylan Boulevard was an observation structure that provided a sweeping view of Raritan Bay. It was the perfect place to watch the sailboats on a summer evening and to enjoy the cool breezes off the bay. Concerts by the South Shore Band were often held there, and it was the final destination of many town parades. (Courtesy of William Carsten.)

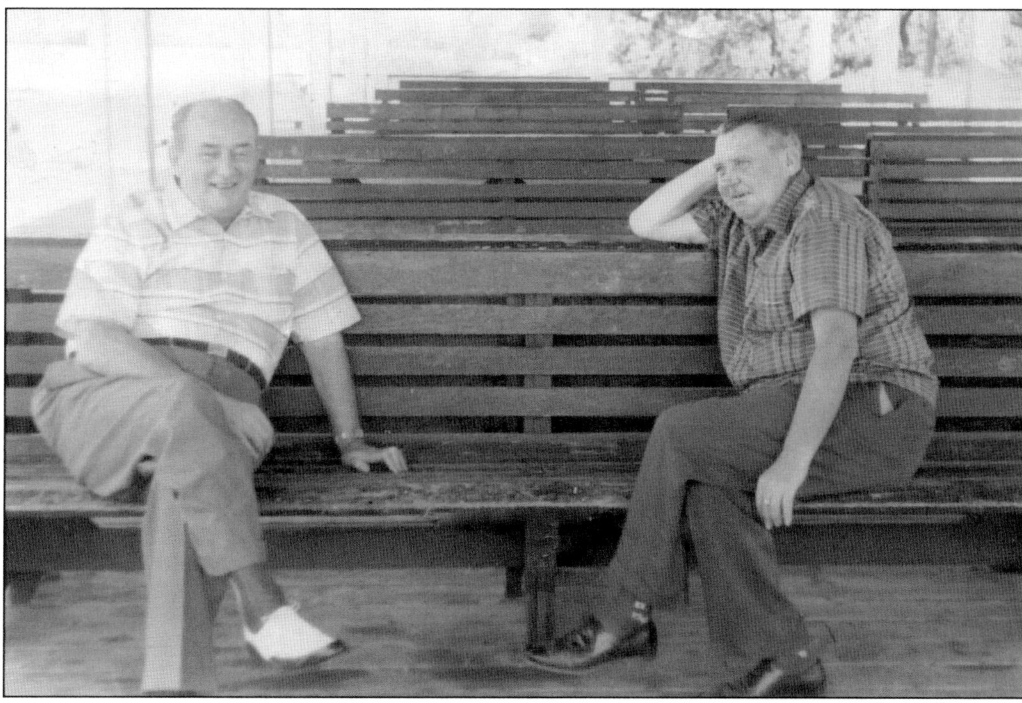

In this *c.* 1955 photograph, Tottenville residents Bill White (right) and Gilbert Dubois, known to many as "Dubee," owner of Dubee's Bar and Grill, enjoy a summer afternoon on the pavilion. (Courtesy of the Leyes and White families.)

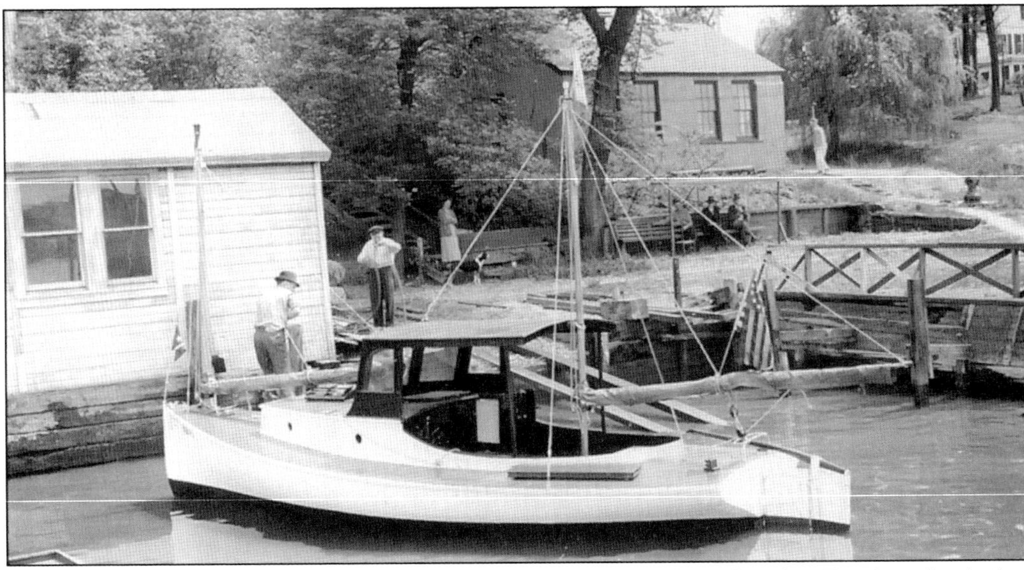

The Bentley Yacht Club, established in 1909, is located near the foot of Amboy Road on the Arthur Kill. The clubhouse, which is pictured on the left, sits on the edge of the bulkhead. Capt. George Kiefer, standing second from the left, founded the club. Muriel (Kiefer) Rössel and Bruce the dog are at the bottom of the stairs, which lead to their home at 79 Hopping Avenue. The building up the hill is the Howat ceramic studio, a family-run business that produced a line of decorative ceramic pieces including vases and figurines. (Courtesy of C. Greg and Carol-Lynn Rössel.)

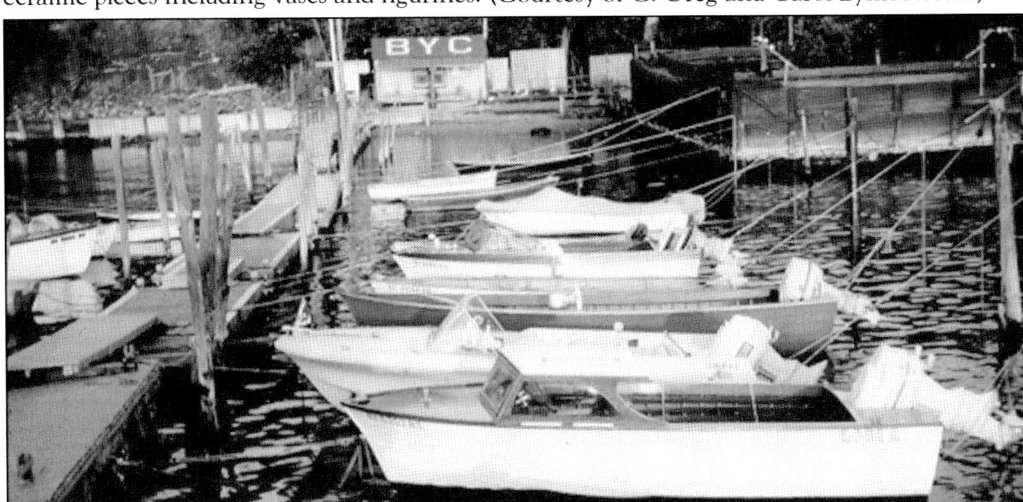

In the 1960s, the Bentley Yacht Club grounds underwent a major renovation and expansion. The length of the pier was doubled, and the clubhouse was moved back and a porch added. A concrete ramp was poured to allow for the hauling and storage of boats. The yacht club was a hands-on collaborative effort of the members. All the carpentry, painting, wiring, plumbing, concrete work, welding, and setting and pulling of the moorings was done by the members at work parties. It was also a place of numerous gatherings, picnics, and celebrations. Young people were not left out of the activities and were included in the work; in return, they were allowed the use of some boats. The barge in this 1967 photograph was used by the Howat ceramic studio. The Bentley Yacht Club proudly celebrated its 100th anniversary in 2009. (Courtesy of C. Greg and Carol-Lynn Rössel.)

Two

Good Times

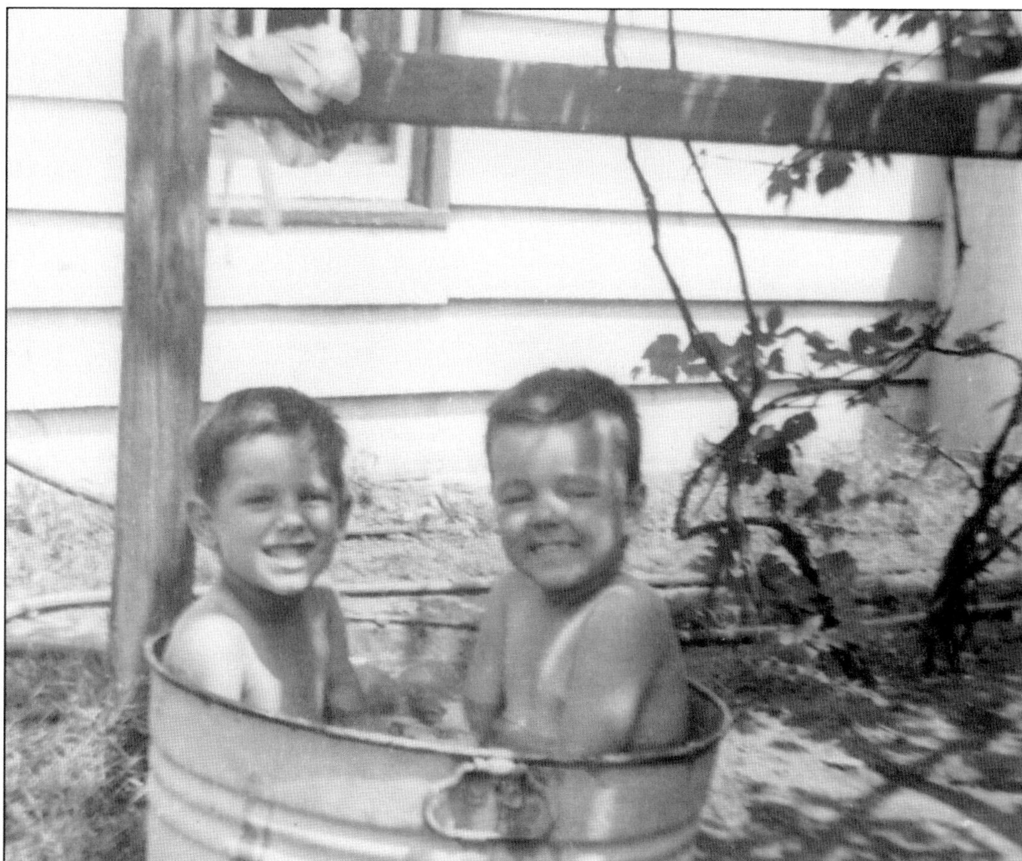

With no air-conditioning and few backyard swimming pools in the 1950s, cousins John Kutko (left) and Wayne Cutler (right) cool off in a galvanized tub on a sultry August day. (Courtesy of the Cutler family.)

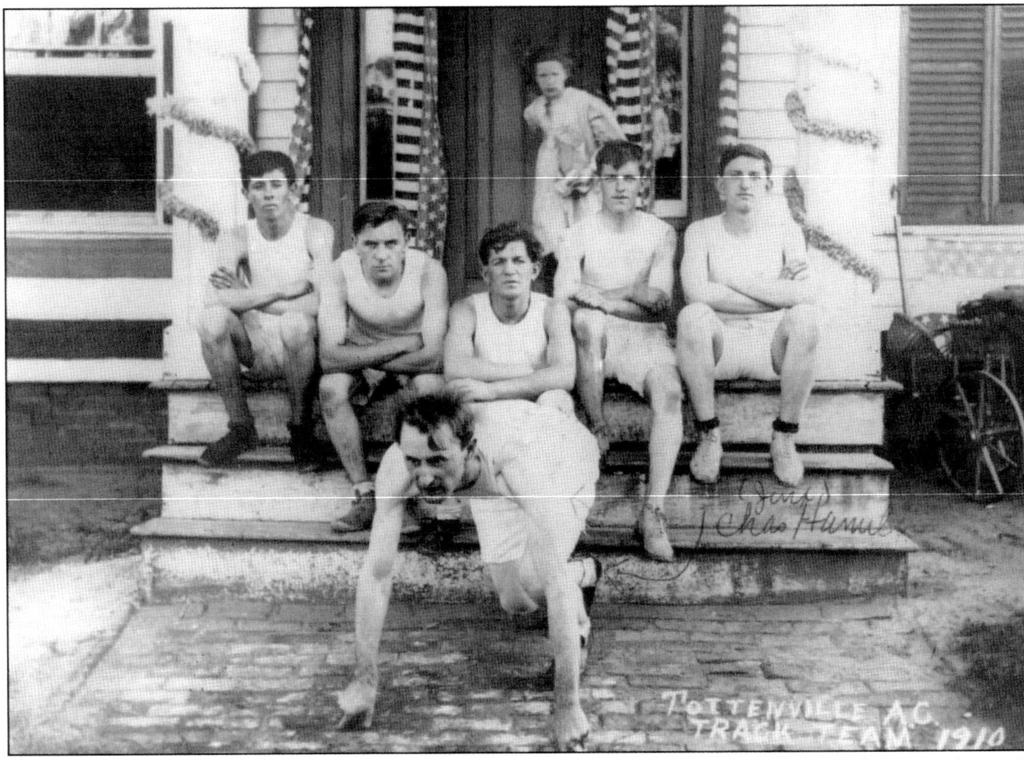

Charles Warren "Jinx" Hamilton is poised in the starting position in this 1910 photograph, with members of the Tottenville Athletic Club track team looking on. Descendants of Jinx Hamilton, a progeny of the Totten family, still reside in the community today. (Courtesy of Linda Cevasco.)

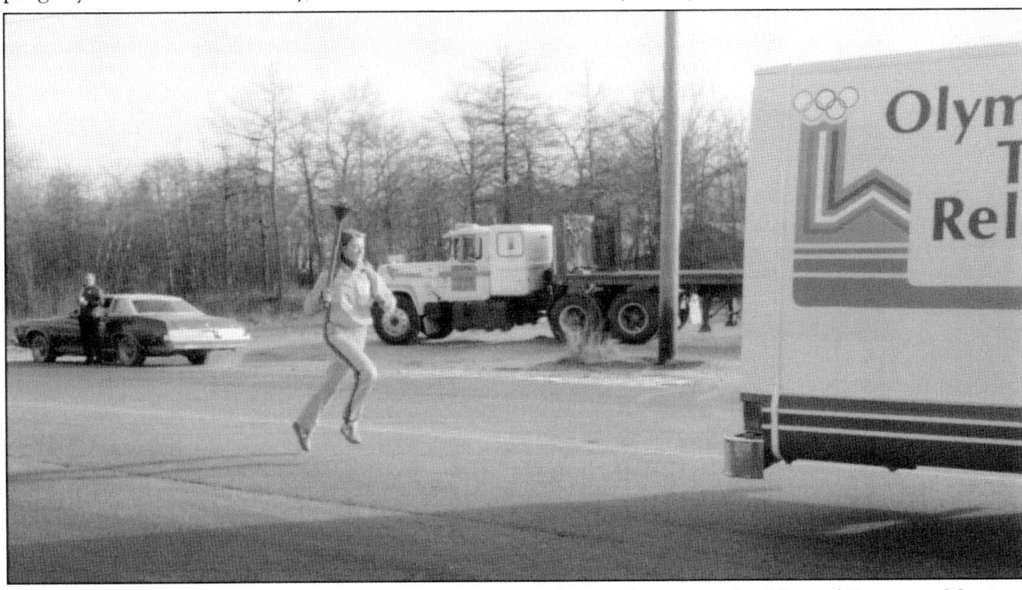

The 1980 Olympic Torch Relay, a nine-day, 1,000-mile run, began in the United States in Virginia and ended at the Winter Olympics in Lake Placid, New York. An American runner carrying the Olympic flame, ignited in Greece a week earlier, passed through Tottenville on February 4, 1980. (Courtesy of the Schaming family.)

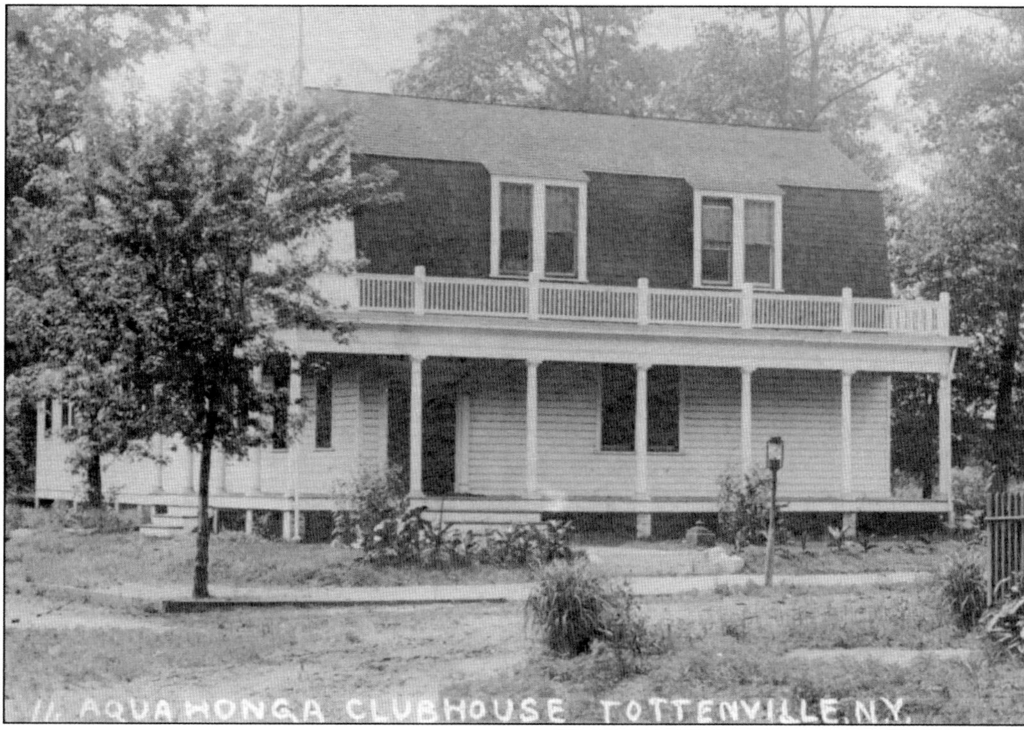

Tottenville was home to several athletic clubs, each organizing competitive teams in a wide variety of sports, including basketball, football, baseball, bowling, and boxing. The Aquehonga Athletic Club was organized in 1889. Their clubhouse on Brighton Street, as seen in this c. 1920 image, had billiard tables, a gymnasium, and a bowling alley. Around 1900, the club opened a home field on Sprague Avenue near Amboy Road. The Aquehonga Field was one of the main baseball diamonds on Staten Island.

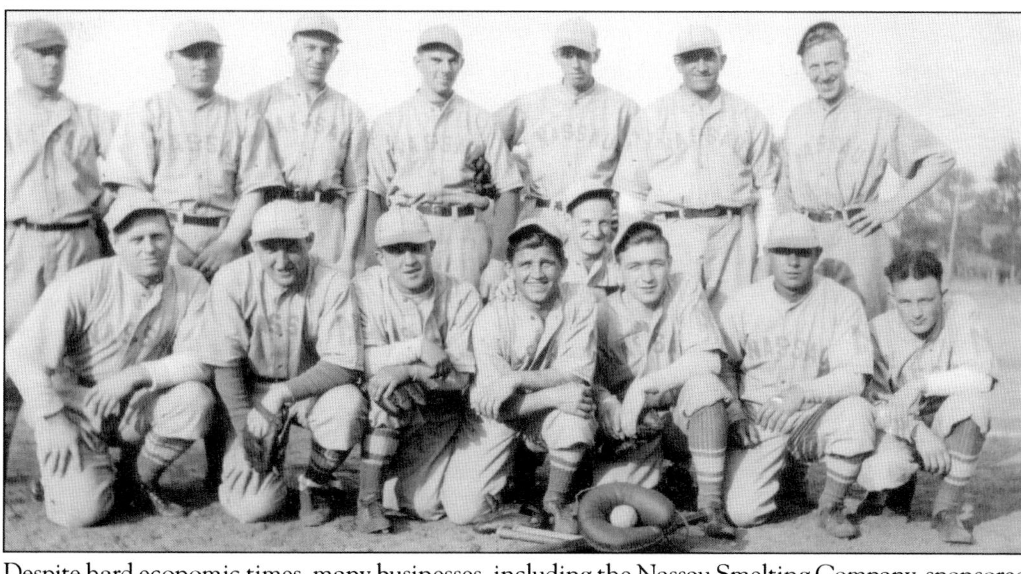

Despite hard economic times, many businesses, including the Nassau Smelting Company, sponsored employee athletic teams, even providing team uniforms and equipment, as shown in this 1934 photograph. (Courtesy of the John Bieser Estate.)

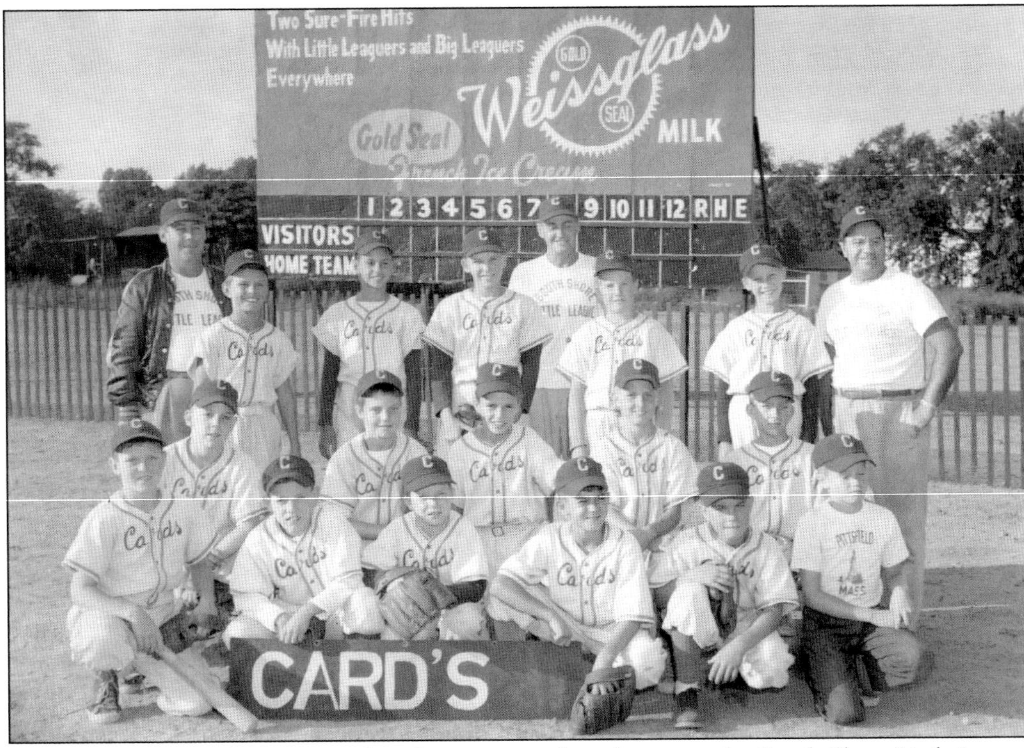

In 1955, with tremendous support from business people and parents, the South Shore Little League was formed at Aquehonga Field. One of the first team sponsors was Beauvais-Hudson American Legion Post 126. Players on the 1956 Beauvais-Hudson team, the Cardinals, are, from left to right, (first row) John Drennan, Thomas Shouldis, Charles Donnelly, Guy Deuel, Pat Tobin, and Brian Sullivan (batboy); (second row) Gary Sloat, Steven Martin, Ronald Fay, William Stasiuk, and Steven Knapp; (third row) John Putnam, Philip Moog, William McCormack, Quinlan Sullivan, and Patrick Lavin. Manager Fred Iversen and coaches Charles Donnelly and Louis Lombardo are pictured in the fourth row. (Courtesy of the Beauvais-Hudson Post 126, American Legion.)

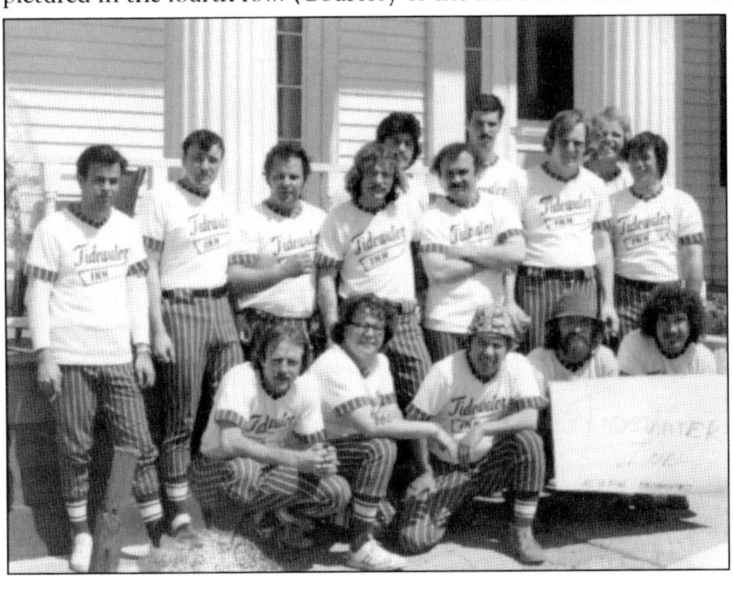

Members of the Tidewater Inn softball team in this 1970s photograph include, from left to right, (first row) Ray Bertsch, Charlie Donnelly, Bobby Imsho, unidentified, and Rocky Biel; (second row) Jackie Baker, Jimmy Cummings, unidentified, Howie Bertsch, Jack Cowan, Tommy Ryan, and Patty Tobin; (third row) Albert Cutler, Greg Thiemer, and Mike Buickerood. (Courtesy of the George Burke Collection.)

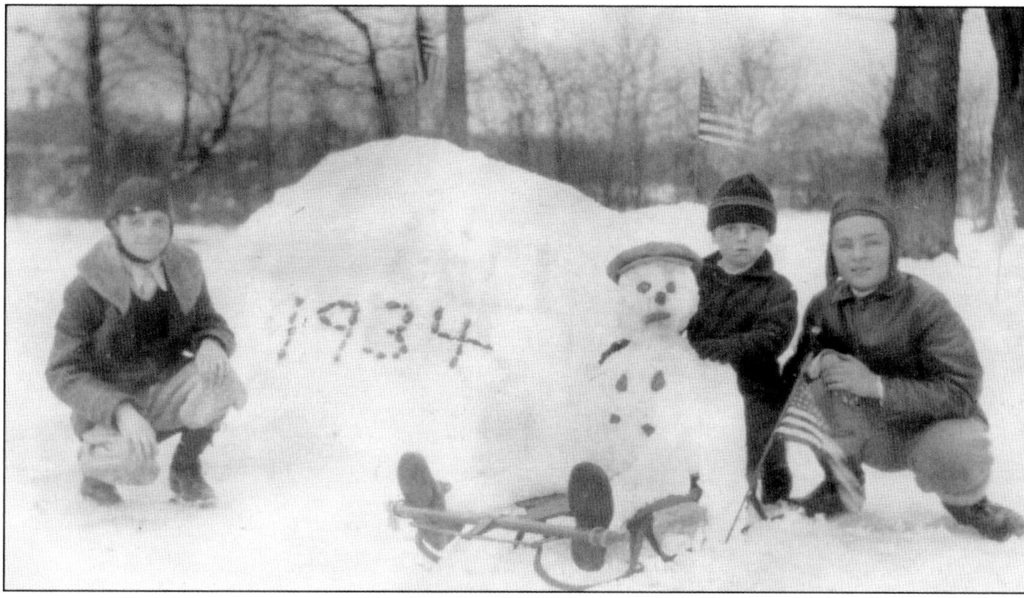

It's a snow day! John Bieser (right) and unidentified friends are having fun in the snow near Mill Creek. In the background are the Barnard Silk Mill and smokestacks from Nassau Smelting and Refining Company. (Courtesy of the John Bieser Estate.)

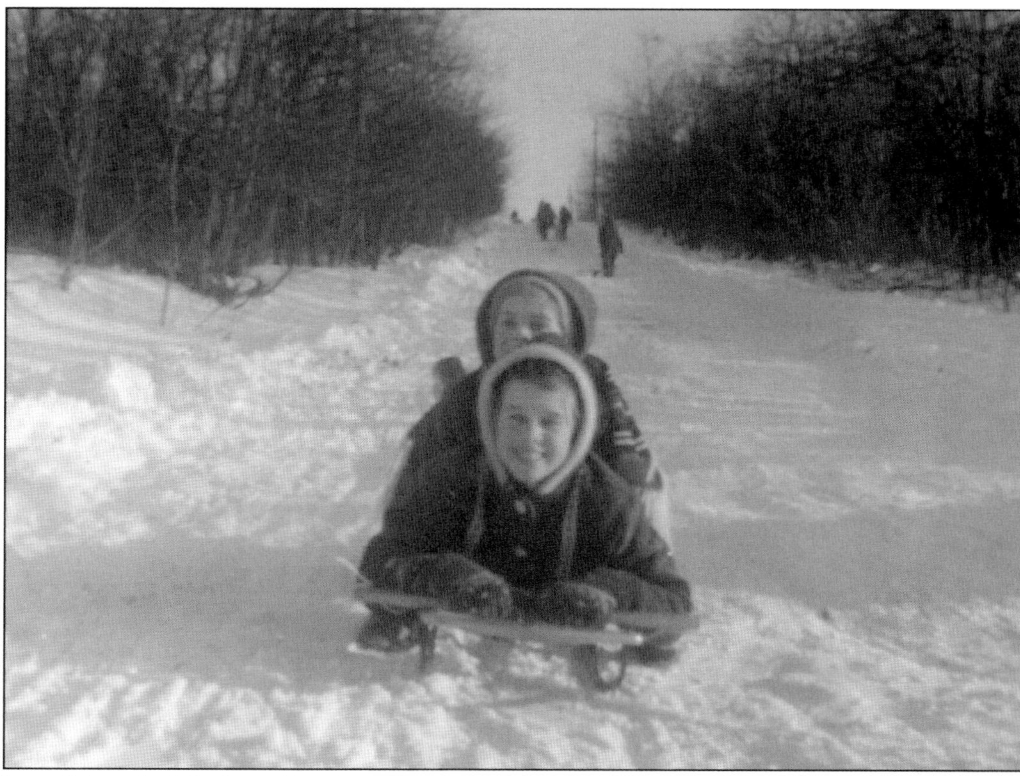

It is all downhill for June (front) and sister Nancy Brennan as they zoom down Nashville Street toward Craig Avenue in 1960. Also known as Dead Man's Hill, this street was one of the best places for sledding in Tottenville. (Courtesy of the Brennan family.)

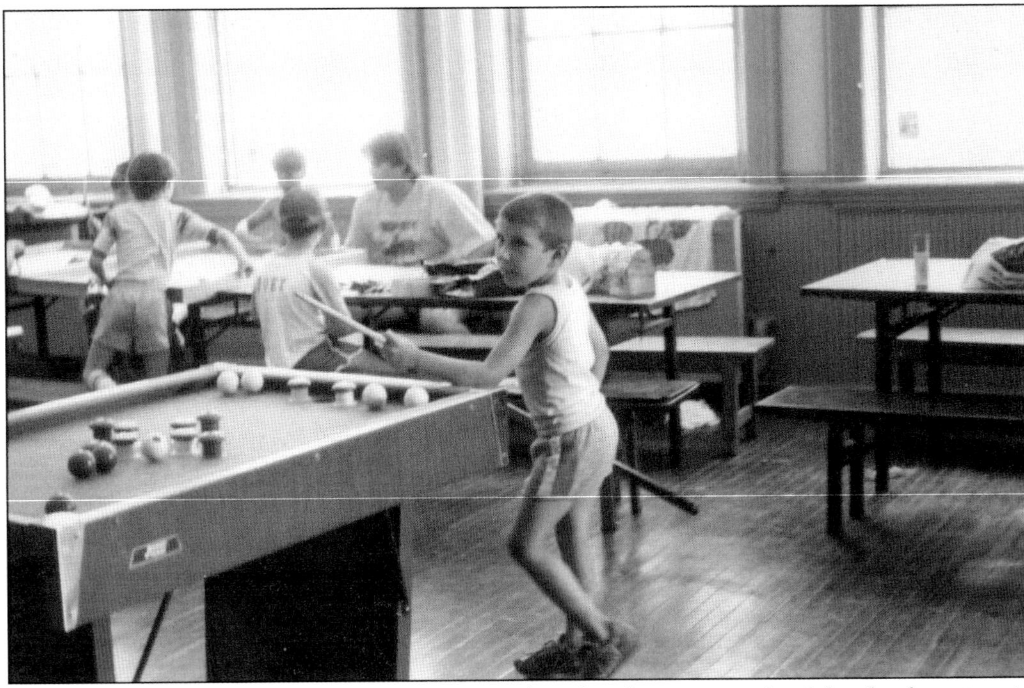

A summer play camp program was implemented at the elementary school for the first time in 1977, providing a wide range of activities for children between the ages of 6 and 13. Indoor and outdoor activities included arts and crafts, gymnastics, hula hoop contests, sports, table games, field trips, and a water sprinkler to cool off on hot summer days. (Both, courtesy of the Janice and June Rose Collection.)

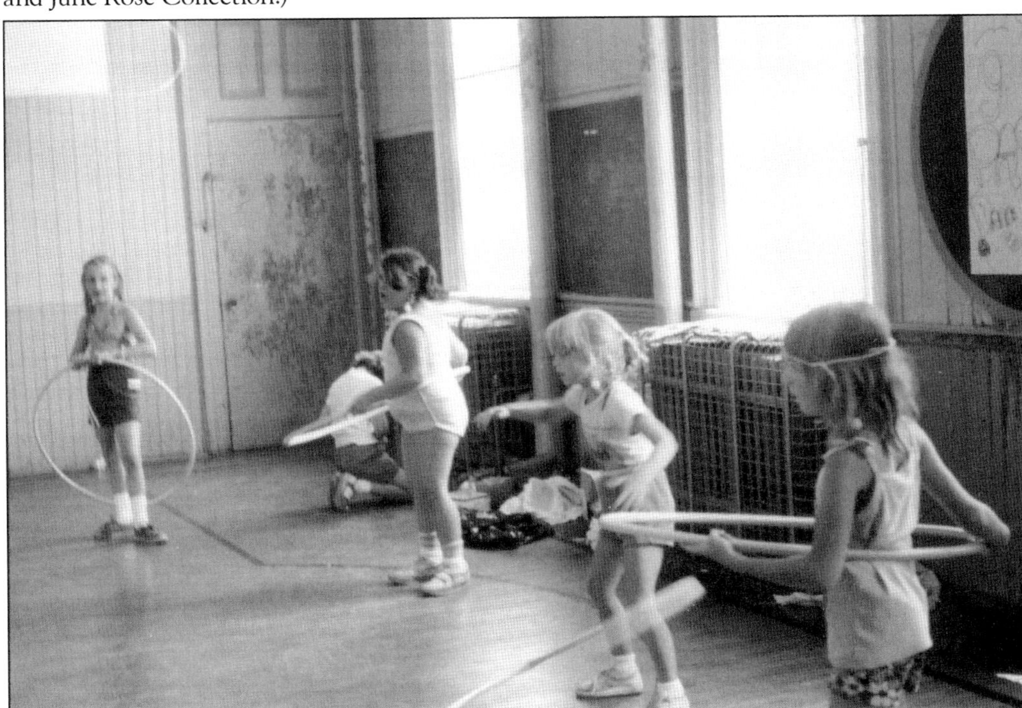

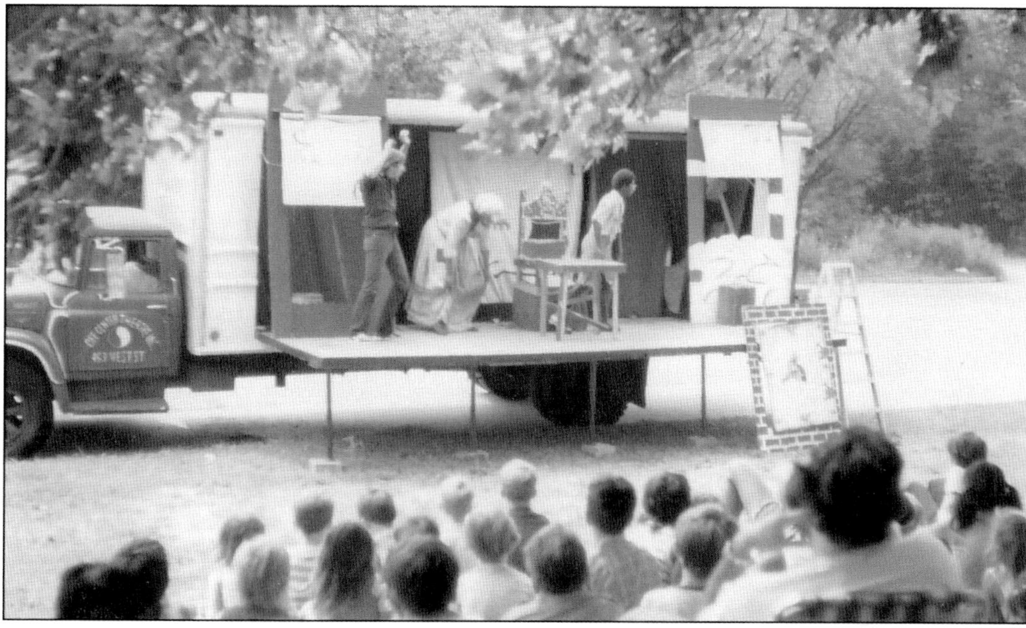

In the early 1970s, the Off-Center Theatre Group of Manhattan provided outdoor summer entertainment, including the marionette show pictured here, to children of all ages. These mobile units were arranged by the Tottenville Improvement Council and provided by the New York City Parks Department. (Courtesy of the Pagliuco family.)

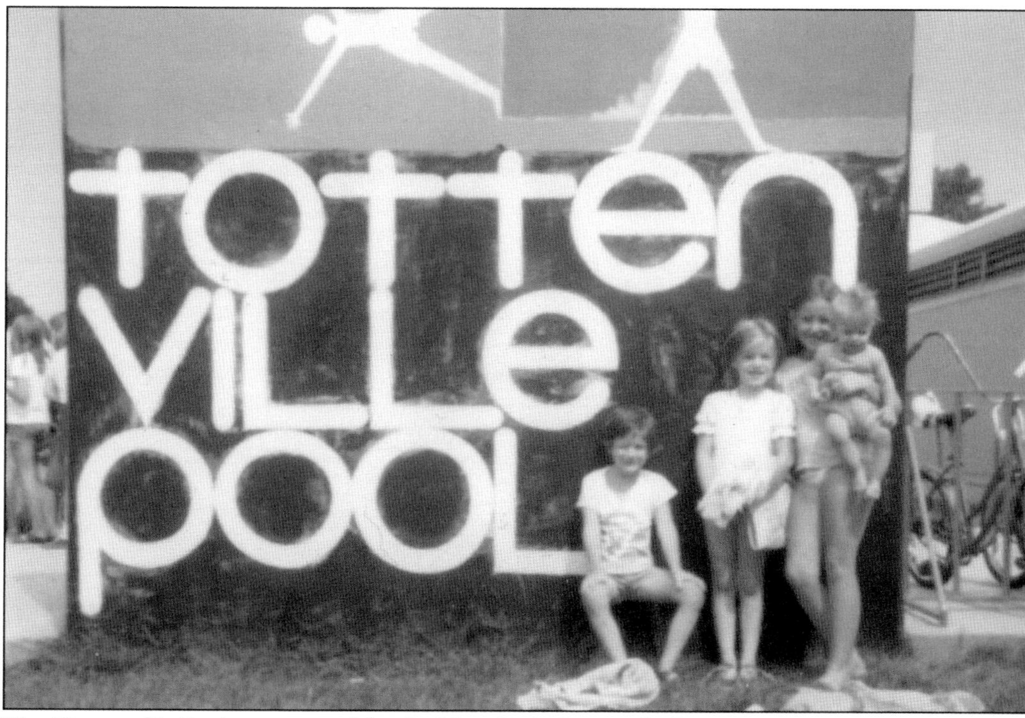

The Tottenville Pool was opened by the New York City Parks Department in 1970. The facility, located at Hylan Boulevard and Joline Avenue, is the only outdoor public swimming pool on Staten Island's South Shore. (Courtesy of the Janice and June Rose Collection.)

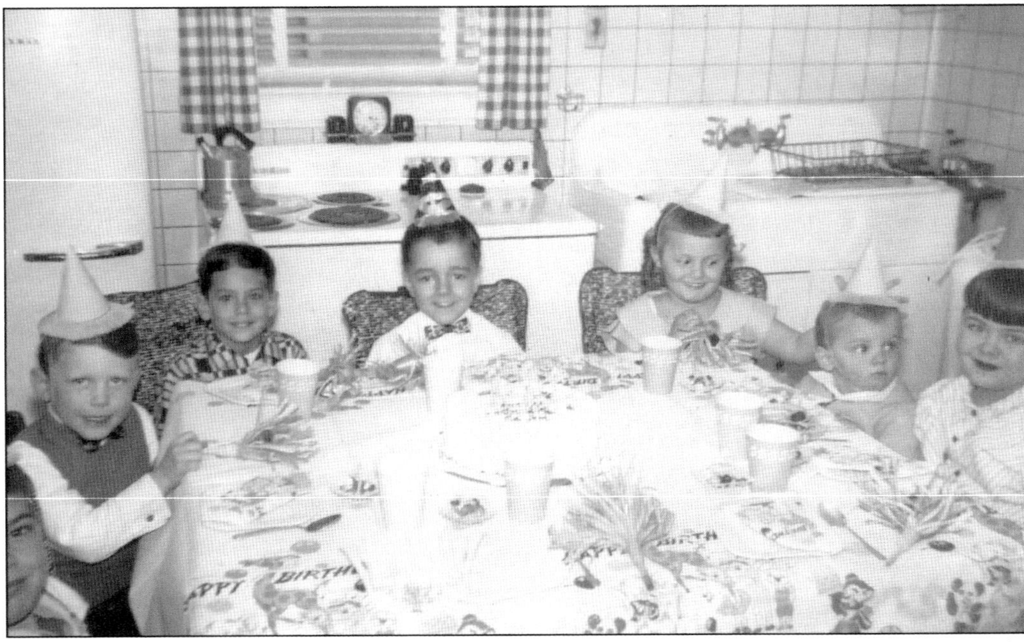

Party hats, candy baskets, and favorite cousins made a birthday memorable in 1954. Wayne Cutler (center) is celebrating his fifth birthday with, from left to right, Albert Cutler, Joseph Swiderski, Barbara Mancini, Robert Mancini, and Margaret Cutler. Birthdays in the 1950s were typically celebrated at home with just family. The retro kitchen helps date this photograph. (Courtesy of the Cutler family.)

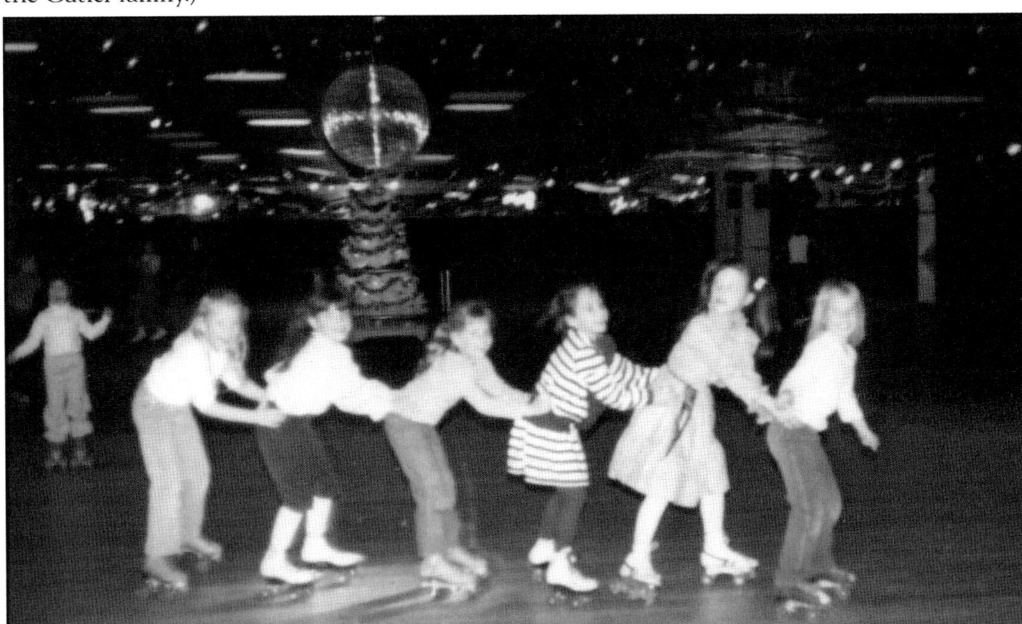

The Rinky Dink Roller Skating Rink opened on February 14, 1975, in the former Stadium Theatre at 217 Main Street. It later became the Fantasy Island Roller Disco Skating Rink and a popular children's birthday party place. These unidentified party girls have formed a soon-to-be-growing conga line under the spinning disco ball. (Courtesy of the Schaming family.)

George Garis (center), scoutmaster of Troop 21, was involved with the Boy Scouts of America for 47 years. During his tenure, 50 Scouts earned the Eagle rank, a testament to George's leadership. This photograph, with Boy Scout Michael Goonan on the right, was taken in 1974. (Courtesy of the Goonan family.)

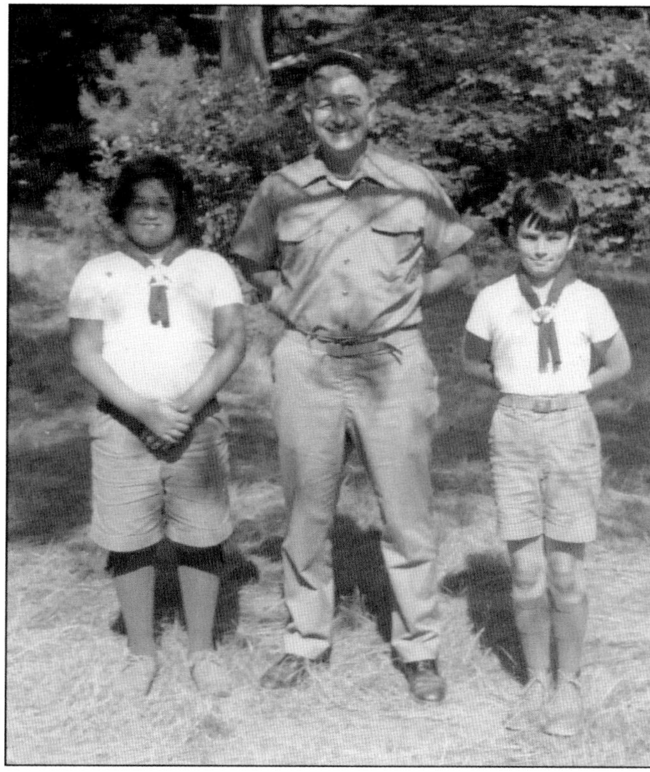

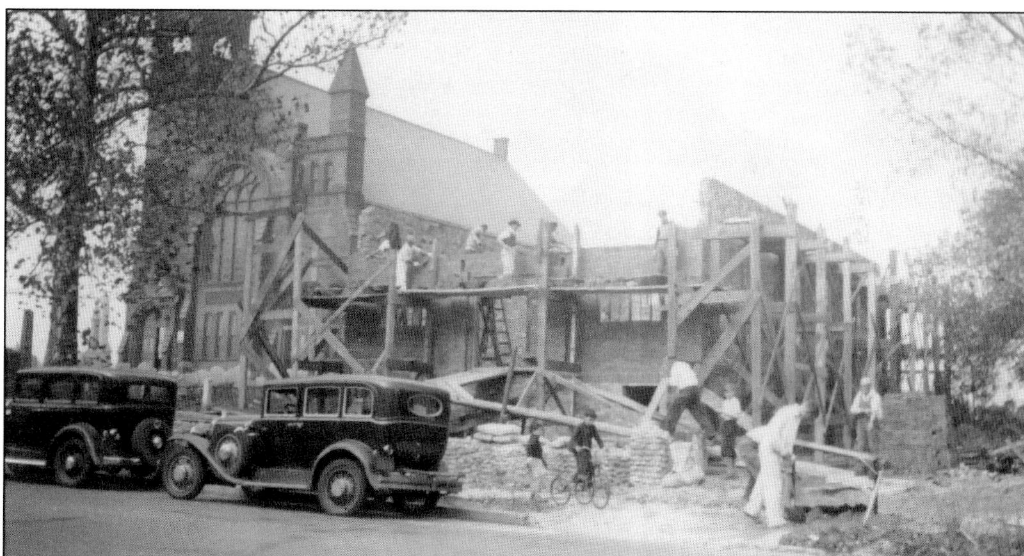

Boy Scout Troop 46 was organized in 1927 by the trustees and official board of Bethel United Methodist Church, on Amboy Road. When the Scouts outgrew their meeting place in the church basement, construction of a Scout shack began on church grounds in the late 1930s with volunteer labor and donated funds and materials. Most of the bricks were salvaged from the abandoned Kreischerville brickworks, located about a mile away. The shack was later named the Guthrie Memorial Scout Shack to honor one of the community's key scout leaders. This photograph was taken in October 1938. (Courtesy of the John Bieser Estate.)

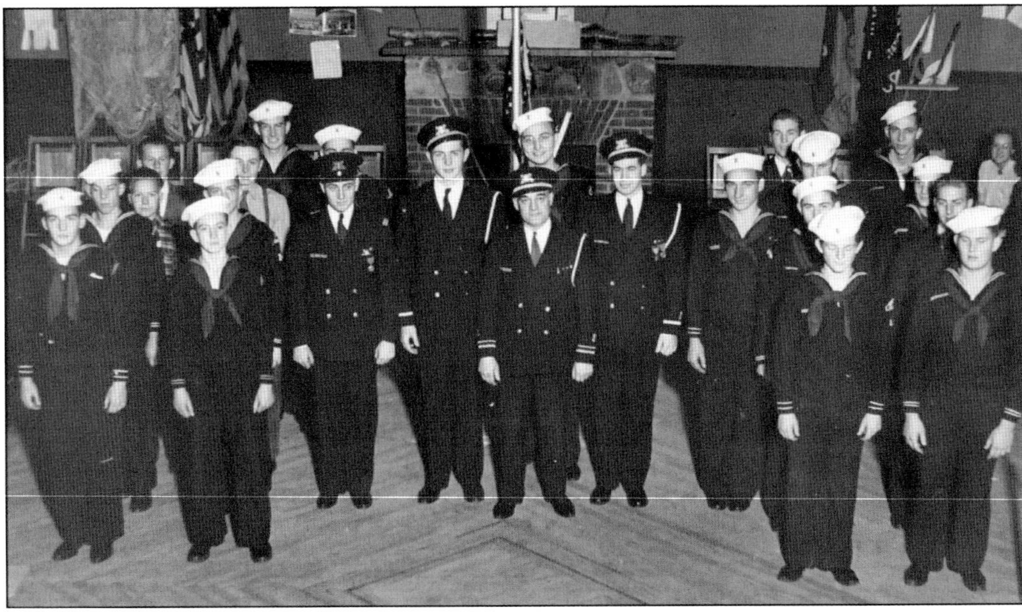

A Sea Scout ship, or unit, was organized in the 1930s. Sea Scouting is a young adult nautical program of the Boy Scouts of America. Sponsored by Bethel United Methodist Church, the ship met regularly in the Guthrie Memorial Scout Shack. In 1937, Harold Blair was the skipper of Sea Scout Ship Rebel No. 46; Helmar Monty was the first mate. (Courtesy of the Margaret Wilson Collection.)

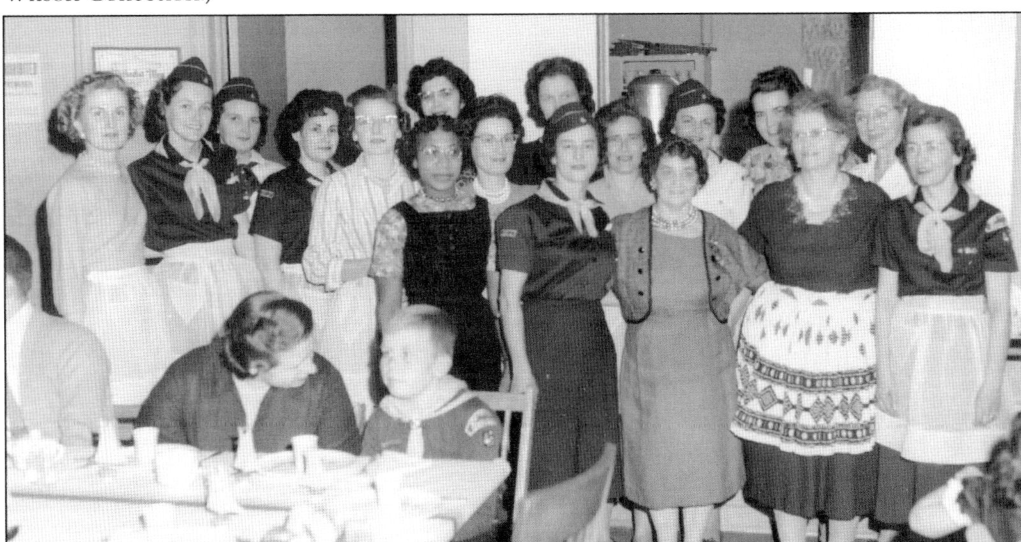

The original Mothers Club of Troop 46 raised funds and prepared picnic-style meals for the weekend volunteers building the new Scout shack. In the mid-1940s, the mothers club reorganized as the "46ers," and the organization was opened to anyone interested in helping the Scouts. Members pose during an awards ceremony in the mid-1960s in the basement of Bethel Church. They are, from left to right, (first row) Anna Josey, Mary Cald, Jean Guthrie, Elizabeth Filimon, and Cora Doty; (second row) Ann Limbert, Marge Flesland, Arlene Klose Schweikert, Hazel Brennan, Eleanor Brown, Roberta Kochon, Jean Mitchell, Frances MacDonald, Juanita Huttar, and Ida Plumb; (third row) Rose Kollar and Beverly Vroome. (Courtesy of Beverly J. Vroome.)

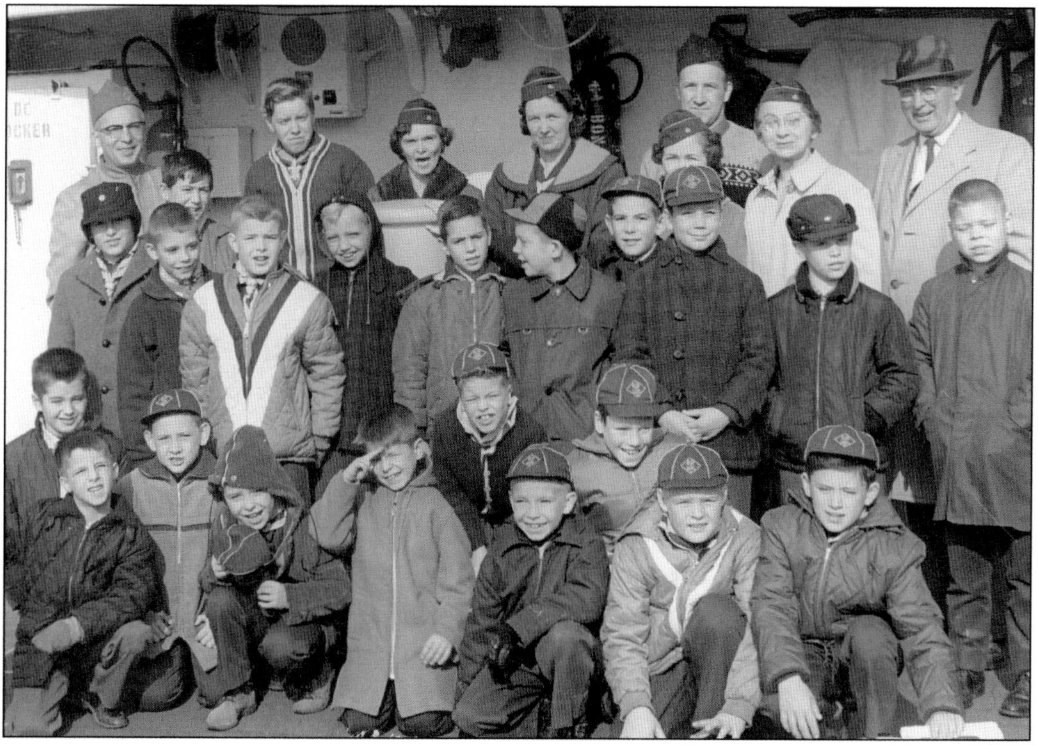

Boys, leaders, and mothers of Cub Scout Pack 46 enjoy a tour aboard a New York City tugboat in 1966. From left to right are (first row) Bobby Doty, John Barrett, Andrew Kuscsik, Alan Cole, Tommy Burnham, Bob Forlie, Tommy Britten, Kurt Bille, Brian Vroome, and Robert Moffit; (second row) George Harrach, Jason Lotvin, Ronald Clohessy, David Vroome, Joseph Werns, Billy Gillespie, Peter Eckel, Terrence Thompson, Billy Shaughnessy, Tommy Csap, and Jeffrey Nemeth; (third row) Frank Mester, Dennis Forlie, Tess Cole, Beverly Vroome, Cora Doty, Irving Britten, Ida Plumb, and John Plumb. (Courtesy of Beverly J. Vroome.)

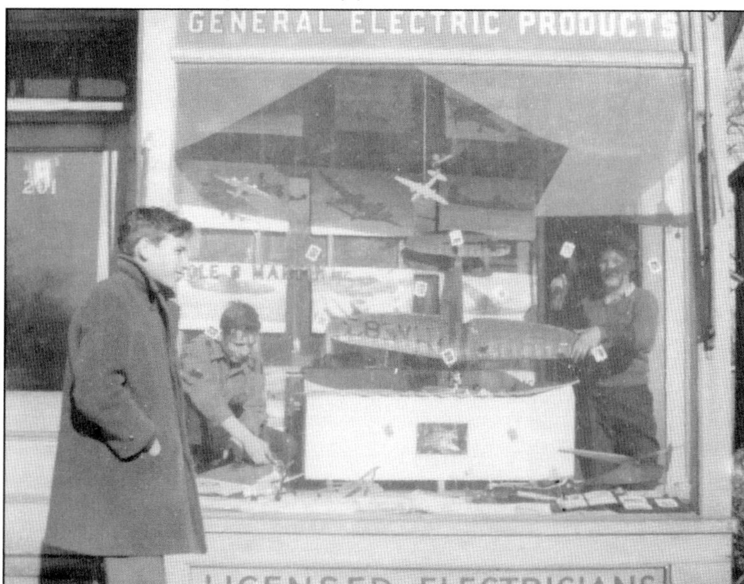

In 1946, members of the Air Scout program assemble an aircraft exhibit in Cole and Martin, an electrical and radio repair shop at 203 Main Street. During Boy Scout Week in February, local businesses would allow the Scouts to place exhibits in their storefront windows. Albert "Pete" Walz is outside the store on the left. Working inside are Bill Seiler (left) and Murray Pine. (Courtesy of Robert P. Ford.)

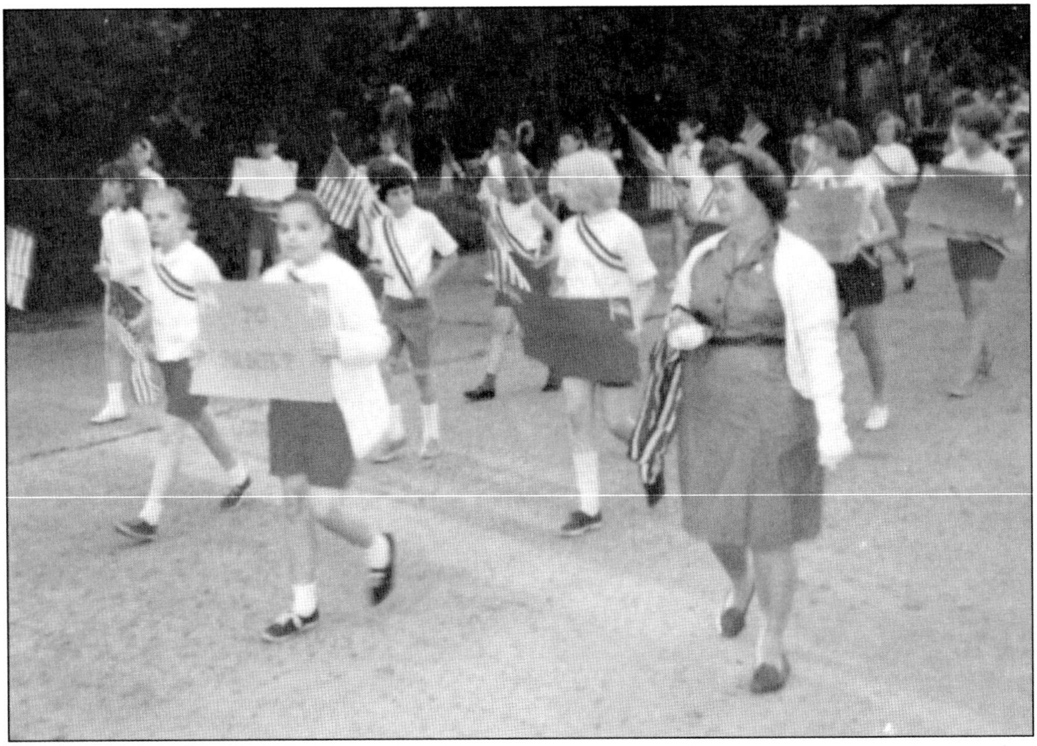

Members of Girl Scout Troop 5-10, uniformly dressed in patriotic colors, march along Amboy Road in the 1966 Flag Day Parade with their leader, Olive Chipman. (Courtesy of Linda Cutler Hauck.)

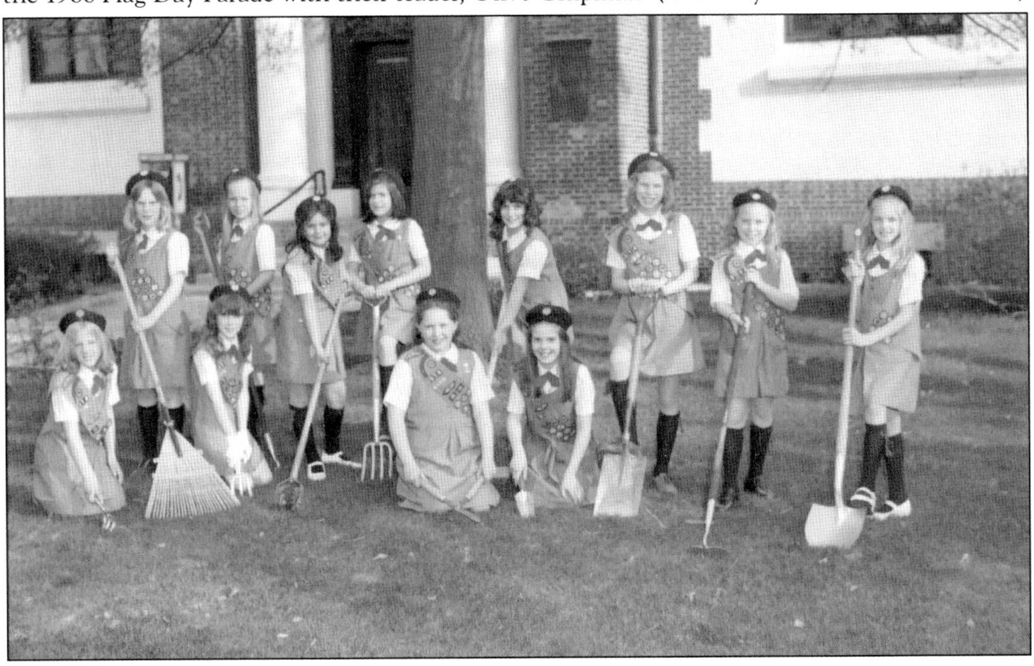

Members of Girl Scout Troop 5-14 in full uniform prepare for the community's annual cleanup around 1971 on the grounds of the Tottenville Branch Library at 7430 Amboy Road. (Courtesy of the New York Public Library.)

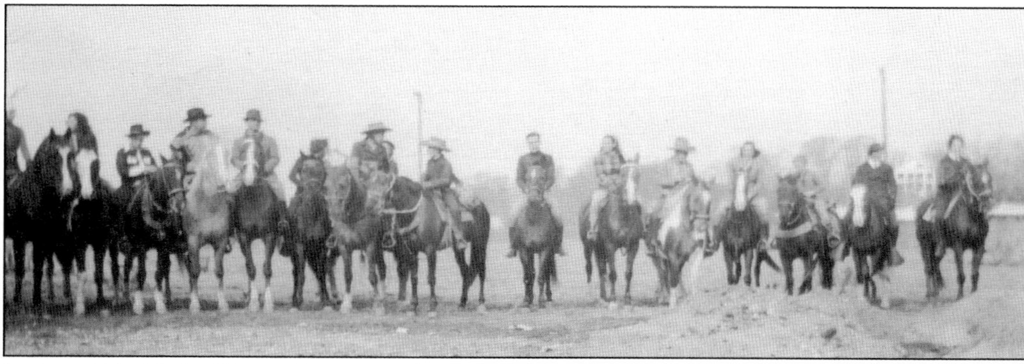

In the 1930s, Philip Xiques Sr., a special game protector, settled in Tottenville on Sprague Avenue and soon began taking in injured wild animals on his 2-acre farm, which quickly turned into a petting zoo and riding academy. Pictured here in this 1937 photograph are members of the Xiques Riding Academy on an early morning excursion from their Tottenville stables to the Princes Bay Inn for breakfast. The Seguine Mansion is visible in the background. (Courtesy of Daphne Brooks; Louise Thompson Collection.)

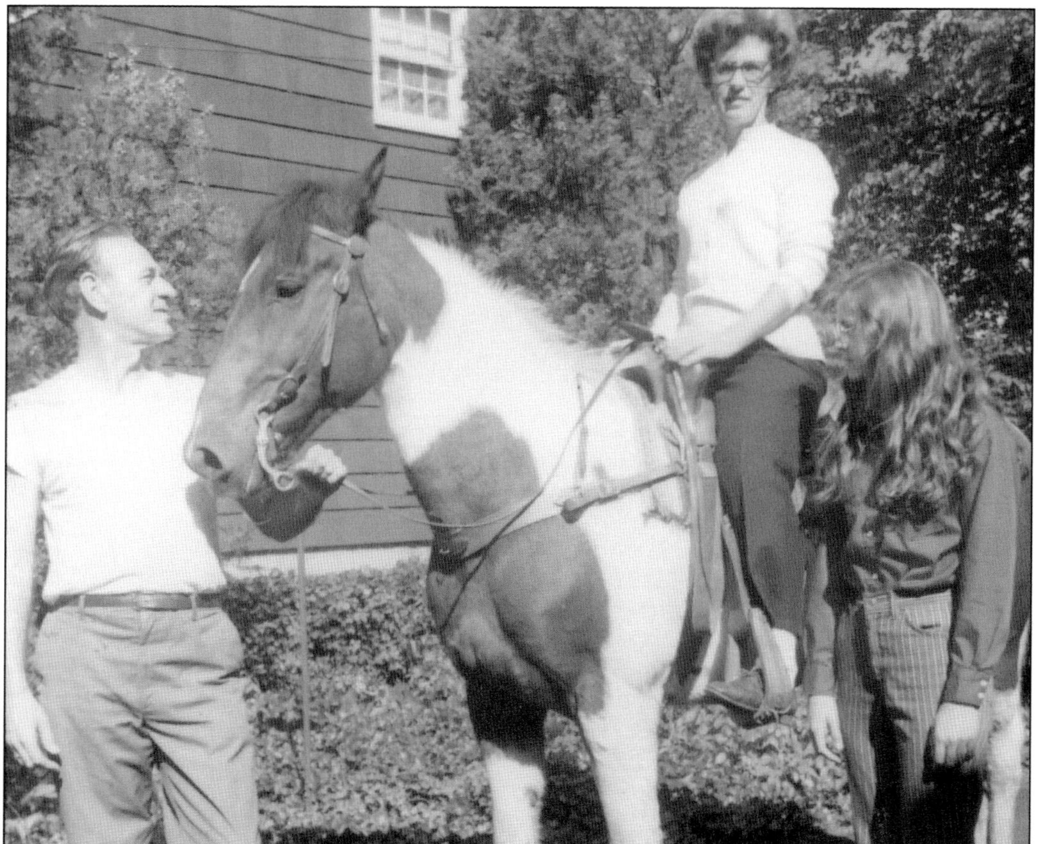

Tottenville was still considered somewhat rural in the 1960s, with many woodland trails and open spaces. Horseback riding was a popular hobby, and many residents, including the Brennan family of Brehaut Avenue, had privately owned horses and backyard stables. In this 1971 photograph, Edythe Brennan gets ready for a ride on her daughter's horse, Tobi, while husband George holds the reins and daughter Nancy looks on. (Courtesy of the Brennan family.)

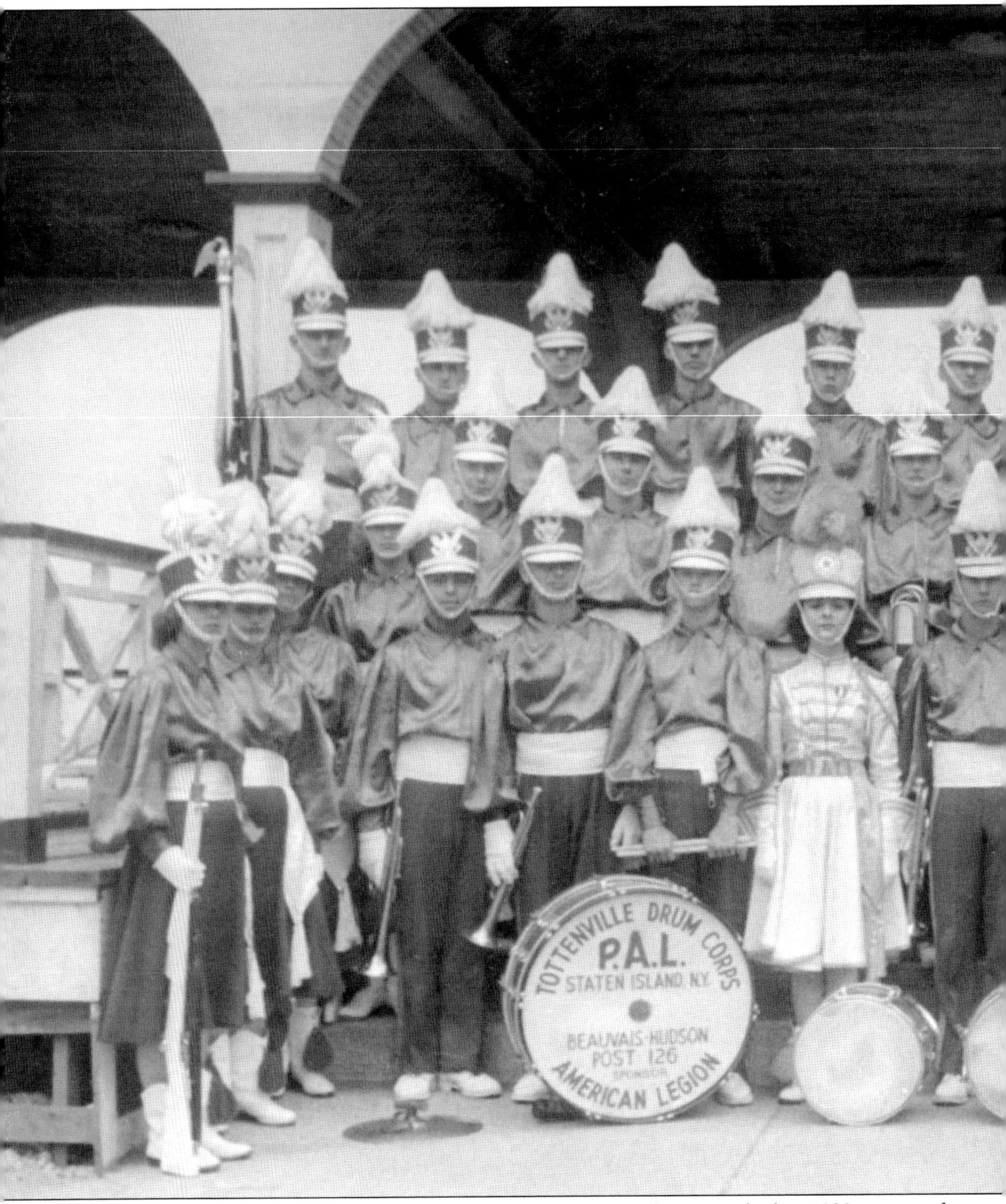

The Police Athletic League (P.A.L.) was organized in New York City in the late 1930s to provide teenagers with sports programs and social activities. In 1941, the 123rd Precinct organized competitive sports programs for basketball, baseball, track and field, volleyball, and boxing but was best known for its drum and bugle corps. Uniforms, instructions, and equipment were provided

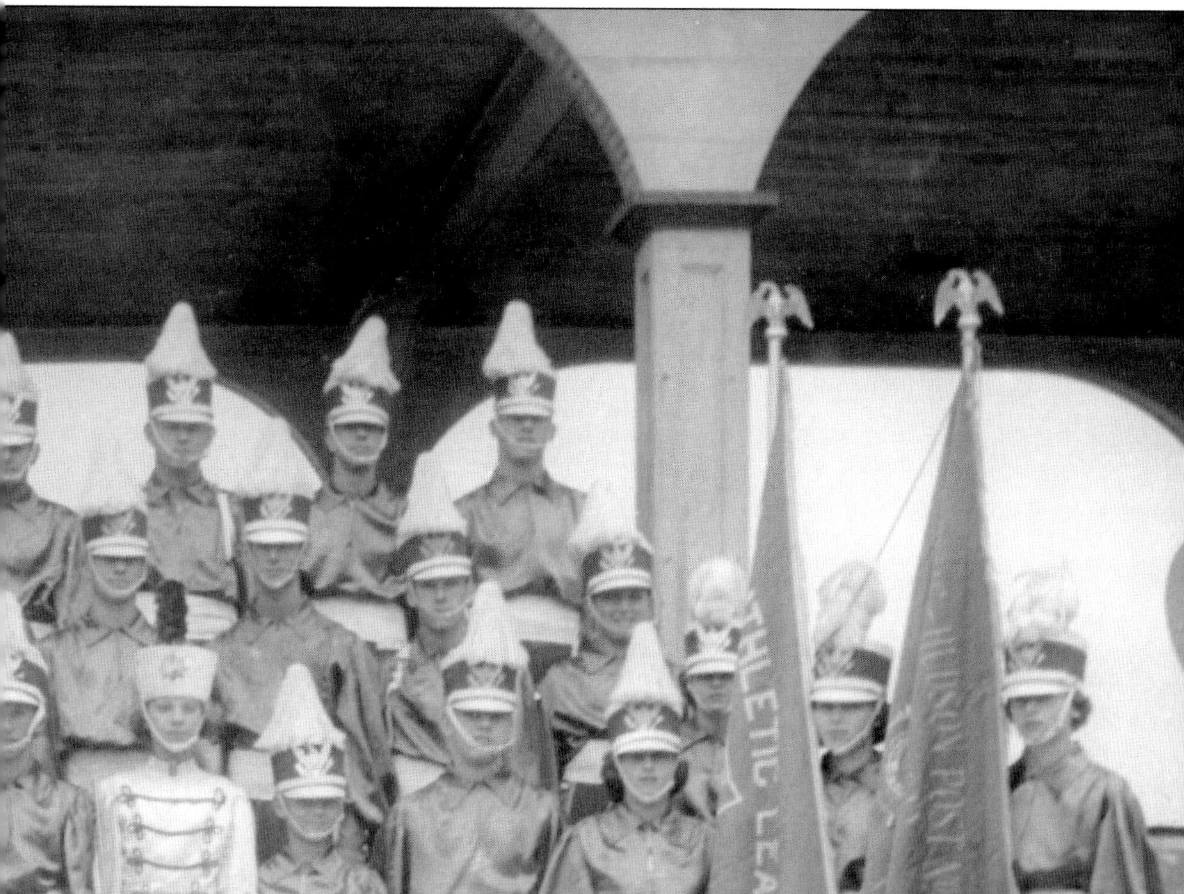

free by the P.A.L. Patrolman William J. White was the precinct's youth coordinator, and he was assisted by Louise Thompson, recreation aide, and a staff of volunteers including Joseph Minichini and Joseph Apignani, corps instructors. The Russell Pavilion provided the backdrop for this 1950s photograph. (Courtesy of the Tottenville Drum Corps Alumni Association Collection.)

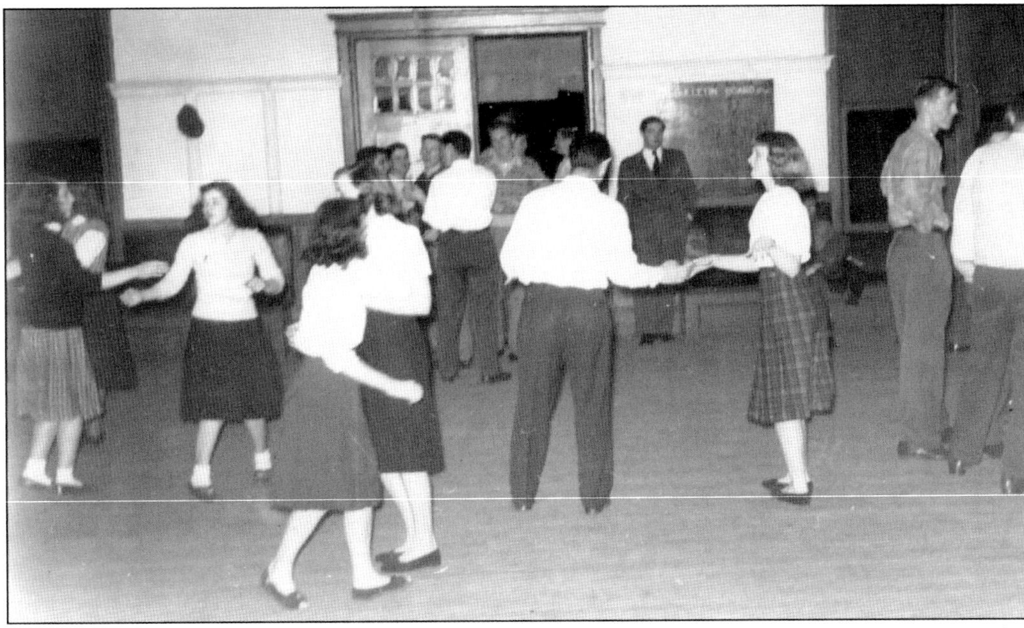

In 1942, a Youth Canteen was established at the American Legion Hall on Main Street. In October 1948, a new youth recreation center, pictured above, was opened in the former waterworks building on Joline Avenue. Open sessions provided group games, skee ball, pool, and deck shuffleboard, but by far the most popular activity for teens was Friday night dances. (Courtesy of Louis Horvath; Louise Thompson Collection.)

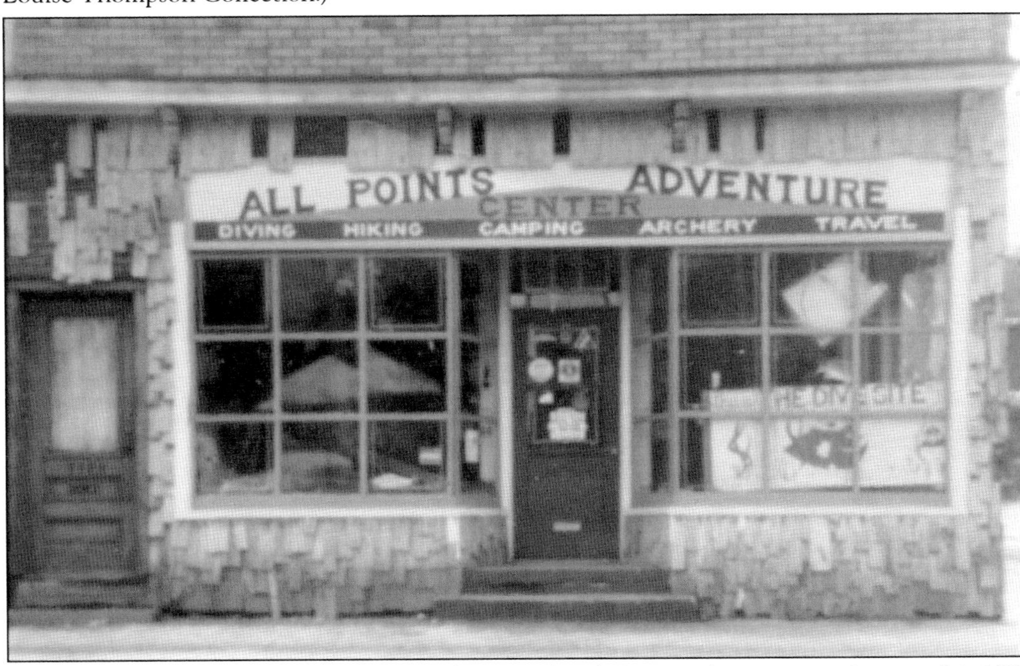

The All Points Adventure Center on Amboy Road and Yetman Avenue, seen here in this 1973 photograph, was a source for hobby and sports instruction and equipment, including scuba diving, archery, and mountain climbing. Previously, in the late 1960s, the building was home to the YWCA. Today it is a pizza parlor. (Courtesy of the Janice and June Rose Collection.)

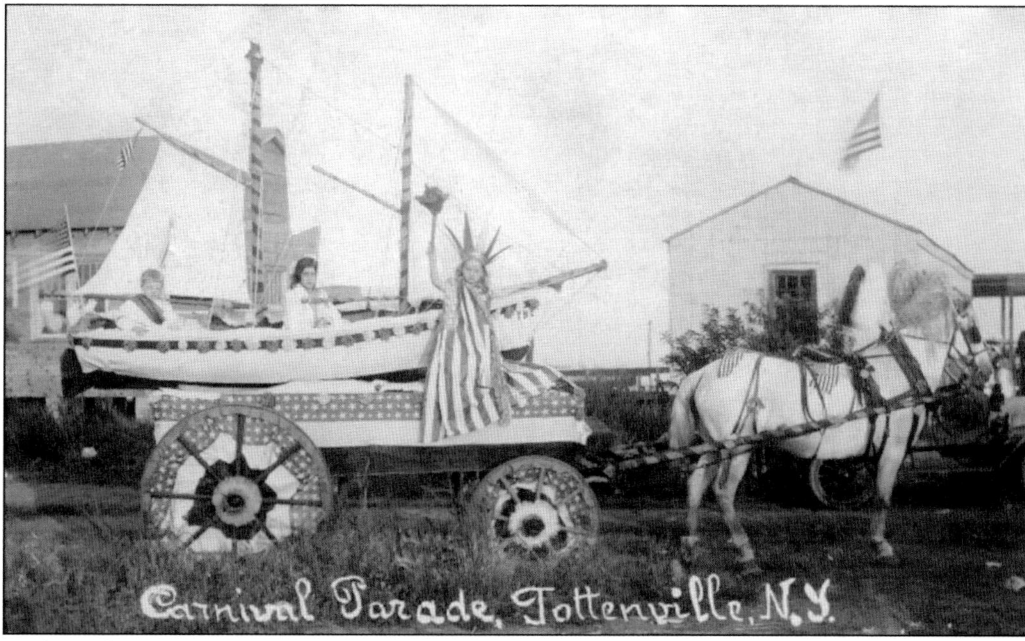

In the early 1900s, Raritan Bay Park, located south of Hylan Boulevard and extending to Raritan Bay, was a popular beach resort for city dwellers. Beginning in 1911, these summer residents organized a three-day, season-ending celebration that featured a carnival parade and swimming and boating competitions. Prizes were awarded for fanciest costumes and floats. The prize-winning float in this *c.* 1914 photograph was built and decorated by Tottenville resident Frank Schult. His son Theodore sits in the rear, and his wife, Grace, who made the costumes, is in the middle. Daughter Lillian portrays the Statue of Liberty. (Courtesy of the Anita Schult Collection.)

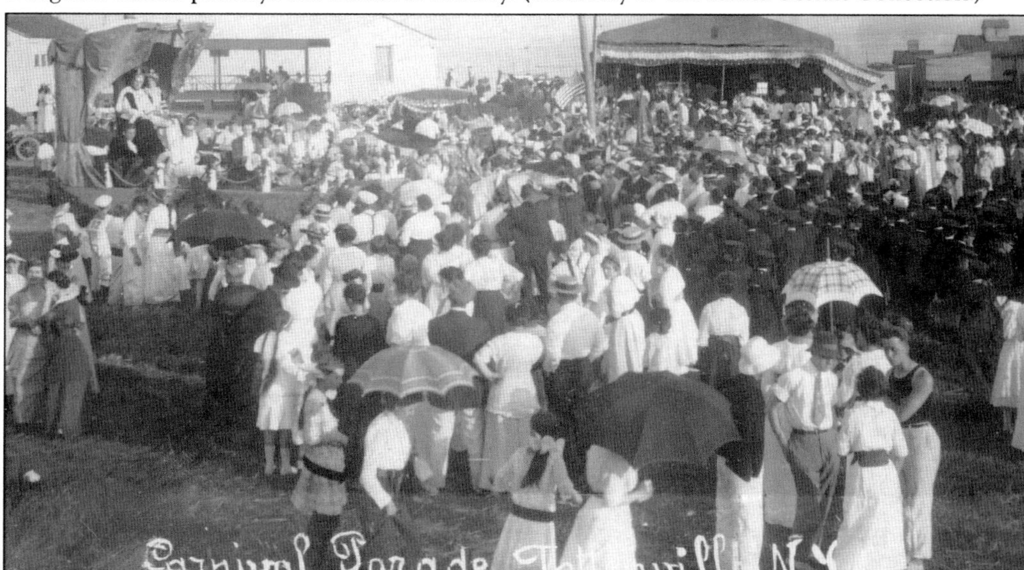

After winding through the streets of Tottenville, the carnival parade ended at the Shore House Hotel on Raritan Bay, where festivities, including the crowning of the king and queen of the carnival, were held, as shown in this 1912 postcard. The unidentified king and queen are seated on their royal throne on the far left.

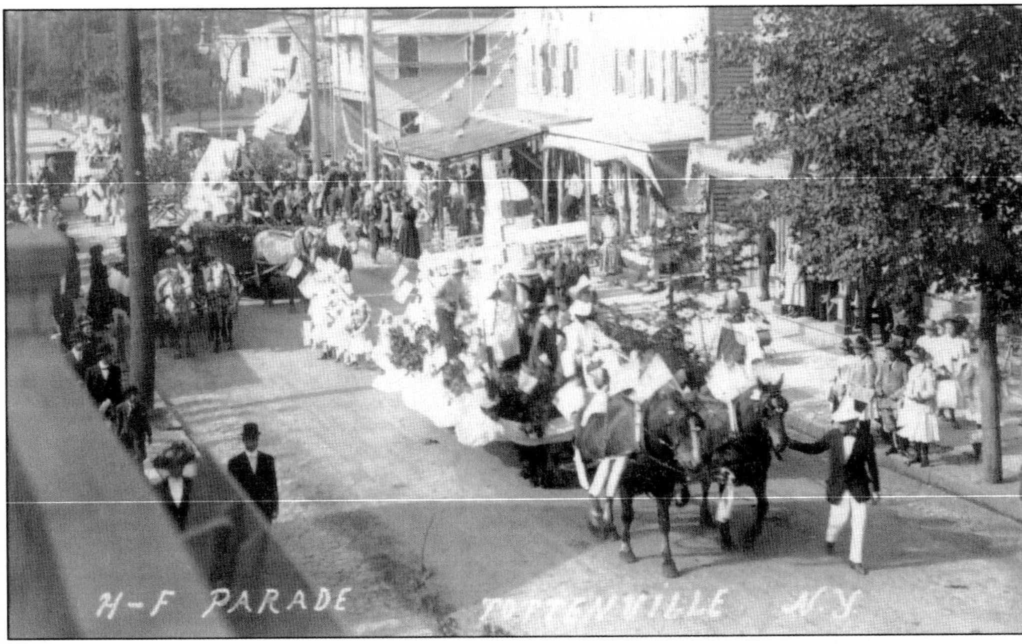

New York City's Hudson-Fulton Celebration in 1909 was an elaborate citywide commemoration of Henry Hudson's discovery of the Hudson River and Robert Fulton's first successful steamboat navigation. Dutch-themed floats travel along Main Street toward Amboy Road as part of this two-week celebration. Obscured behind the trees on the right is the South Baptist Church.

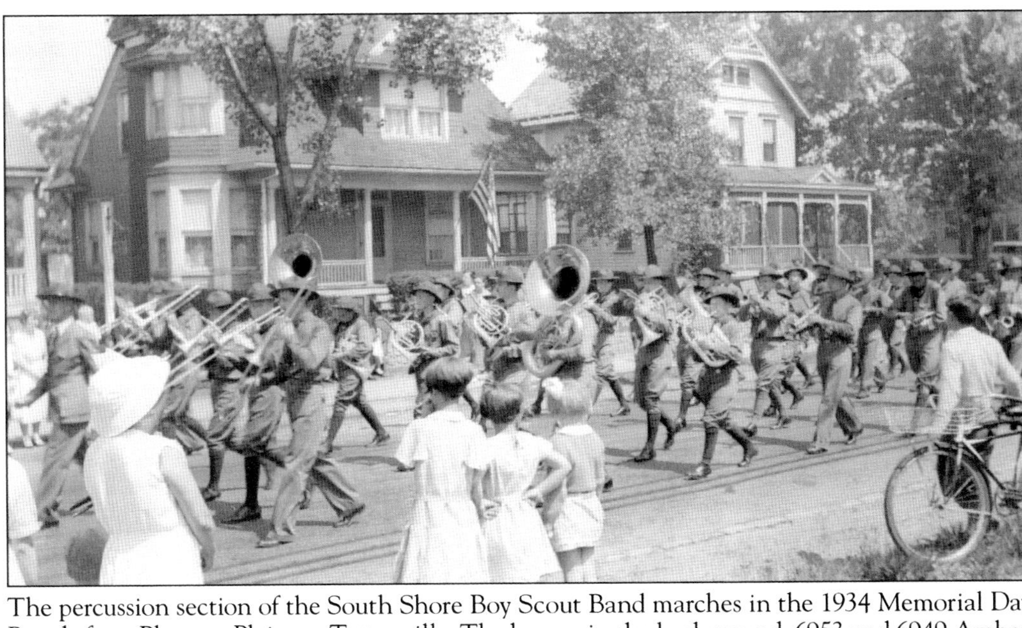

The percussion section of the South Shore Boy Scout Band marches in the 1934 Memorial Day Parade from Pleasant Plains to Tottenville. The houses in the background, 6953 and 6949 Amboy Road, located between Page Avenue and Murray Street, remain standing today. (Courtesy of the John Bieser Estate.)

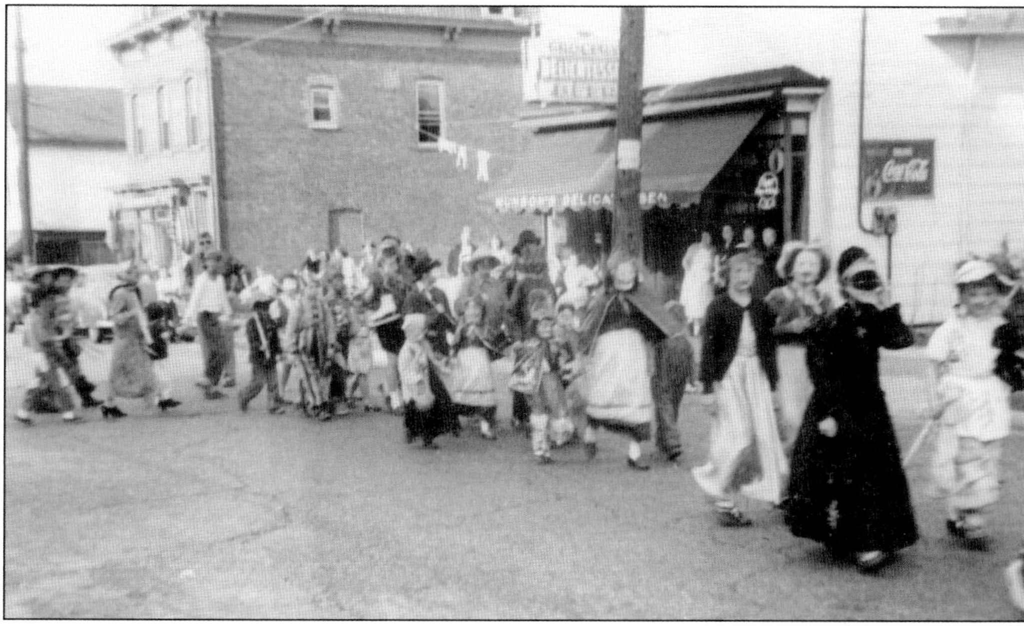

Boys and girls line up along Main Street in the third annual Halloween Ragamuffin Parade in this 1950 photograph. The event was sponsored by the Tottenville Precinct Police Athletic League . The two-story brick building in the background (left) housed Lehman's Pharmacy. The awning of the smaller store to its right reads "Bedell's Grocery." (Courtesy of the Alice Williams Collection.)

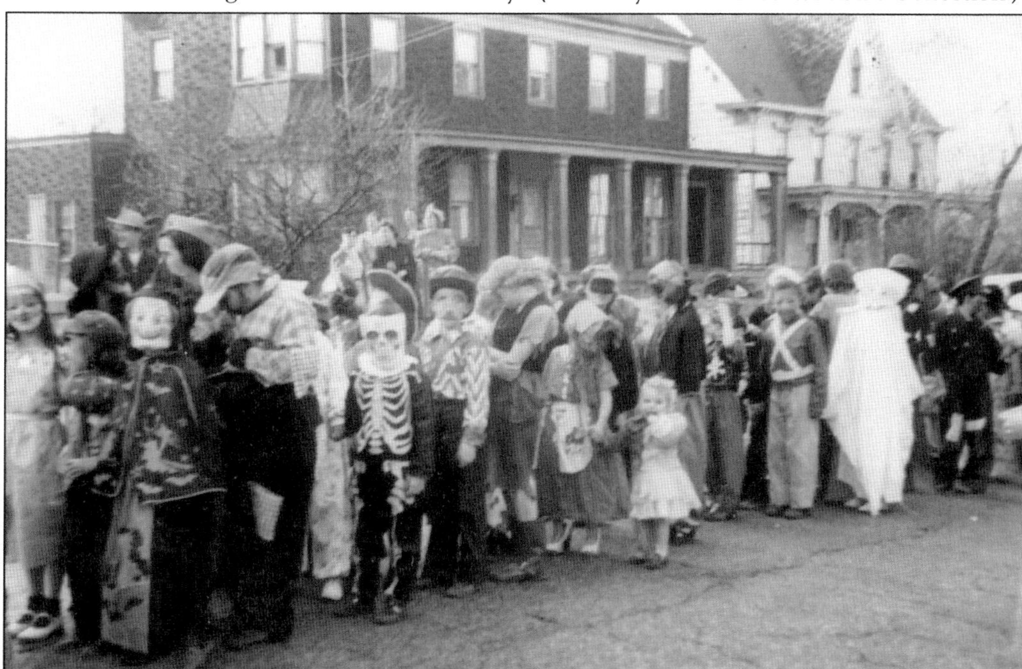

The 1950 children's Ragamuffin Parade, sponsored by the Police Athletic League, began at Arthur Kill Road and Main Street and ended at the P.A.L. Center on Joline Avenue, where prizes were awarded for most original, fanciest, funniest, and spookiest costumes. (Courtesy of the Alice Williams Collection.)

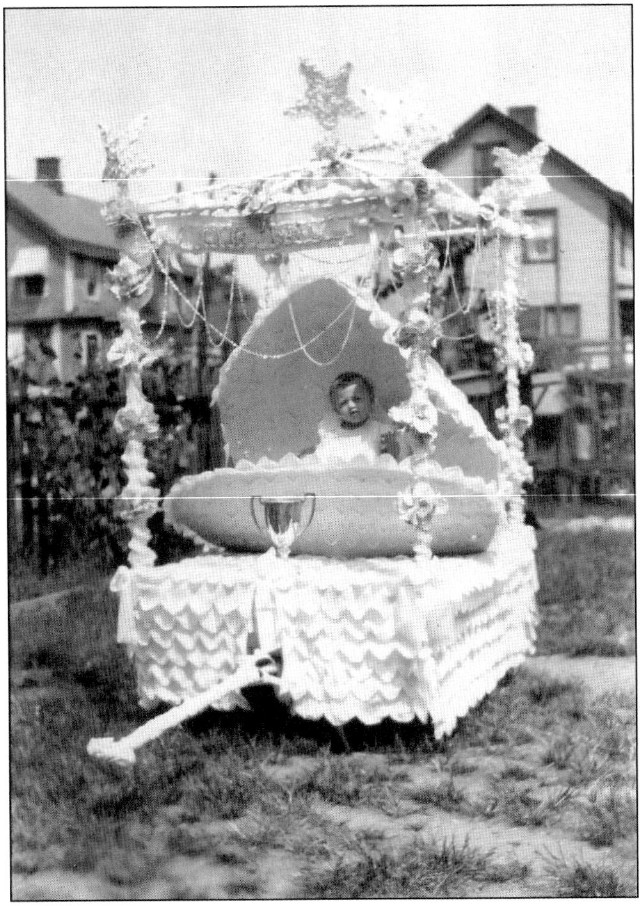

Baby parade contests were popular from the early 1900s through the late 1920s and were often a featured opening or closing event at fund-raising carnivals to benefit a local organization. Baby Marie Covell is pictured on this lavishly decorated winning float in this c. 1929 photograph with her loving cup proudly displayed. (Courtesy of the John Bieser Estate.)

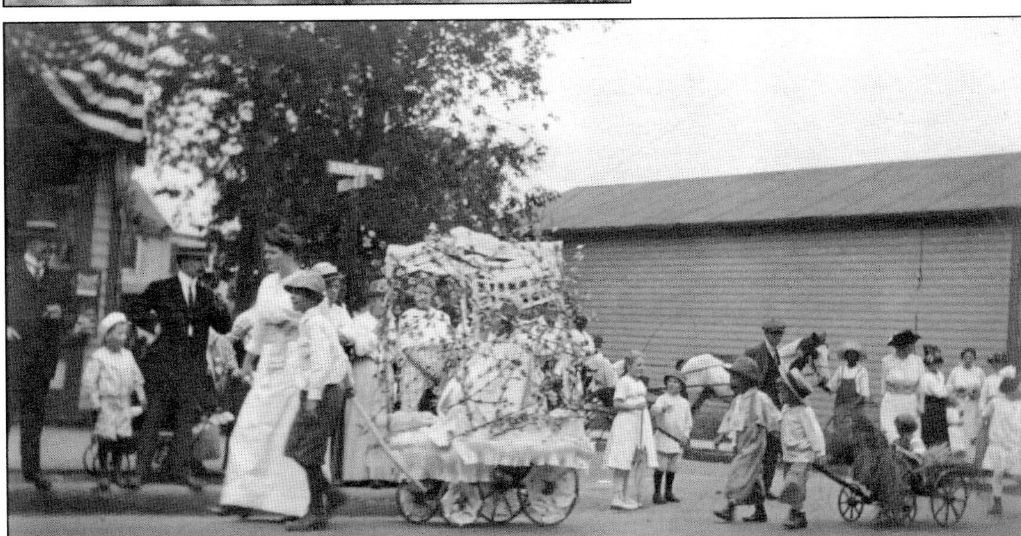

Spectators line the streets in this c. 1915 image to watch the caravan of decorated strollers and wagons go by carrying adorable children dressed to impress. (Courtesy of the John Bieser Estate.)

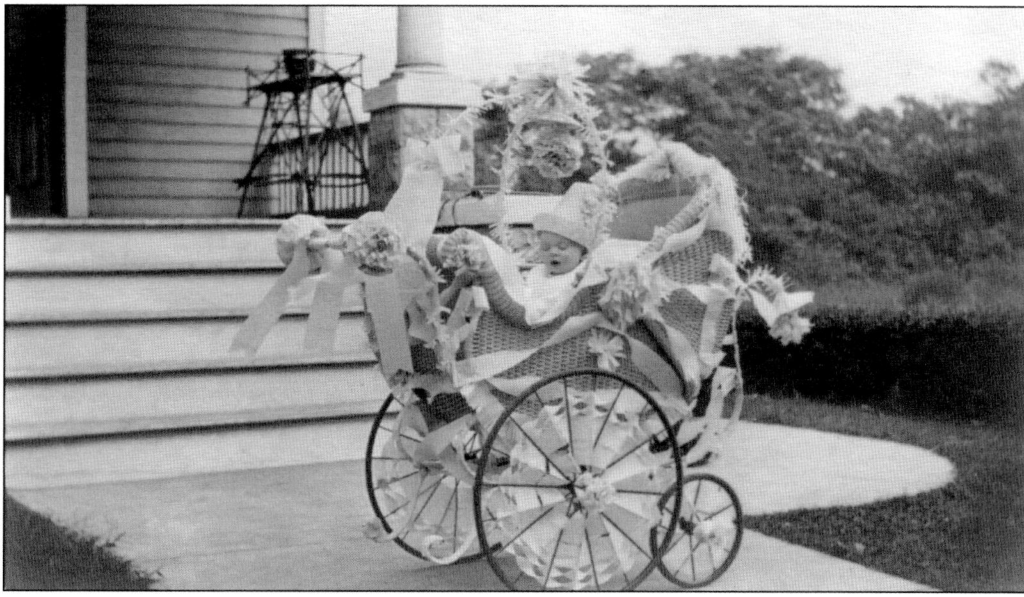

This large-wheeled, high-sided pram was surely a prize-winning entry in the baby parade contest. This *c.* 1915 photograph was taken at 353 Sleight Avenue. (Courtesy of the John Bieser Estate.)

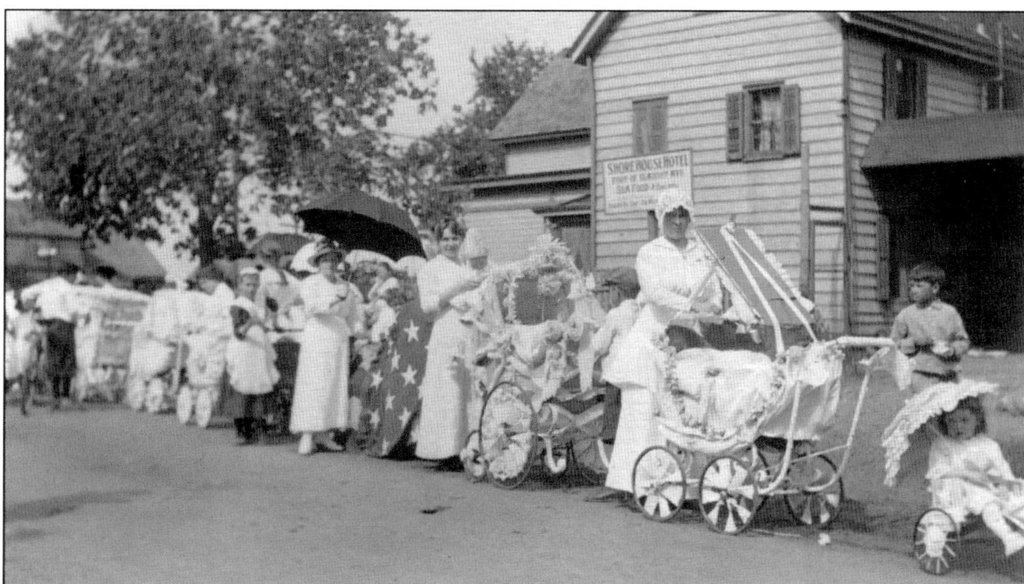

Women dressed in fancy costumes and children riding in gaily decorated baby carriages line up for the baby parade in this 1915 photograph. The sign in the background advertises the Shore House Hotel, where "Seafood [is] A Specialty." (Courtesy of the John Bieser Estate.)

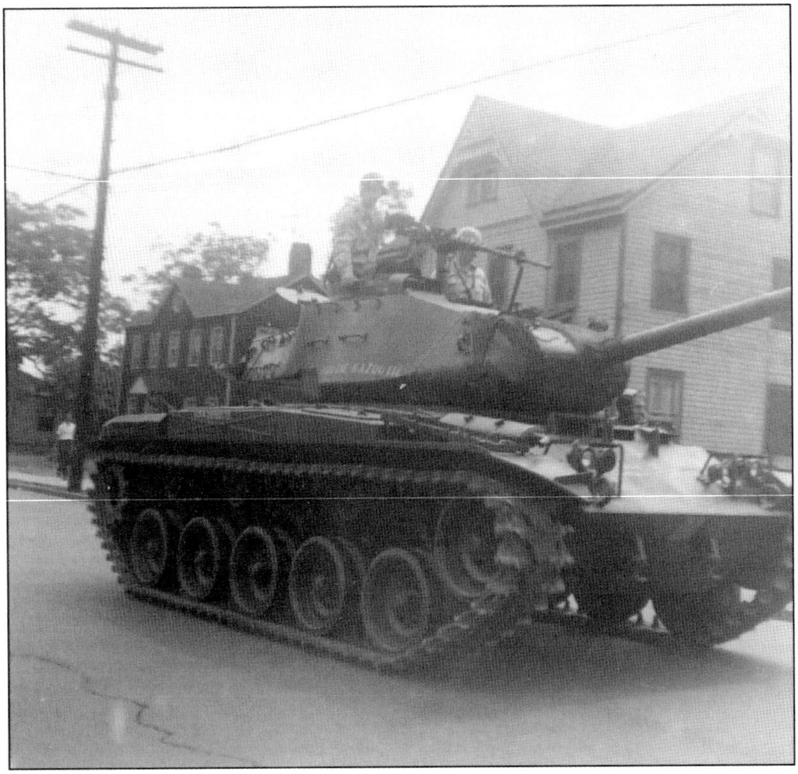

Pictured in this 1957 photograph is one of the highlights of the Memorial Day parade—a military tank. When the ground began to vibrate and a low rumbling noise grew louder and louder, spectators knew the tank was approaching. (Courtesy of Jane Schaaff Cole.)

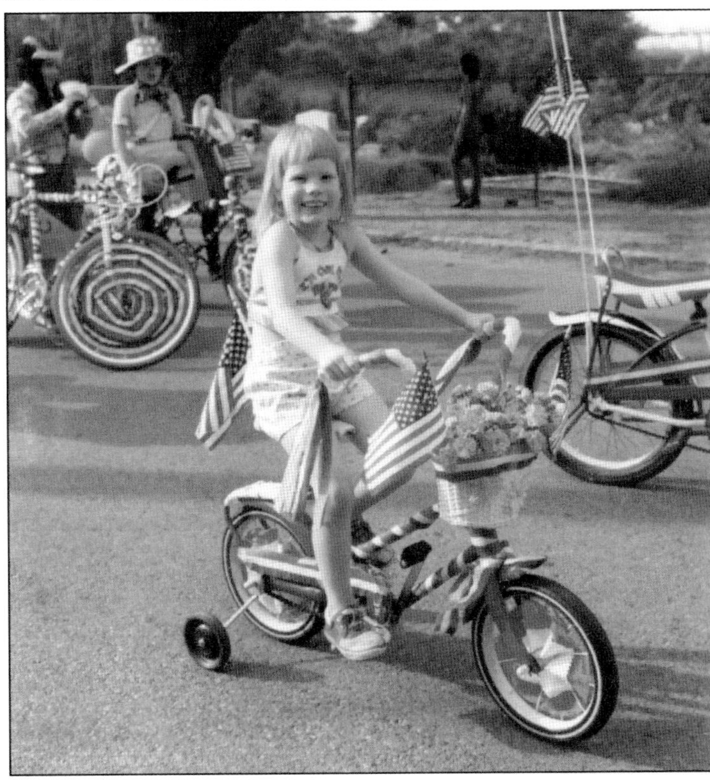

The South Shore Flag Day Parade Association was formed in 1939 for the purpose of "renewing loyalty and affection for the stars and stripes." Edward Clinchy was the first honorary president, and Harry Ekstrand was the first honorary grand marshal. The parade formed on Page Avenue and marched along Amboy Road to the end of Hylan Boulevard, where an awards ceremony for the best decorated float, bicycle, and marching group was held. The grand prize was an American flag. Suzanne Schaming is all smiles as she joins other parade bicyclists in this 1981 photograph. (Courtesy of the Schaming family.)

Three

SCHOOL DAYS

The P.S. 1 Colonial Marching Band was formed in 1972 by teacher Frank DeJulio, seen here leading the band during one of its many parade appearances. "Mr. D" got the inspiration for the band while teaching third graders to play the song flute. Later, xylophones and drums were added to the flute band. DeJulio began his teaching career at P.S. 1 in 1962 and retired from teaching there after more than 35 years. (Courtesy of the Frank DeJulio Collection.)

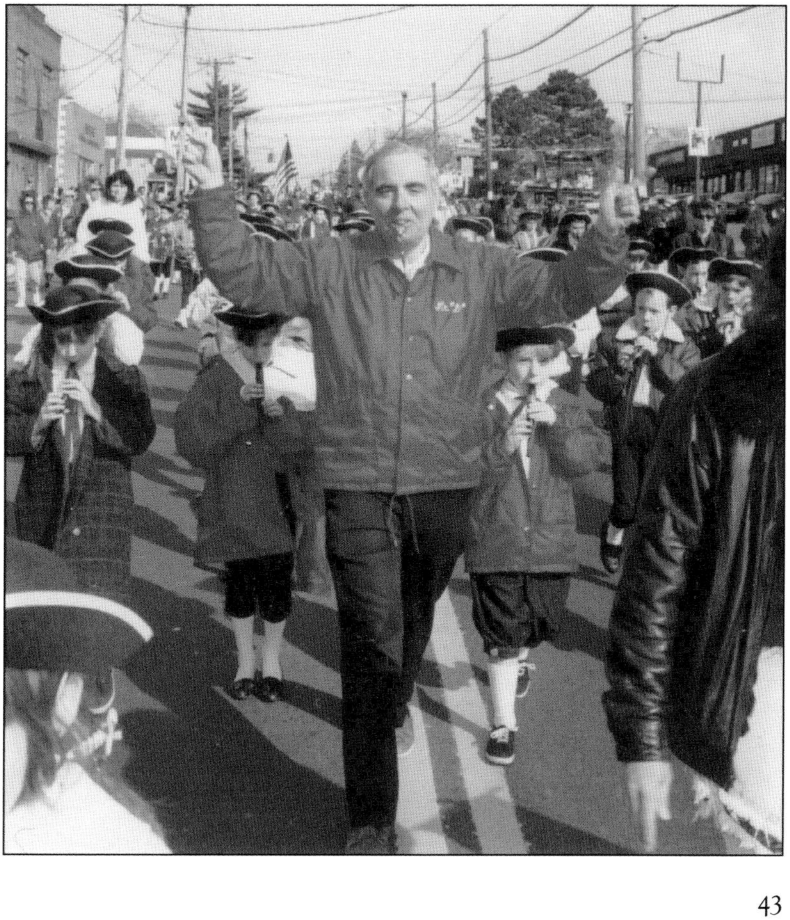

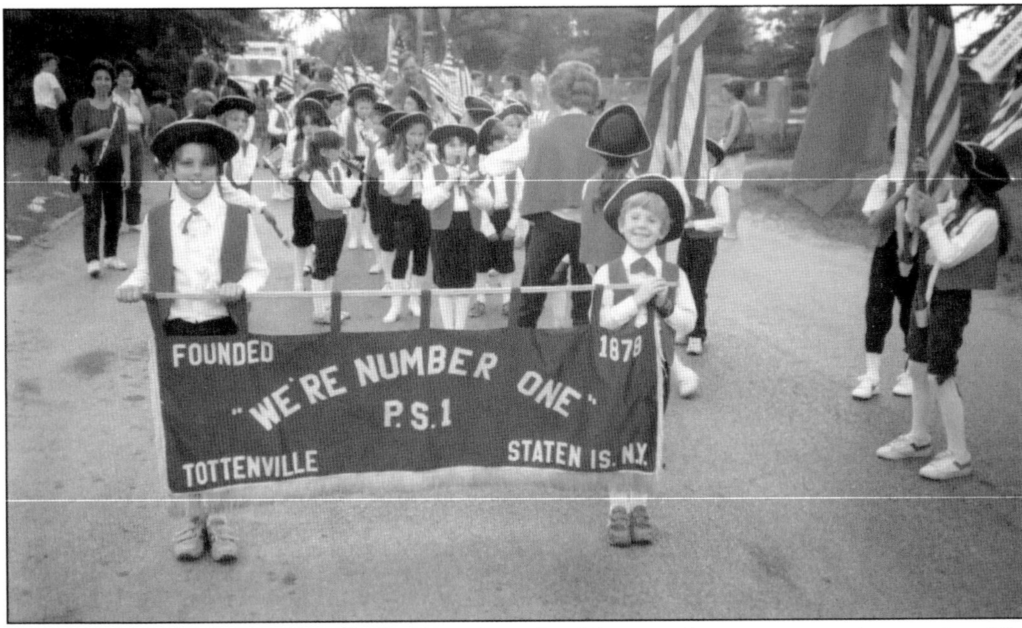

John W. Leary III (right) proudly displays the school banner during pre-parade practice. The marching band's colonial theme was inspired by the Conference House, a local historic landmark. Costumes were made by parent-volunteers. (Courtesy of the Leary family.)

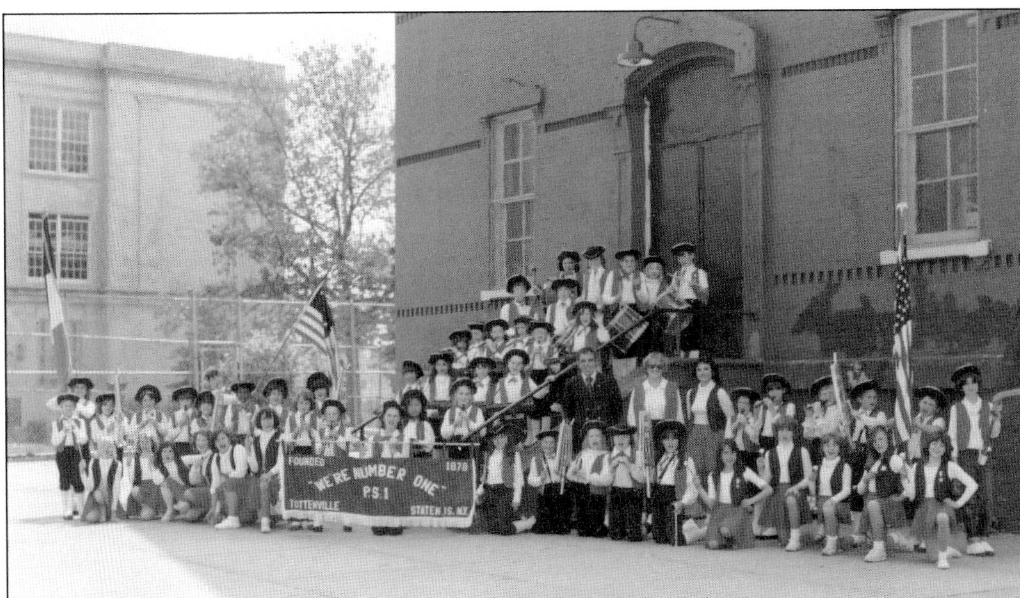

The P.S. 1 Colonial Marching Band poses for a group portrait on the steps of the P.S. 1 Annex, originally named Bay View Academy. A New York City designated landmark, the former academy was built in 1878 and is the oldest building still in use in the New York City public school system. Band director Frank DeJulio is in the center. (Courtesy of the Frank DeJulio Collection.)

Members of the P.S. 1 glee club perform in the school auditorium during the 1966 winter concert. The choral group was organized as part of the after-school program which provided indoor and outdoor activities for boys and girls throughout the year. Pictured are, from left to right, (first row) Deborah Dahlstrom, Joan Carstensen, and unidentified; (second row) JoAnne Lucas, Lori Harper, Brenda Degon, unidentified, and Jill Sweetman; (third row) Susan Tufte, Linda Cutler, and Carol Harris. (Courtesy of Linda Cutler Hauck.)

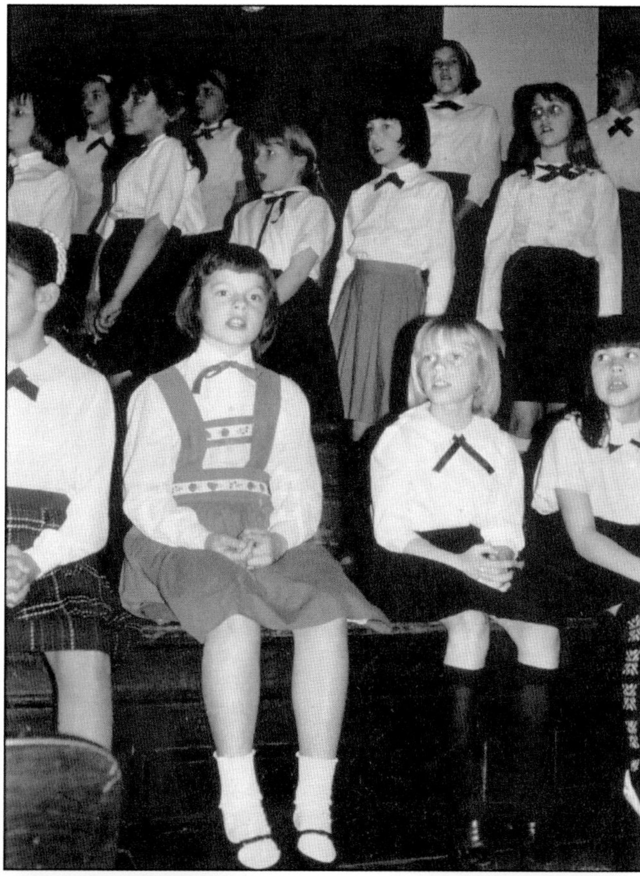

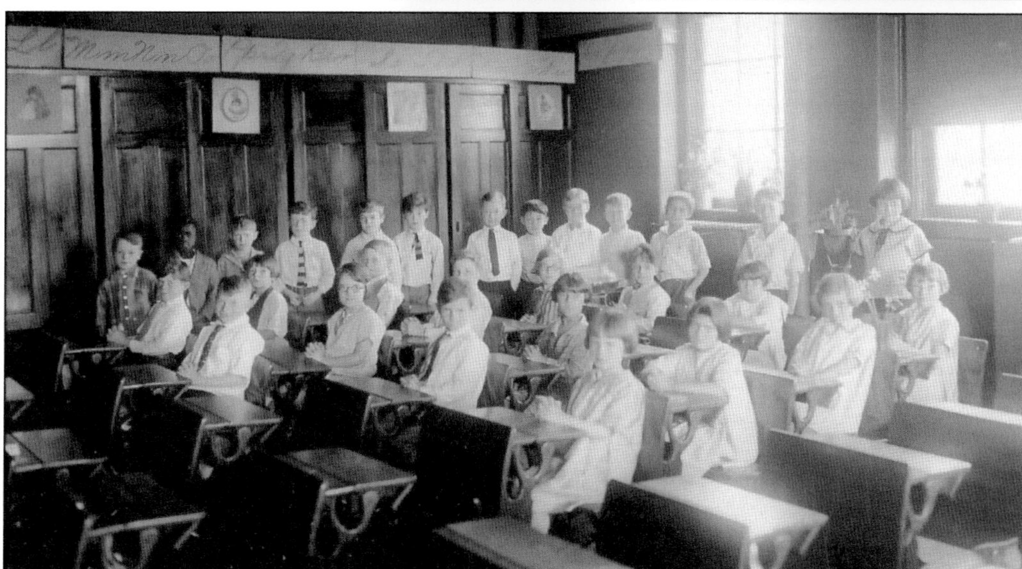

The desks, closets, and tall windows in this 1928 classroom would be familiar to those who attended P.S. 1 even in the 1950s. Edwin R. Peterson is standing in the back row center with his hands in his pockets and wearing a dark tie. (Courtesy of Ingrid Peterson.)

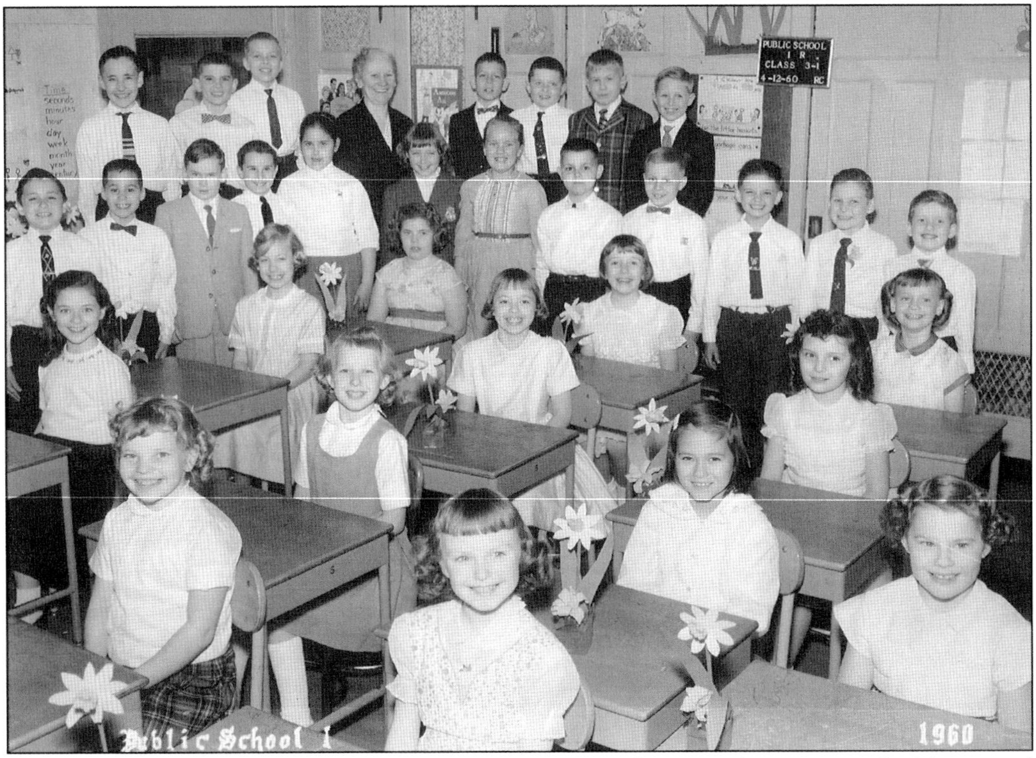

A major modernization of P.S. 1 began in the late 1950s. In this 1960 classroom are freshly painted walls and woodwork and freestanding desks that are no longer bolted to the floor. Greg Rössel, standing in the back row and wearing a plaid jacket, is among the students in Katherine Blette's third-grade class. (Courtesy of C. Greg and Carol-Lynn Rössel.)

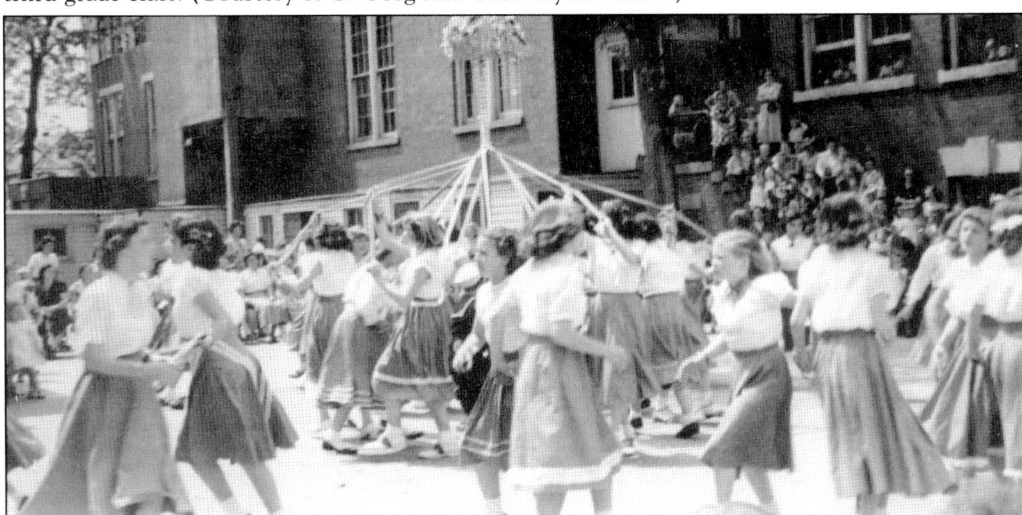

The traditional maypole dance, celebrating the first day of May, was incorporated into the spring elementary school program during the 1950s. The girls dance around the pole holding colorful streamers, winding and braiding them as they circle the pole. The dance was choreographed to music and practiced to perfection. This photograph was taken in the Yetman Avenue courtyard in 1950. (Courtesy of the Alice Williams Collection.)

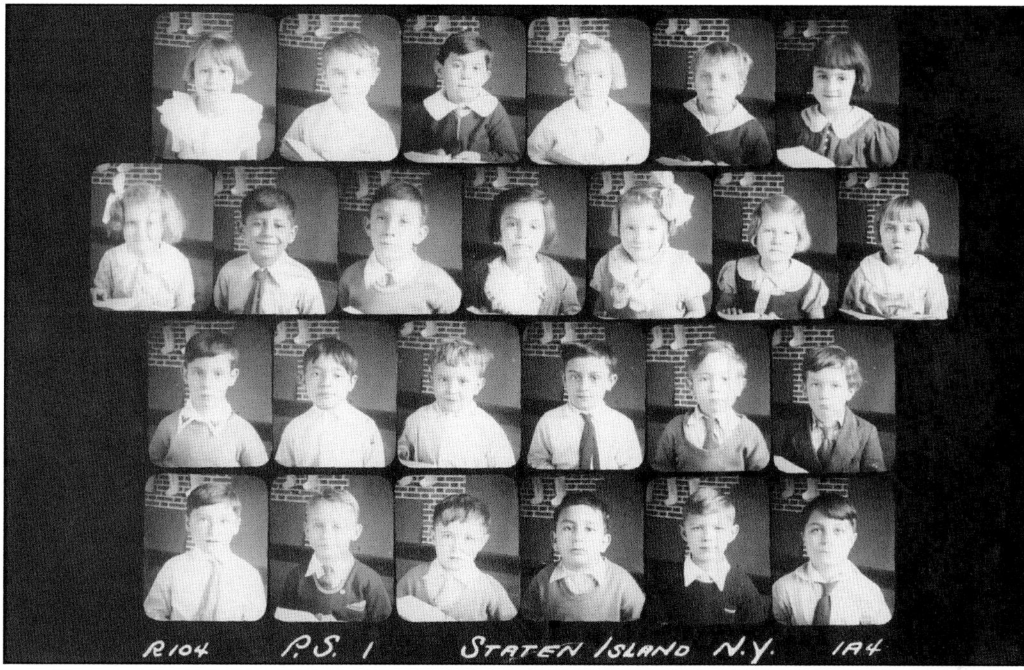

Pictured in the second row from the top are first-graders Jean Hawke (far left) and Alva E. Schulz (fourth from the left). A lifelong Tottenville resident, Alva taught at P.S. 1 for more than 32 years. In 1982, she became the first recipient of the Teacher of the Year Award presented by the Staten Island Continuum of Education in recognition of her devoted and outstanding service to school and community. (Courtesy of the Alva E. Schulz Collection.)

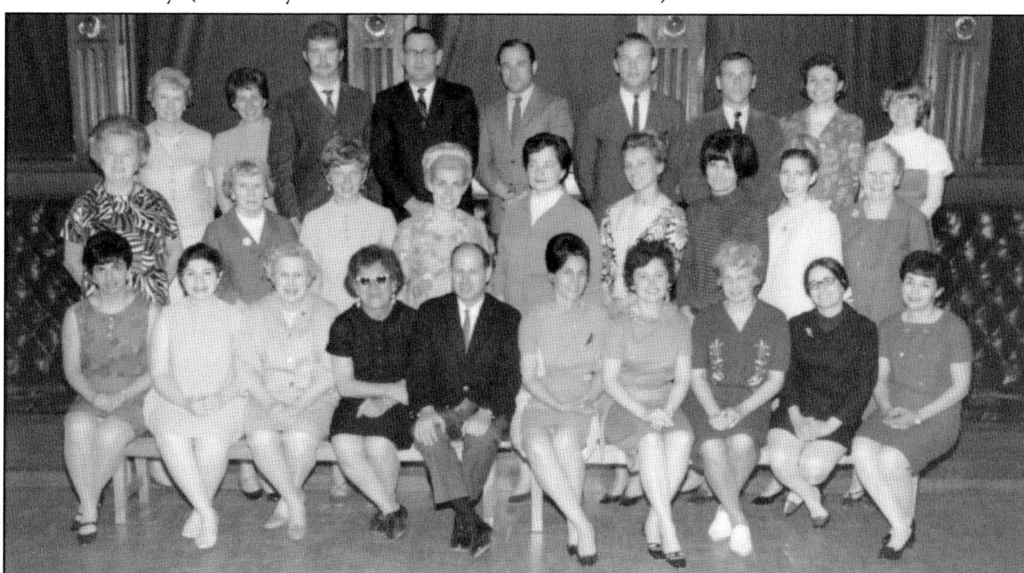

The faculty of P.S. 1 poses in this 1960s photograph. They are, from left to right, (first row) two unidentified, Elvira Cunningham, Mattie Adler, Robert Burger (principal), Dorothy Dunkle, Alva E. Schulz, Anne Ogilvie, and two unidentified; (second row) Loretta Lewis, Ethel Paugh, Caroline Morgan, unidentified, Elleneva Weening, unidentified, Gerry LaBuzza, unidentified, and Katherine Blette; (third row) Mary McGeehan, Anna May Guinn, and seven unidentified.

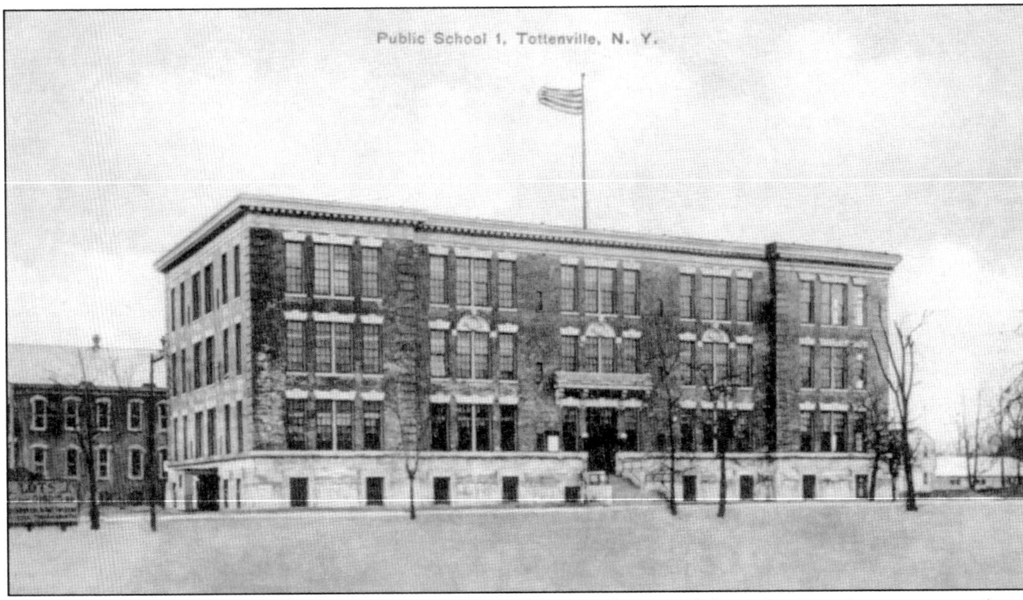

With flourishing industries and a growing population, the need for a larger elementary school was realized by 1900. A three-story brick building, designed by prolific architect Charles B. J. Snyder (1860–1945) and trimmed with locally made terra-cotta, was completed in 1906. P.S. 1 had 27 classrooms for grades kindergarten through eight. A glimpse of the earlier school, Bay View Academy (back left), is visible in this 1909 postcard.

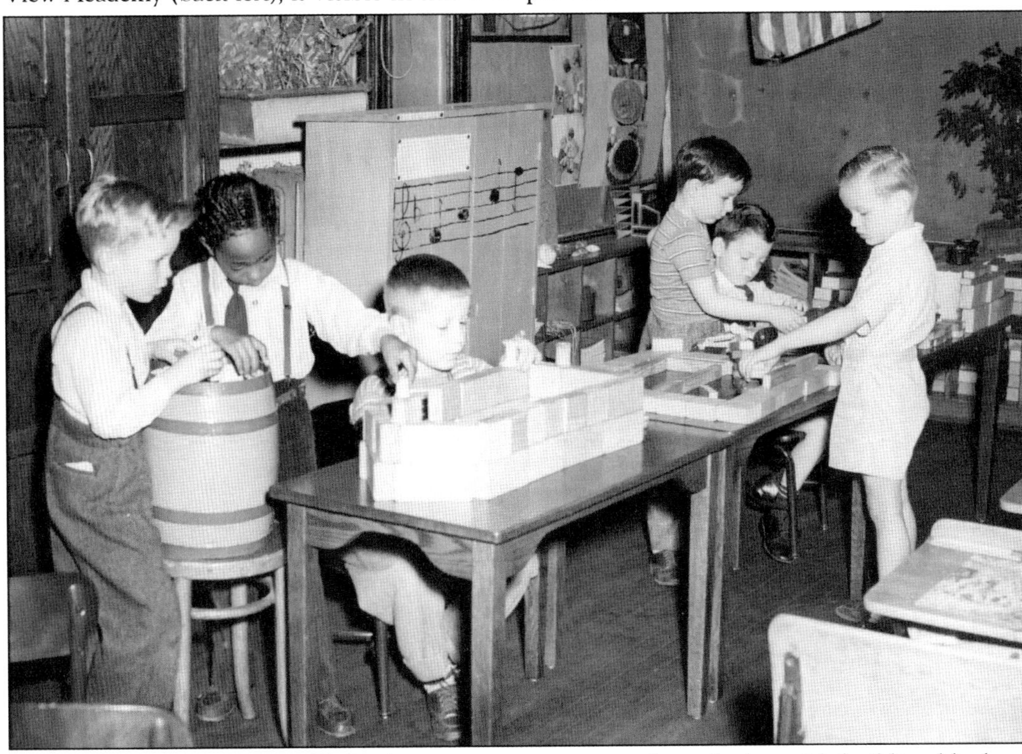

Today first graders are more likely playing computer games than playing with building blocks as the children in this 1947 photograph are doing.

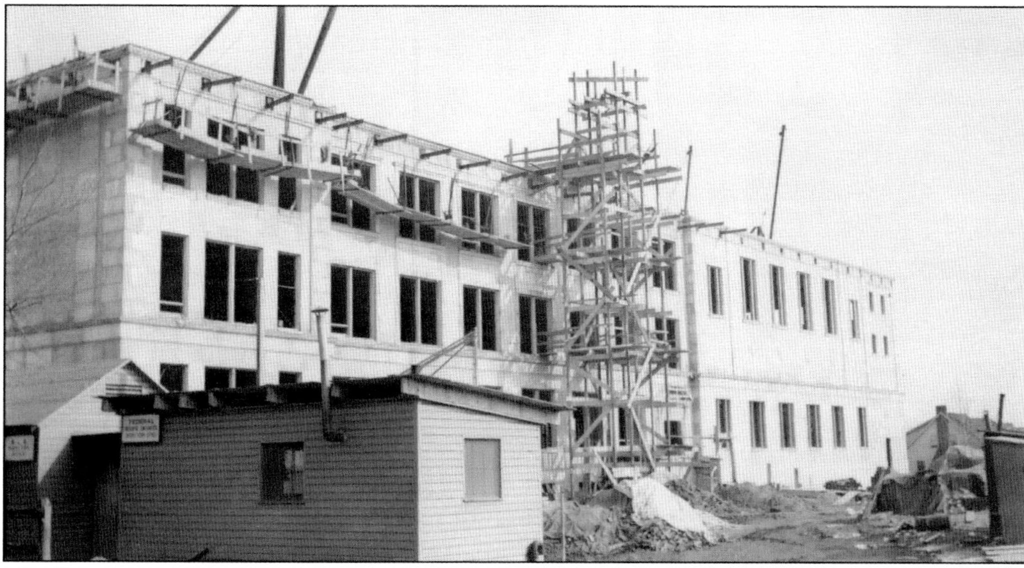

The Beauvais American Legion Post and Auxiliary were instrumental in securing a site for a new high school, and after an 11-year battle, construction finally began in 1935. Tottenville High School was dedicated on May 30, 1936. (Courtesy of the John Bieser Estate.)

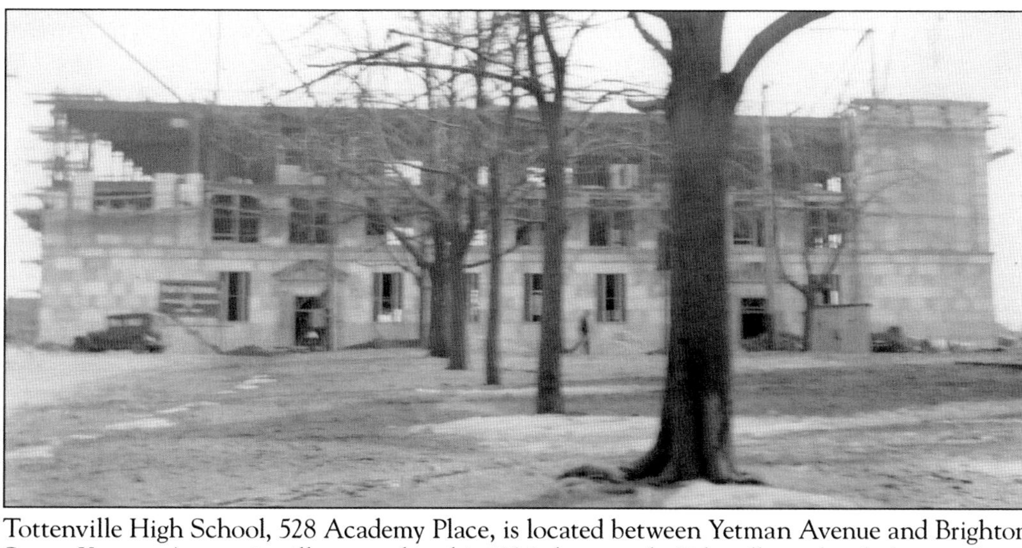

Tottenville High School, 528 Academy Place, is located between Yetman Avenue and Brighton Street. Yetman Avenue is still unpaved in this 1936 photograph. Sidewalks and curbs later replaced the row of trees. (Courtesy of the John Bieser Estate.)

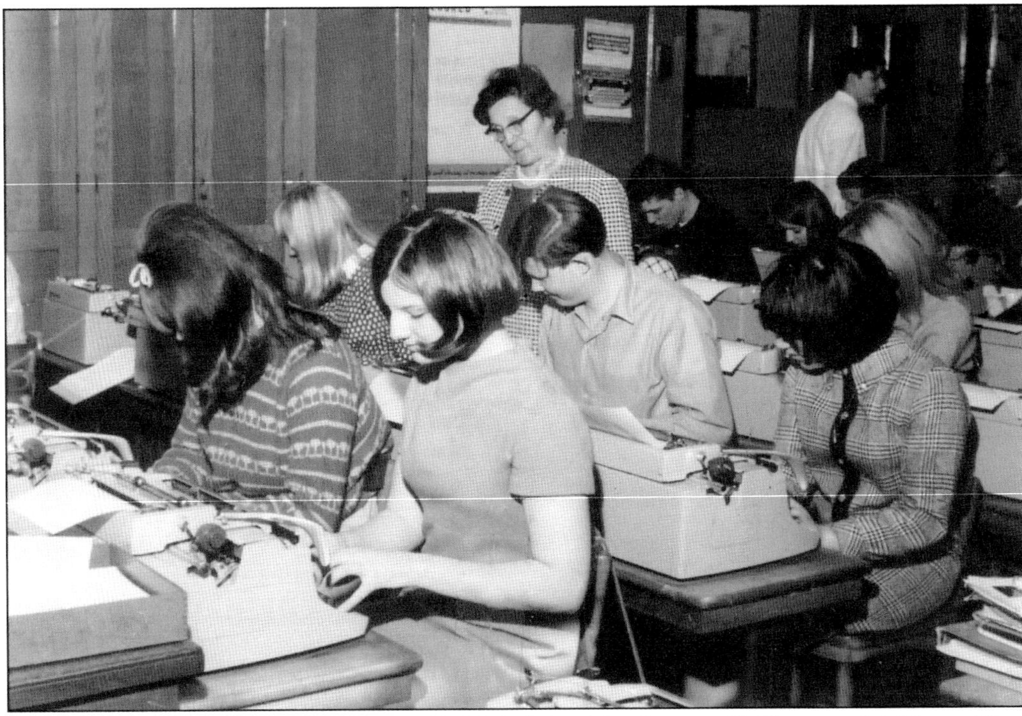

Throughout its 100-year history, Tottenville High School has been staffed by many highly qualified, dedicated teachers. Among them was Gene B. Drill (1908–2008), a teacher of business studies at the school for 40 years. She started the first future teachers club, headed the Commercial Club for students, and served as acting head of the business department. (Courtesy of the Gene B. Drill Collection.)

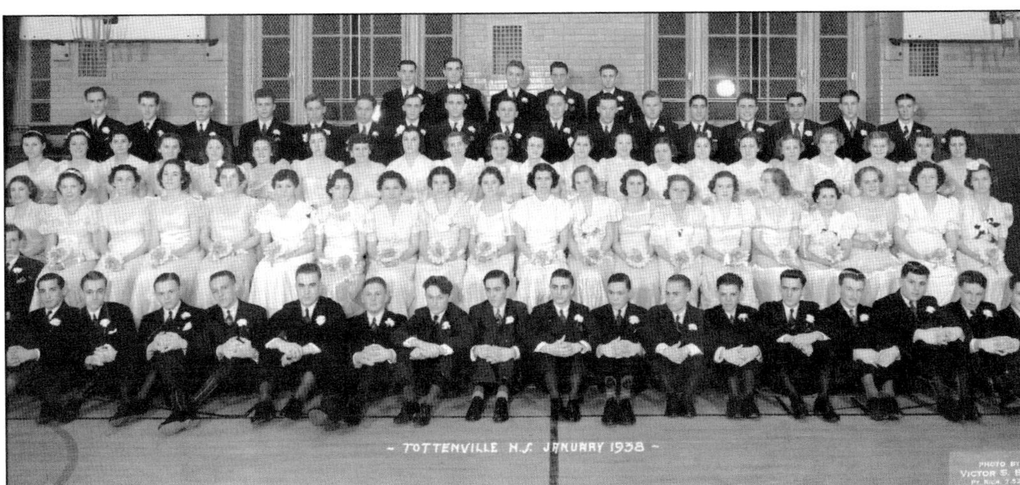

This January 1938 photograph of the graduating class of the new Tottenville High School was taken in the school's gymnasium. Norma Grodzinsky is seated in the second row, far left. Dorothy Schaaff is standing in the third row, sixth from the left. (Courtesy of Jane Schaaff Cole.)

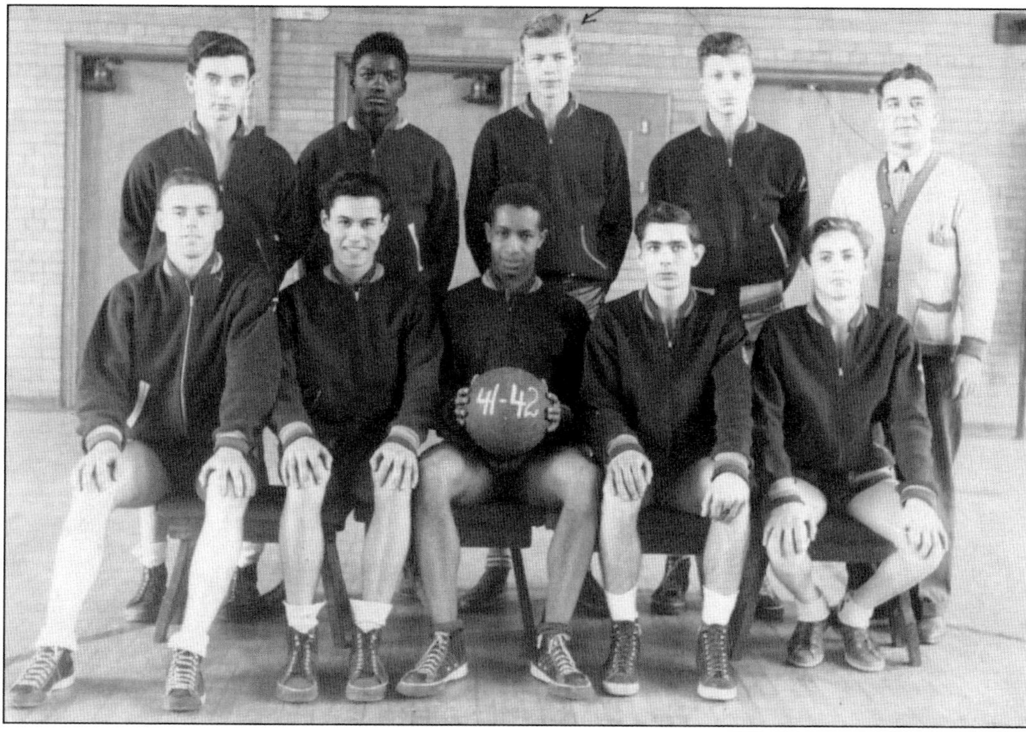

Since its earliest days, Tottenville High School has had a proven track record of excellence in competitive high school sports. Walter Stolzenthaler began his career as a boys' physical education teacher and soon began coaching the baseball and basketball teams. Members of the 1941–1942 basketball team include Frederick Cutler, John Kutko, "Jesse" Owens, Julie Bowers, Daryl Smith, and William Wilson. Coach Stolzenthaler is standing in the back row, far right. Stolzenthaler retired as dean in 1966 after serving the school for more than 25 years. (Courtesy of the Cutler family.)

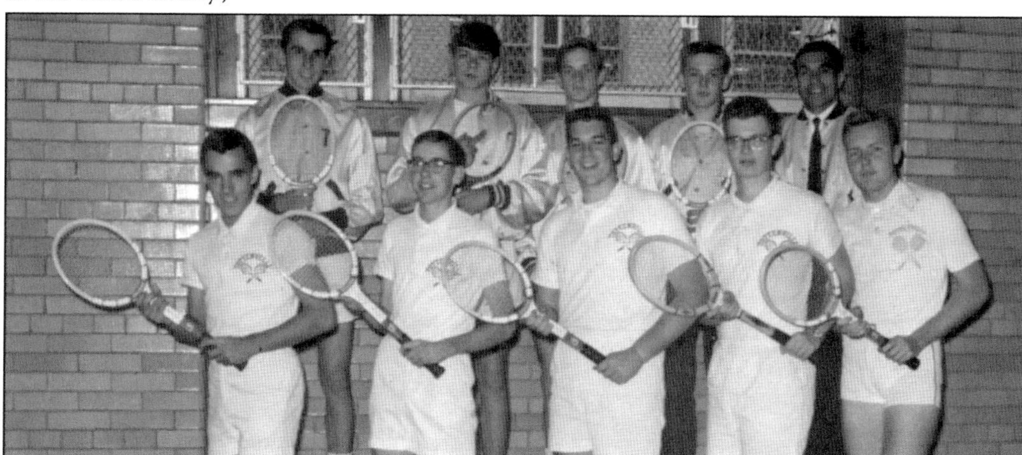

Under the leadership of Leo Katz, the Tottenville High School tennis team won several island and city championships and made the school name legendary in New York City tennis. This photograph of the 1966–1967 team includes, from left to right, (first row) Wayne Cutler, Rich Wilburn, Russ Kiefer, Ken Dangman, and Dave Johnson; (second row) Dave Birchard, Mike Reilly, Steve Bang, Dave Boardman, and coach Leo Katz. (Courtesy of the Schaming family.)

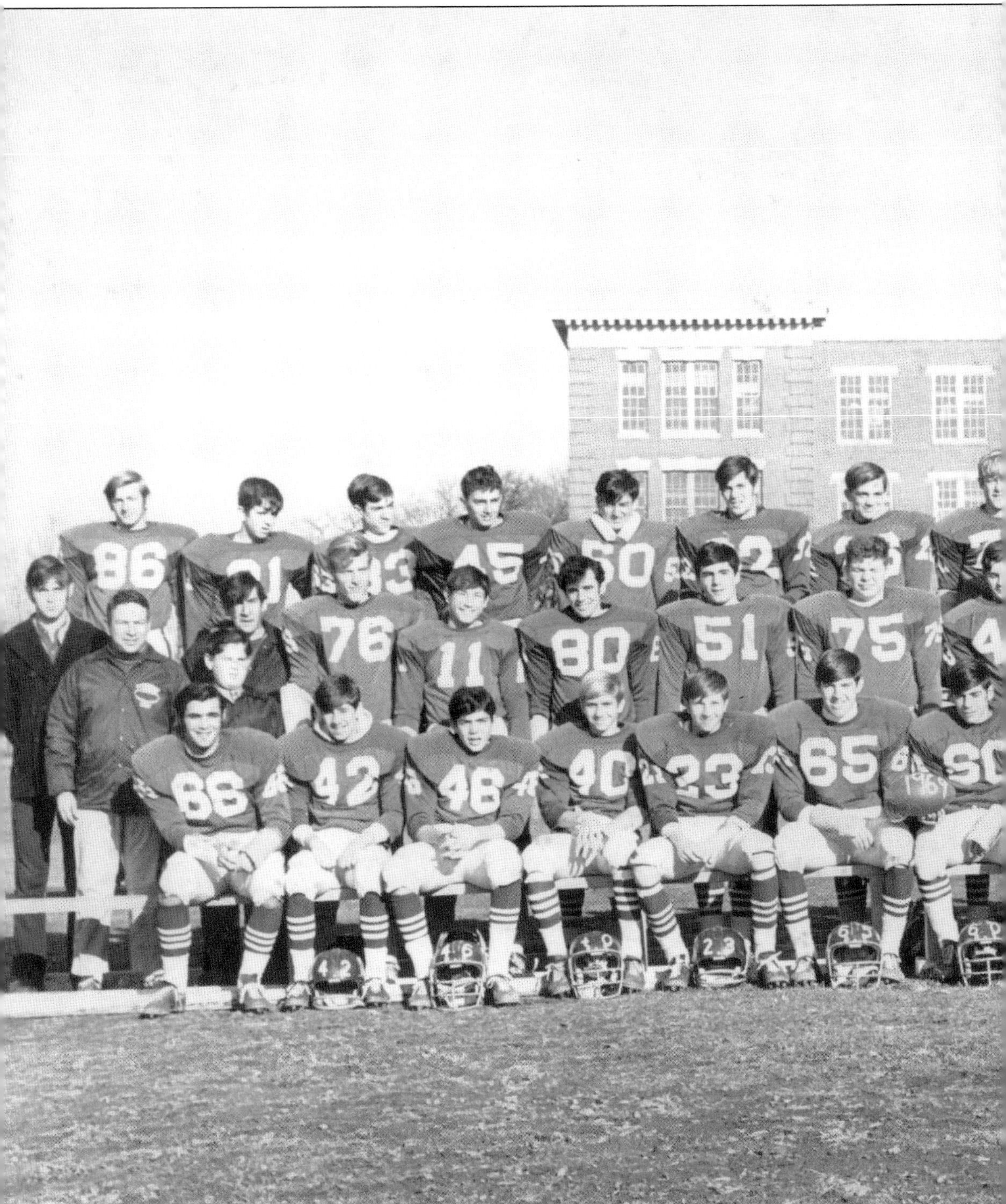

It was not until 1969 that a high school football team from Tottenville played on the gridiron. Coach Marty Spielman, assistant coach Tom Tierney, the Fathers Club, and countless faculty, students, and parents can be credited with making the dream a reality. The team's first game,

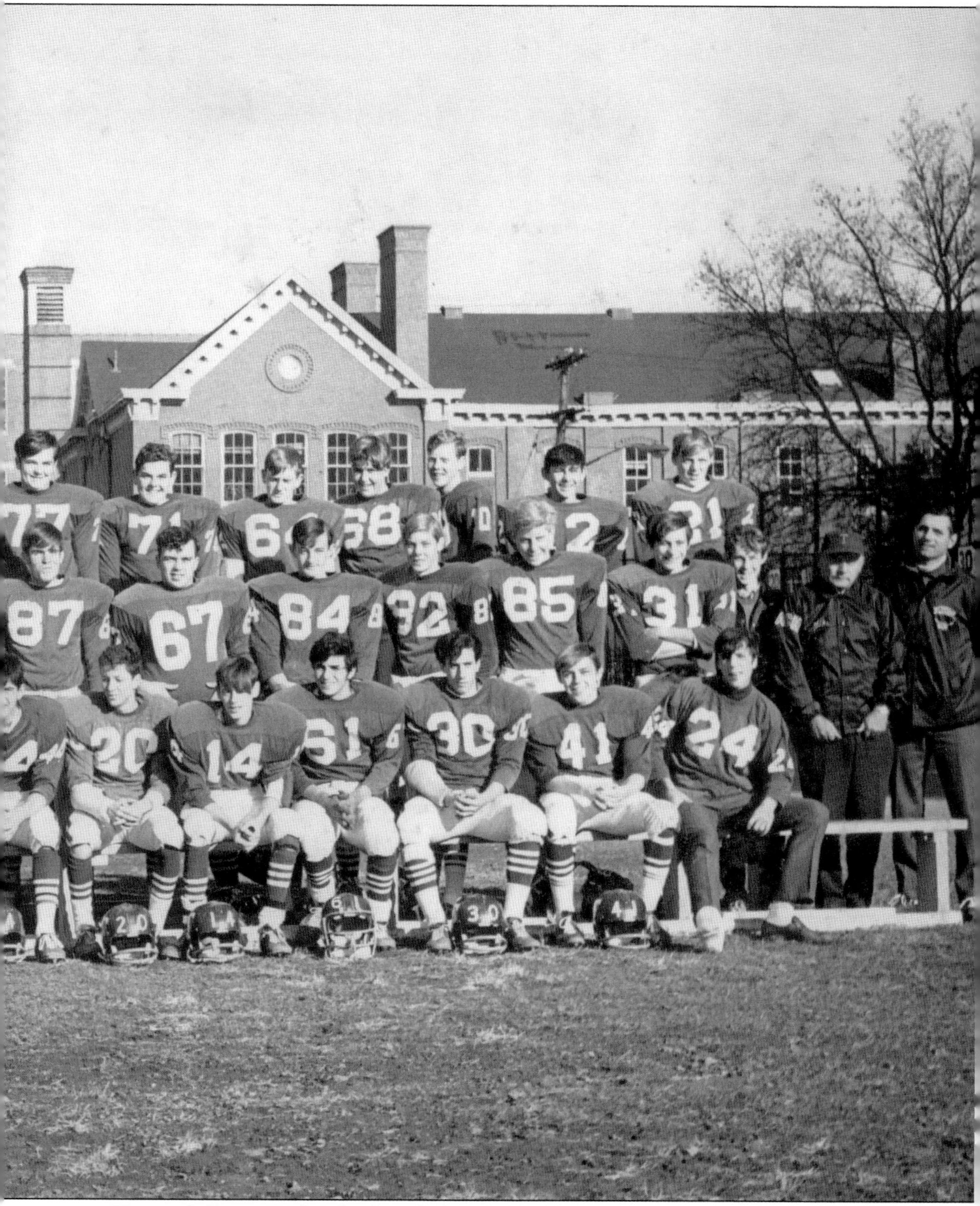

against Thomas Jefferson High School, took place on the home field on October 4, 1969, and the home team proved victorious. (Courtesy of the family of Robert C. Eysel Sr.)

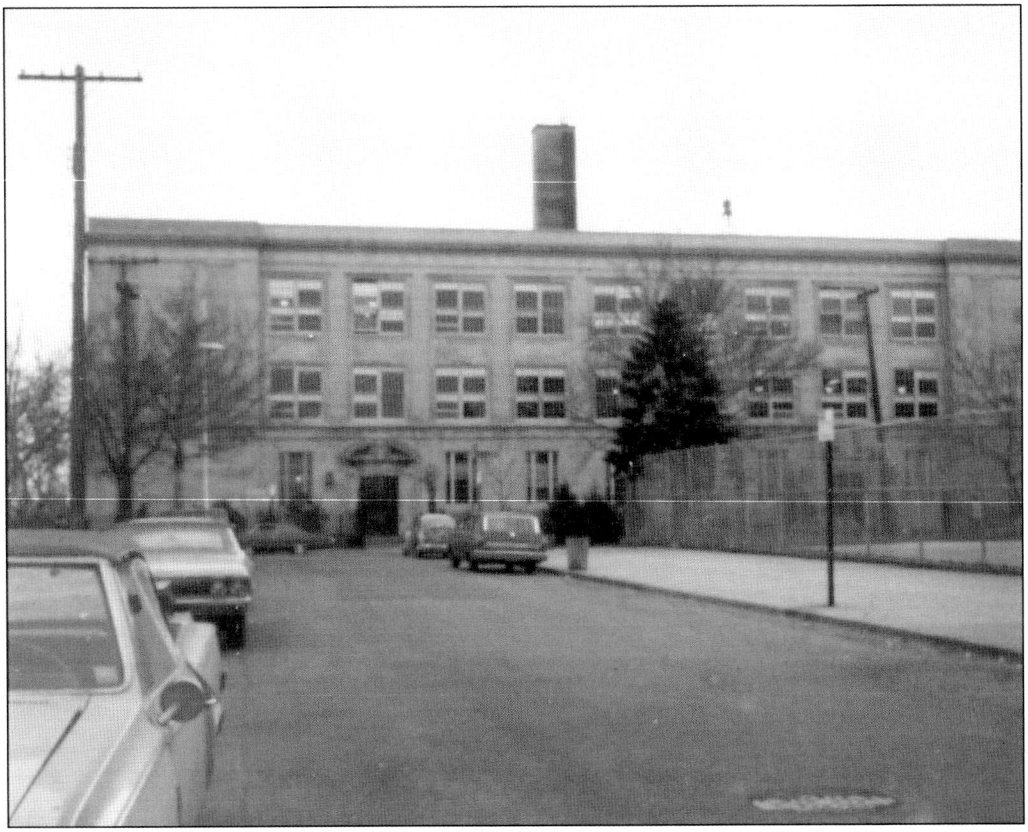

This photograph was taken in 1973 during the building's transition from high school to intermediate school. Number 528 Academy Place became Totten Intermediate School 34 when Tottenville High School moved to its new, larger quarters 3.8 miles away in Huguenot. (Photograph by Francis X. Schweikert.)

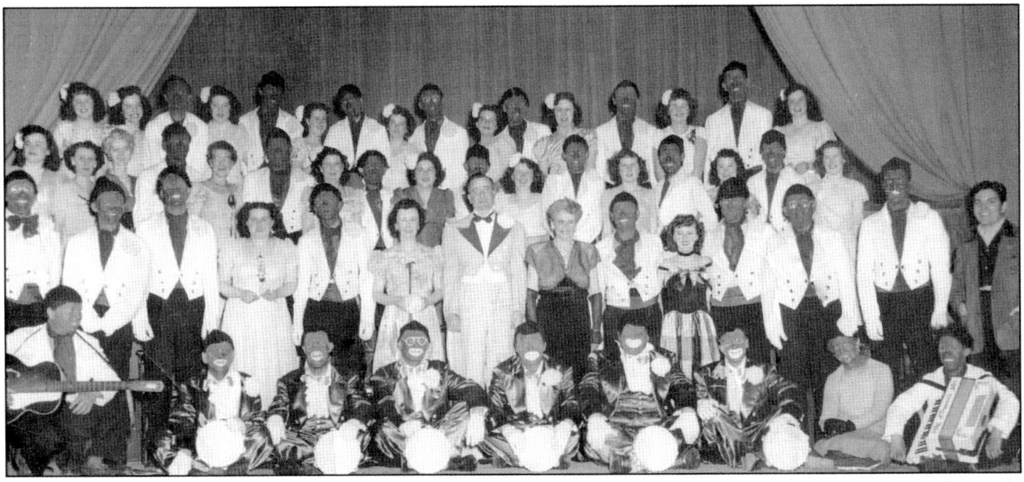

The blackface minstrel act was a popular form of entertainment from the 19th century through the mid-20th century and included comedy skits, dancing, and music. These performers pose for a group portrait after the show on the Tottenville High School stage. (Courtesy of the Margaret Wilson Collection.)

The first community preschool was started at Bethel United Methodist Church in 1974. Teacher Bonnie Grimes DiMauro, known as "Miss Bonnie," is pictured with some of the children in this late 1970s photograph. (Courtesy of B. DiMauro.)

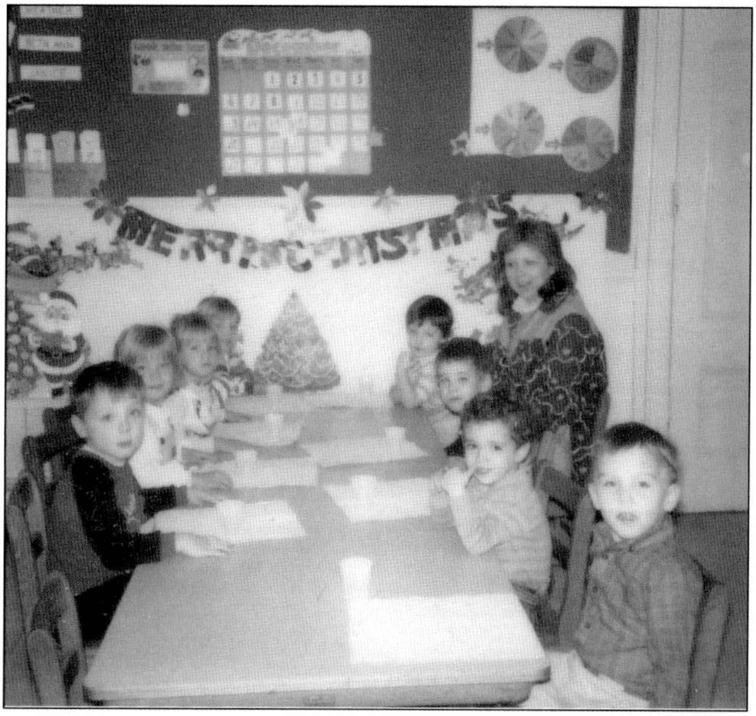

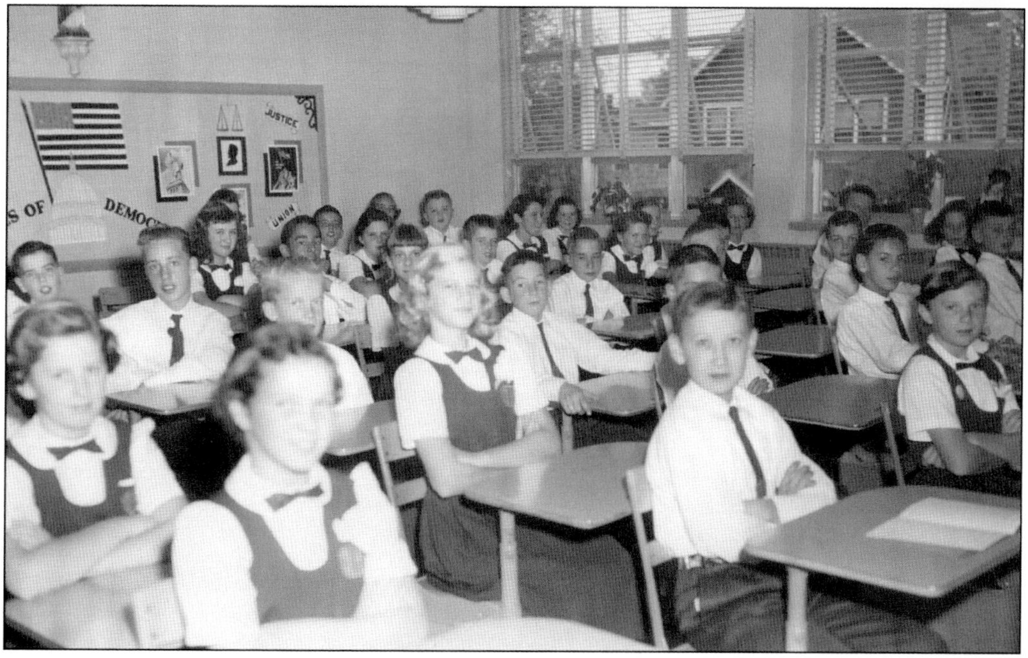

Catholic education in Tottenville began in a convent chapel at 222 Main Street in 1904. In 1910, a parochial school was opened on Yetman Avenue behind Our Lady Help of Christians (O.L.H.C.) Church. In 1954, O.L.H.C. began a fund-raising campaign for a larger facility with more classrooms and an auditorium, and in 1955, ground-breaking ceremonies took place. Francis Cardinal Spellman, Archbishop of New York, officiated at the blessing of the new parochial school, seen here in this 1956 photograph. (Courtesy of Our Lady Help of Christians.)

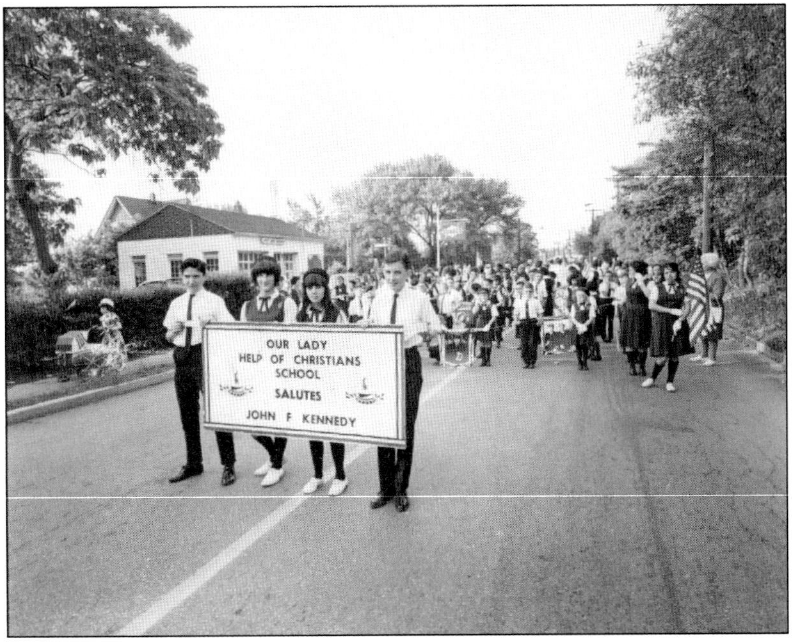

School children from Our Lady Help of Christians have chosen to honor Pres. John F. Kennedy, the first Roman Catholic president of the United States, for their parade theme in 1965. (Courtesy of the Eckel family.)

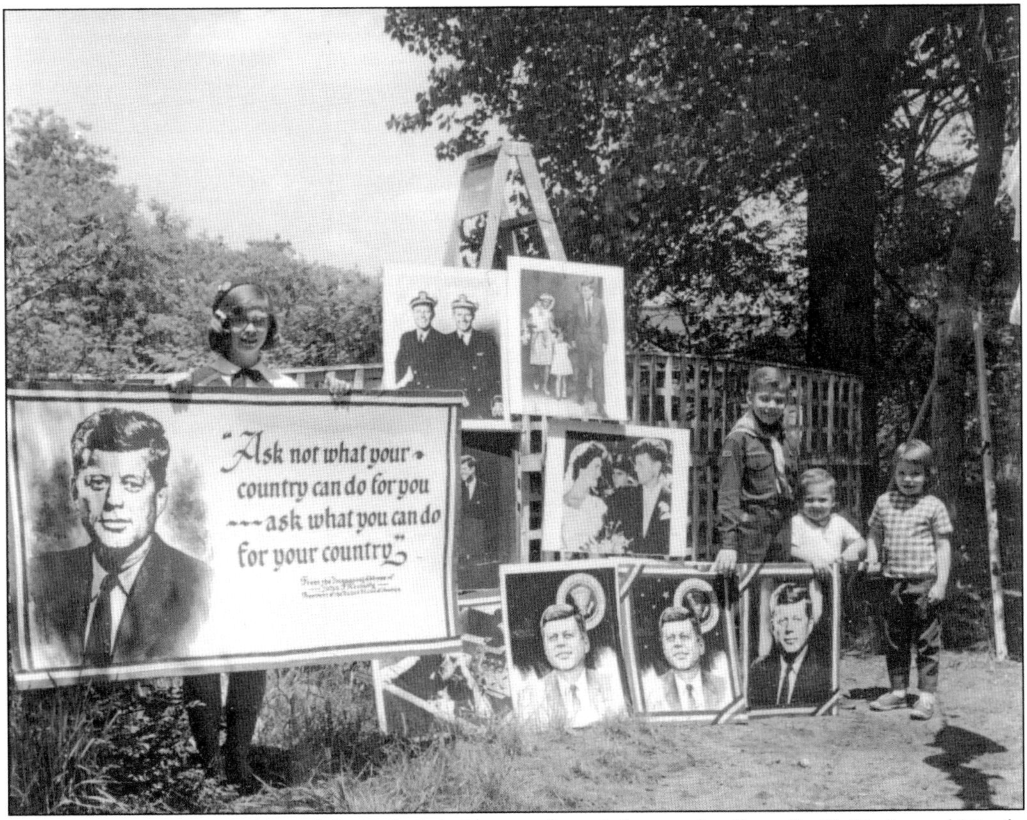

Ann Marie Browne (left) and the Eckel children—from left to right, Peter J., Philip J., and Cindy L.—help photographer Peter Eckel (the children's father) organize parade photographs for Our Lady Help of Christians school at their Butler Avenue home. (Courtesy of the Eckel family.)

Four

Religious Life

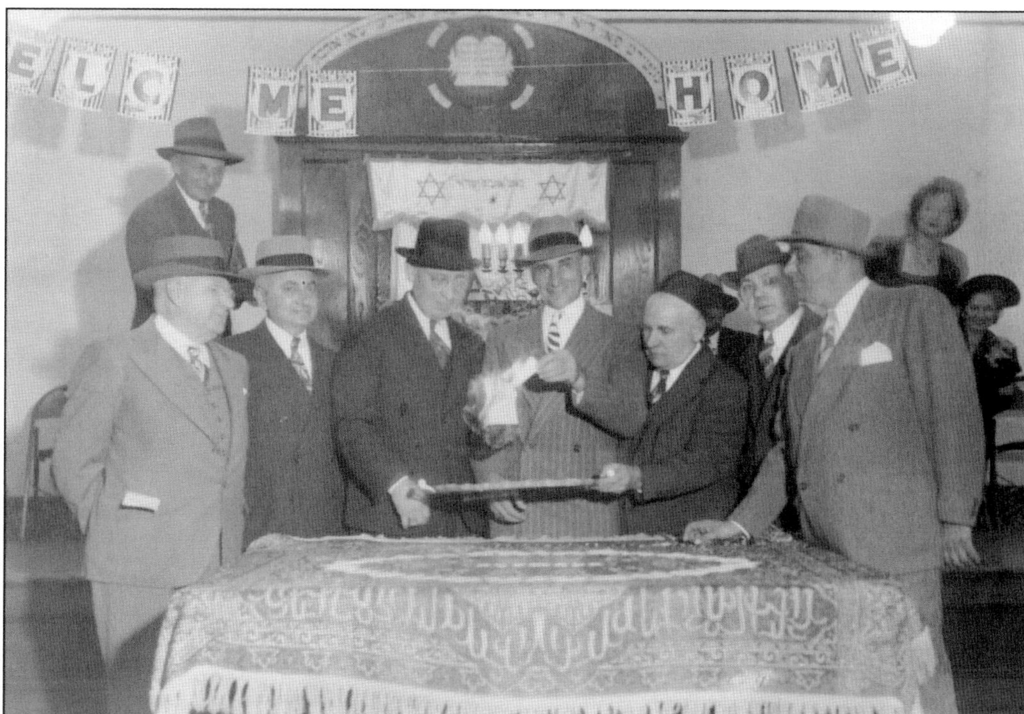

Congregation Ahavath Israel was organized in 1914, and its synagogue has been located at 7630 Amboy Road since 1932. The burning of the mortgage is celebrated in this October 13, 1945, photograph. Members of the congregation pictured include Julius Getz, Julius Cohen, Barnet Schulman, Abraham Goldberg, a Mr. Levenson, David Becker, and Emanuel Honig. (Courtesy of Congregation Ahavath Israel.)

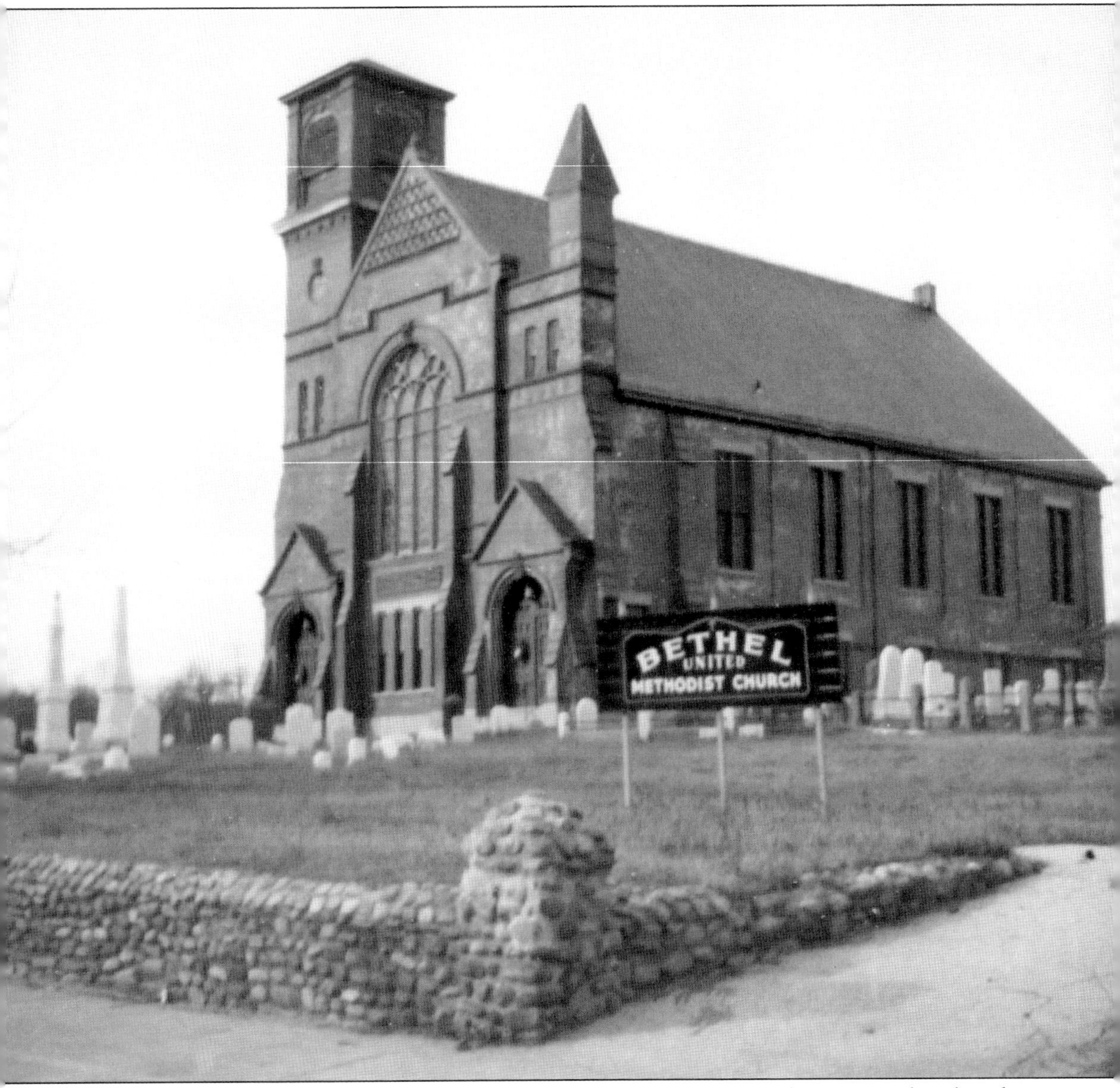

Bethel United Methodist Church is located at 7033 Amboy Road. In 1841, the church was established when John Totten Sr. donated 1 acre of his farm, and a structure was built by local carpenter Isaac P. Bedell. After the original structure burned, a new brick church was constructed in 1886, as shown in this 1973 photograph. (Courtesy of Robert Schweikert.)

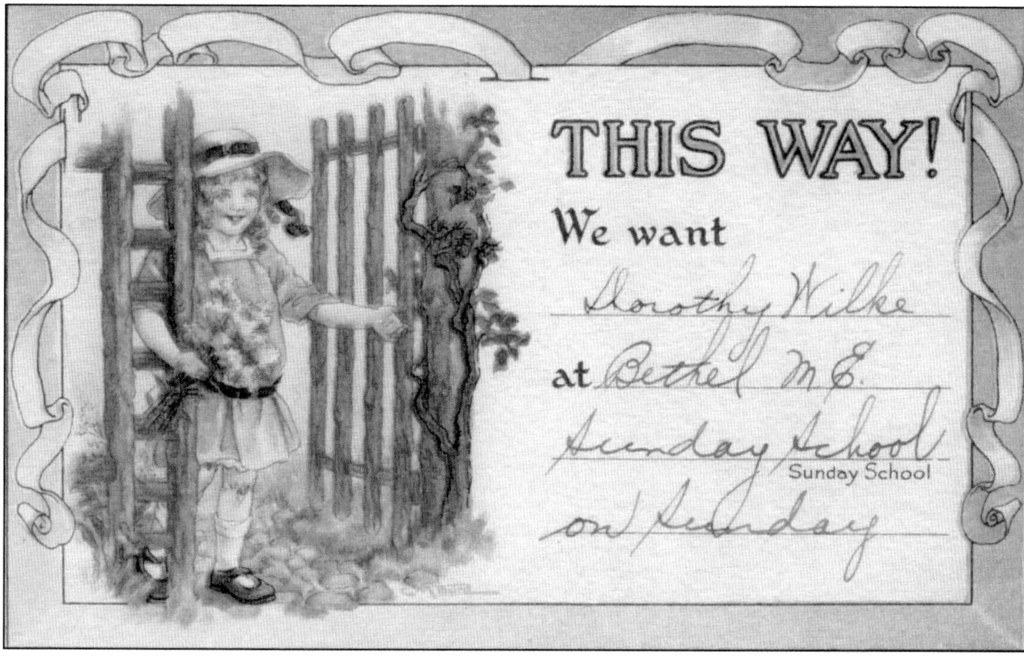

Whenever a child missed Sunday school at Bethel United Methodist Church, a little reminder was sent. This colorful 1922 postcard is an example. (Courtesy of the Wilkie-Farina family.)

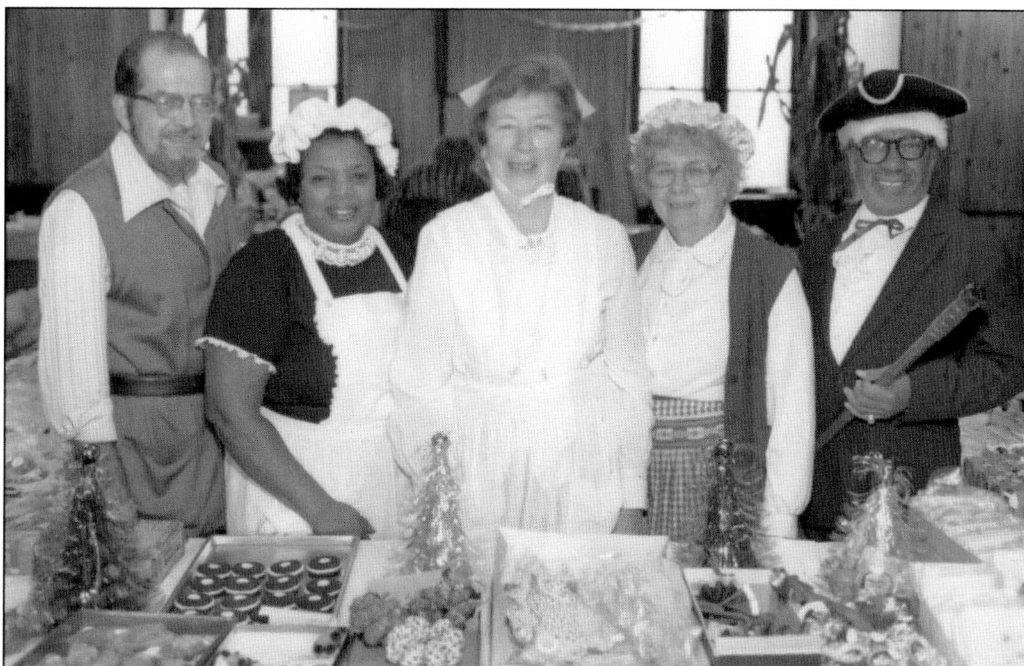

From left to right, George Gierman, Naomi Washington, Florence Spence, Solway Hannan, and James Josey are all decked out for a fair at Bethel United Methodist Church. (Courtesy of Arlene Spence Schweikert.)

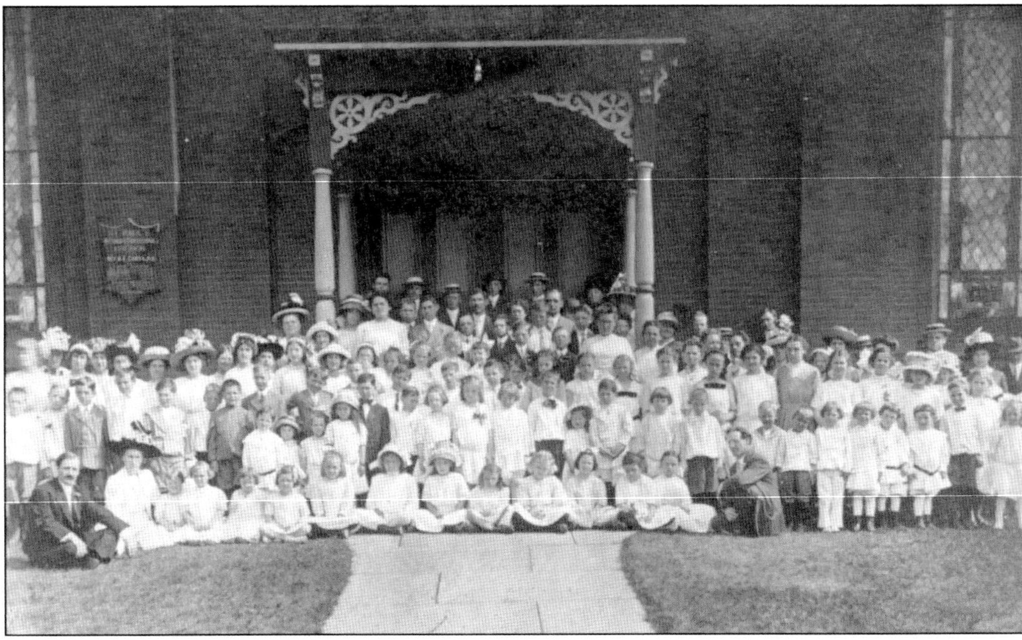

St. Paul's United Methodist Church, located at 7558 Amboy Road, was originally a small two-story chapel constructed in 1859. In 1862, a new, larger brick church was dedicated. The congregation poses in this late-19th-century photograph in front of the ornate wooden entranceway. (Courtesy of the Brennan family.)

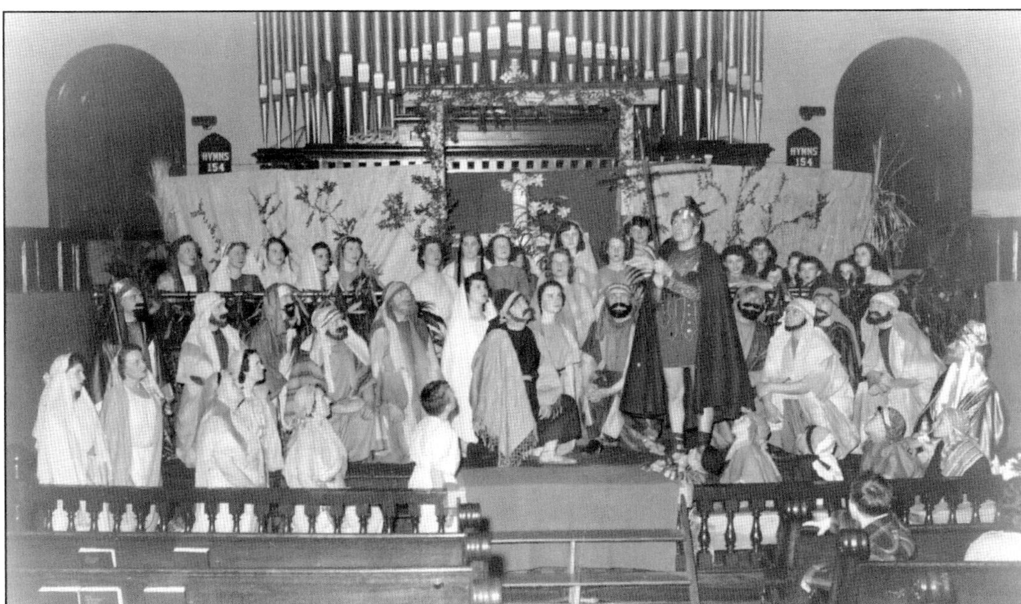

Men, women, and children of St. Paul's congregation are participating in an Easter pageant in the mid-1940s. (Courtesy of St. Paul's United Methodist Church.)

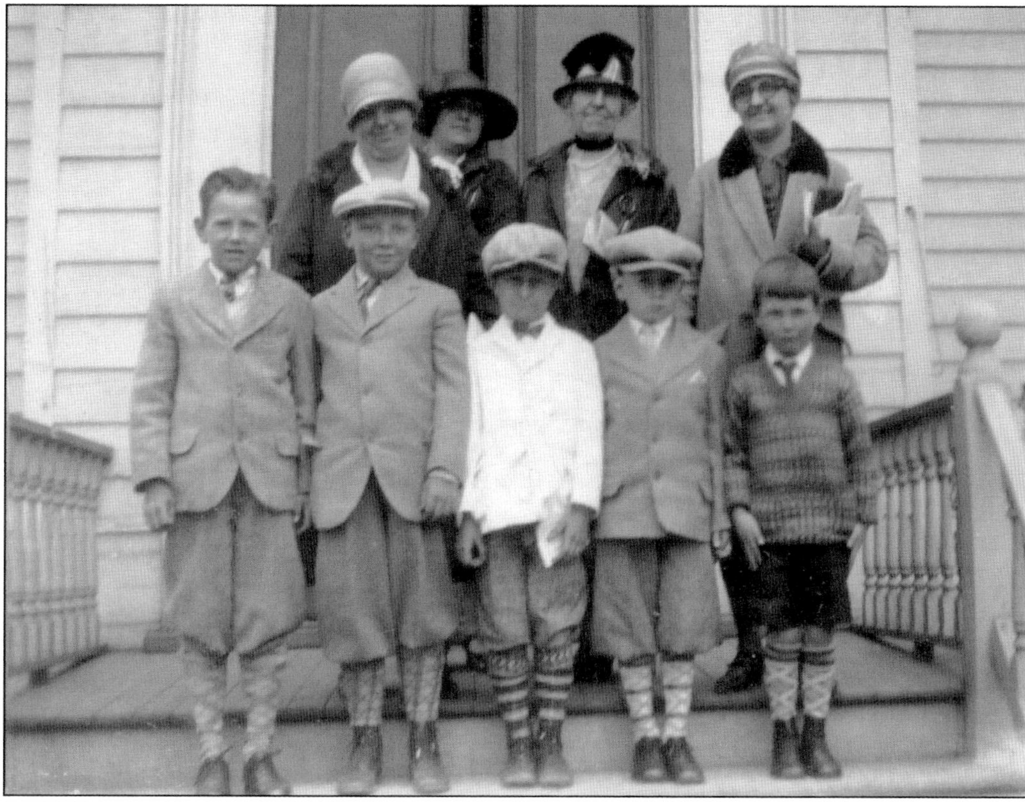

South Baptist Church, located today at 197 Main Street, started holding meetings in a private home on Johnson Avenue in 1856. A cornerstone was laid in 1860, after John Turner gave a plot of land on Main Street to construct a church building. This *c.* 1928 photograph was taken outside the church. (Courtesy of the Biller family.)

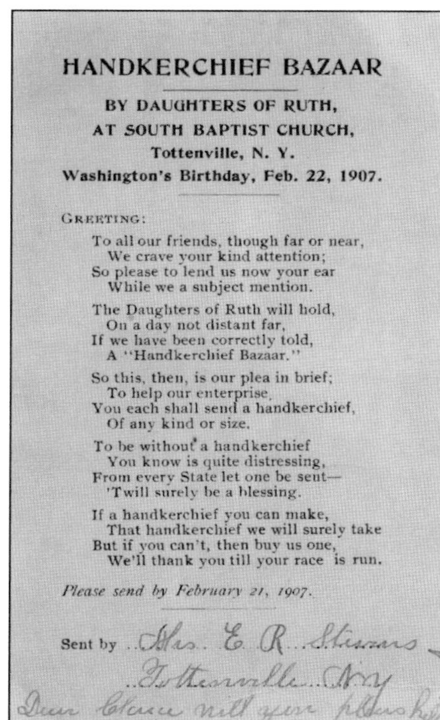

HANDKERCHIEF BAZAAR

BY DAUGHTERS OF RUTH,
AT SOUTH BAPTIST CHURCH,
Tottenville, N. Y.
Washington's Birthday, Feb. 22, 1907.

GREETING:

To all our friends, though far or near,
We crave your kind attention;
So please to lend us now your ear
While we a subject mention.

The Daughters of Ruth will hold,
On a day not distant far,
If we have been correctly told,
A "Handkerchief Bazaar."

So this, then, is our plea in brief;
To help our enterprise,
You each shall send a handkerchief,
Of any kind or size.

To be without a handkerchief
You know is quite distressing,
From every State let one be sent—
'Twill surely be a blessing.

If a handkerchief you can make,
That handkerchief we will surely take
But if you can't, then buy us one,
We'll thank you till your race is run.

Please send by February 21, 1907.

Sent by Mrs. E. R. Stevens
Tottenville N.Y.

In 1907, the Daughters of Ruth of South Baptist Church organized an unusual fund-raising event—a handkerchief bazaar. Members were notified by postcard and asked to send a handkerchief "of any kind or size."

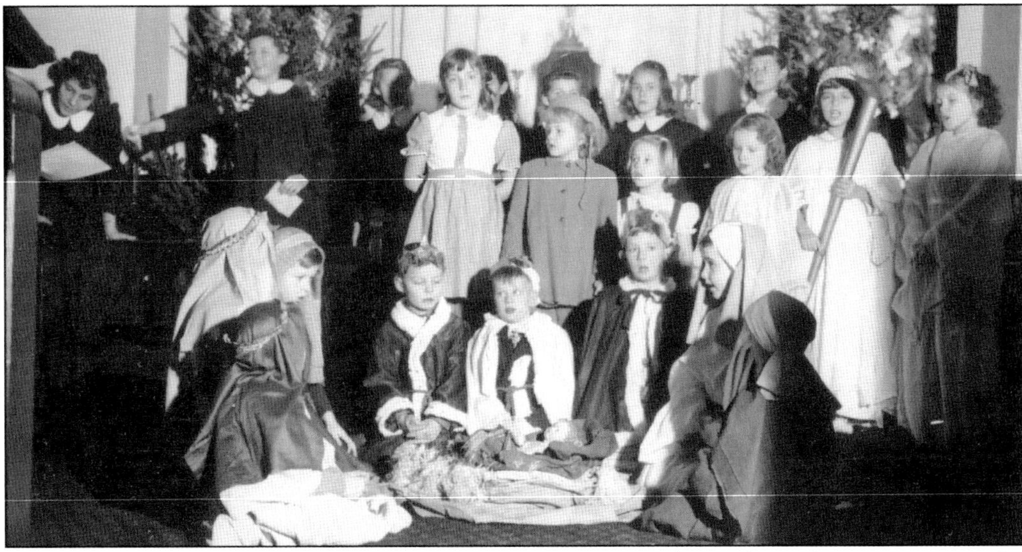

St. Stephen's Episcopal Church, located at 7516 Amboy Road, was formed in 1883. In 1965, a fire destroyed the old frame church. A new church building was dedicated in 1967. The Sunday school is seen here putting on a Christmas pageant in this 1950 photograph. (Courtesy of C. Greg and Carol-Lynn Rössel.)

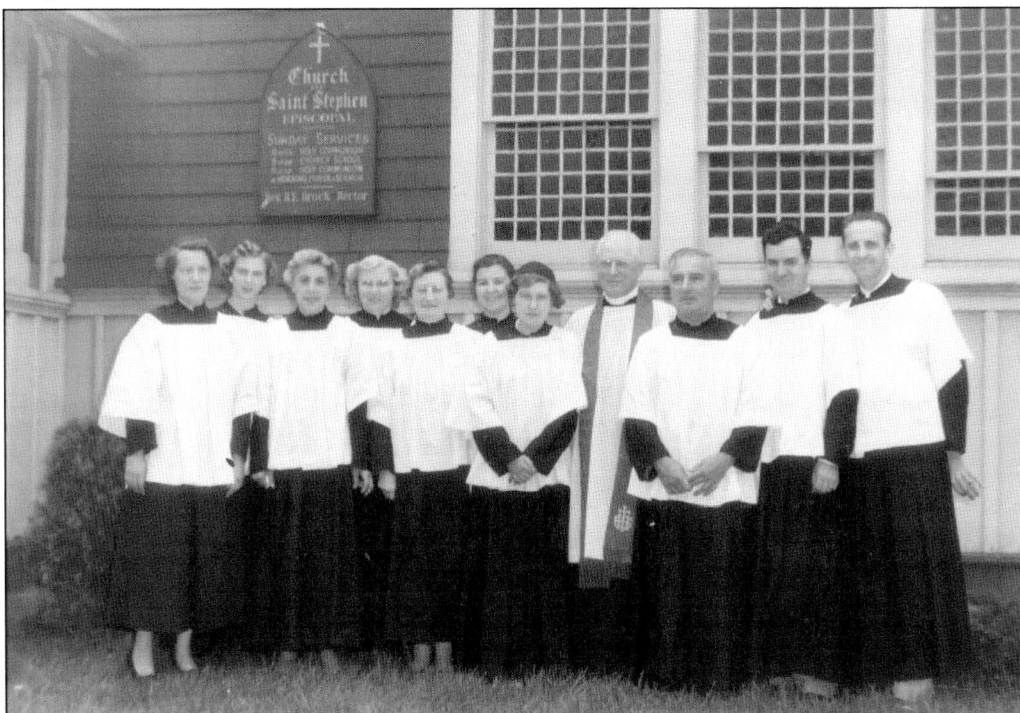

The adult choir of St. Stephen's Episcopal Church is shown outside the wooden church in this photograph with the Reverend Raymond E. Brock, who served as rector for 20 years. In this 1950s photograph are, from left to right, two unidentified, Hazel Polhemus, Dorothy Lea, Alice Hollowell, Kitty Bausch, Barbara Olsen, Father Brock, Everett Polhemus, Raymond Eisengrein, and Harold Hollowell. (Courtesy of C. Greg and Carol-Lynn Rössel.)

Terence Cardinal Cooke, Archbishop of New York (center) concelebrates the 75th Anniversary Mass of Our Lady Help of Christians Roman Catholic Church on October 14, 1973, along with, from left to right, Fr. Victor Buebendorf; Fr. Frederick Miller; Deacon Edward Wetherall; Monsignor McCarrick; Msgr. Jeremiah Brennan, pastor of the church; and Fr. Lawrence O'Connor. (Courtesy of Our Lady Help of Christians.)

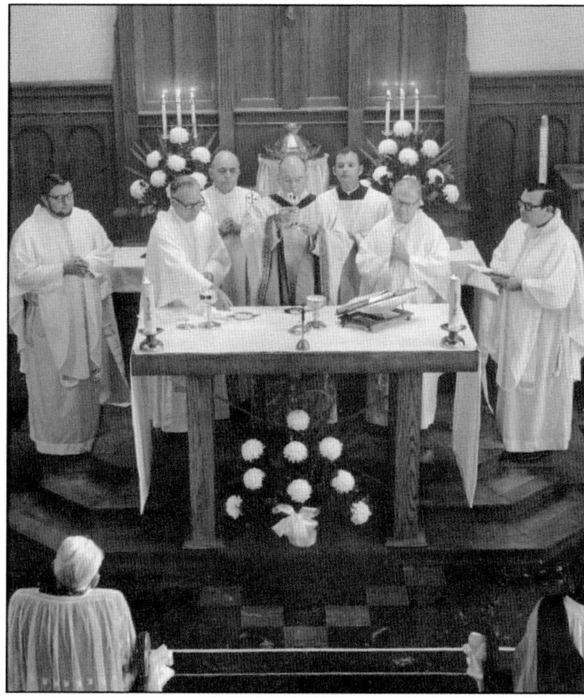

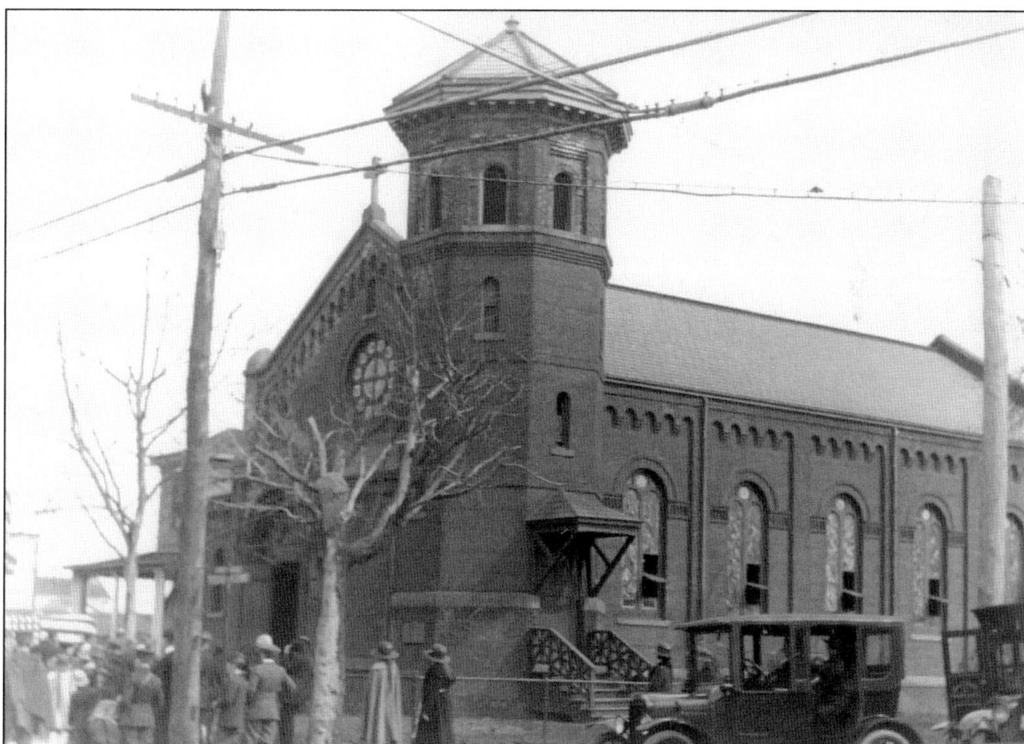

Built in 1898, Our Lady Help of Christians Church is shown here in a 1919 photograph. The image shows people arriving for the funeral mass for Sgt. John W. O'Meara Jr., who was killed in action during World War I. (Courtesy of the John Bieser Estate.)

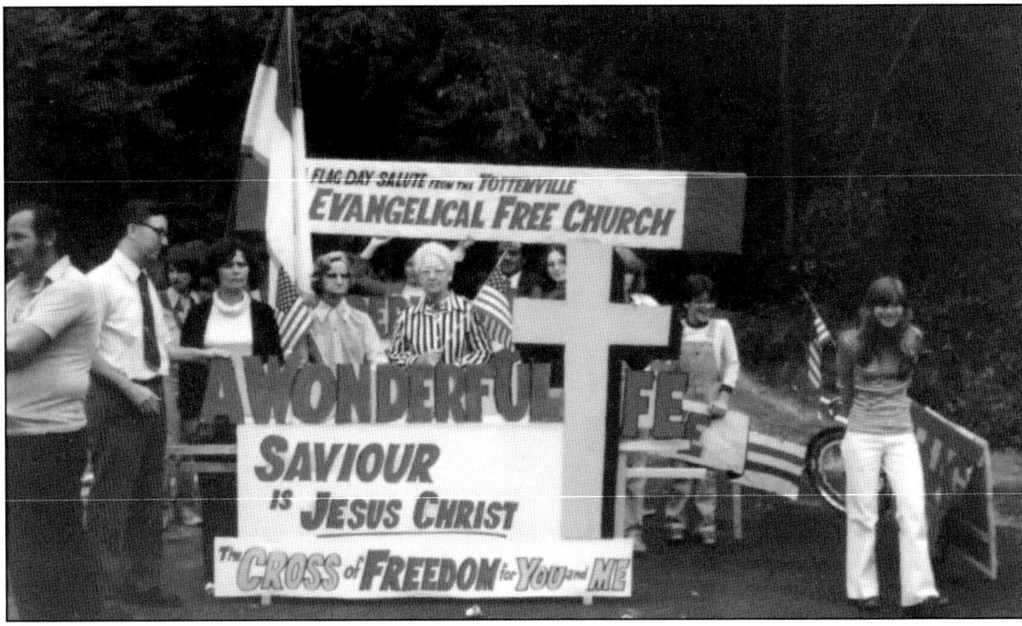

The Tottenville Evangelical Free Church began in 1915, when 13 men and women of Norwegian ancestry came together for worship. In 1924, the present church building was erected. The congregation constructed this award-winning float for a 1970s Flag Day parade. (Courtesy of Arnold J. Kroeger.)

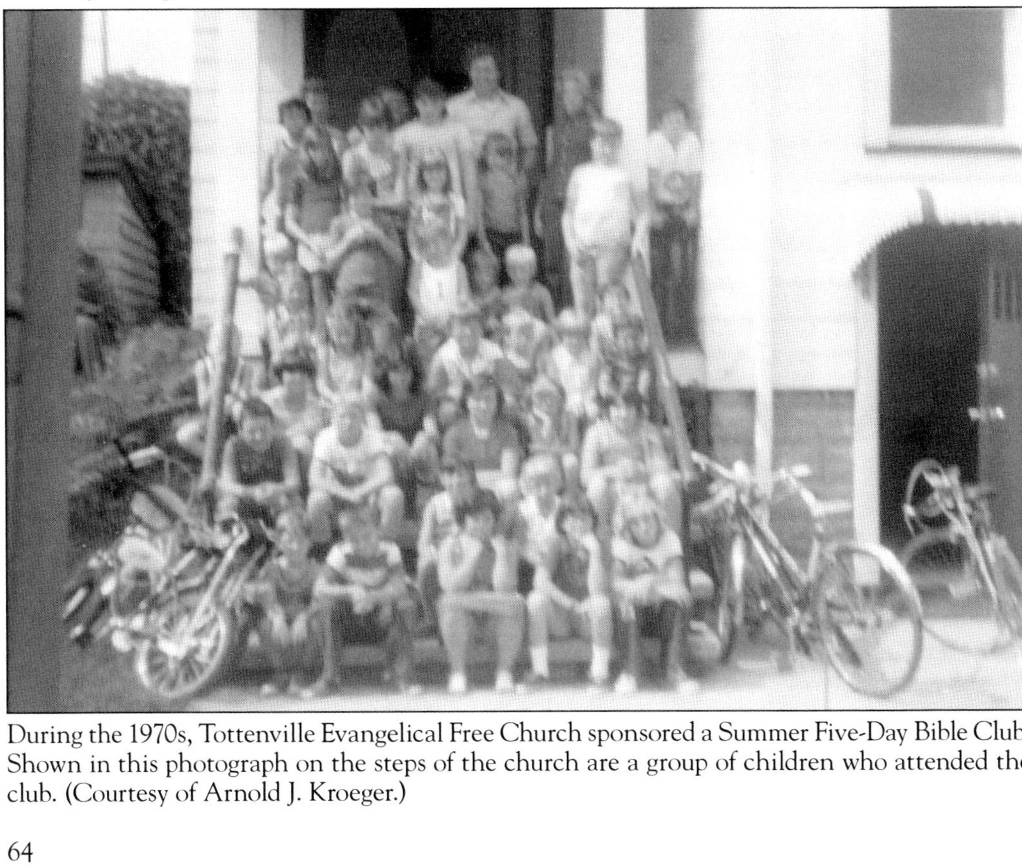

During the 1970s, Tottenville Evangelical Free Church sponsored a Summer Five-Day Bible Club. Shown in this photograph on the steps of the church are a group of children who attended the club. (Courtesy of Arnold J. Kroeger.)

Five

BUSINESS AND INDUSTRY

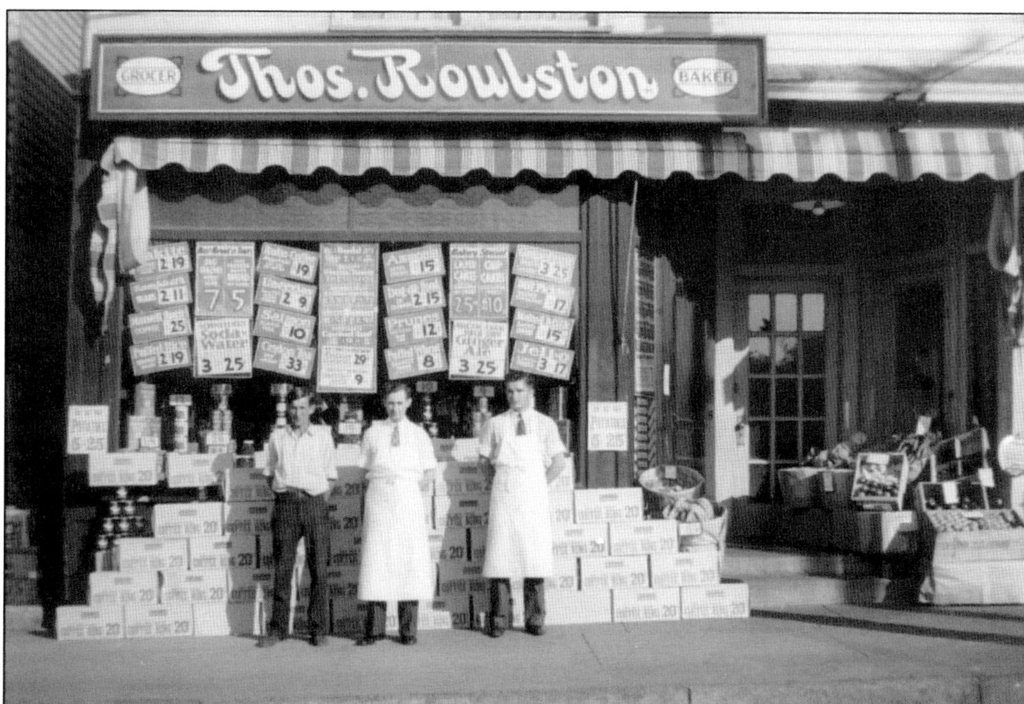

Thomas Roulston was a New York–based grocery store chain that began in the 1920s and operated through the 1940s. The Roulston location shown in this 1937 photograph was at 5264–5266 Arthur Kill Road. The building would later house Cutting's Furniture Store and the popular Standard Club, a bar. Pictured on the left is Louis Maklari, and on the right is John Grzeskowiak Sr. (Courtesy of the Grzeskowiak family.)

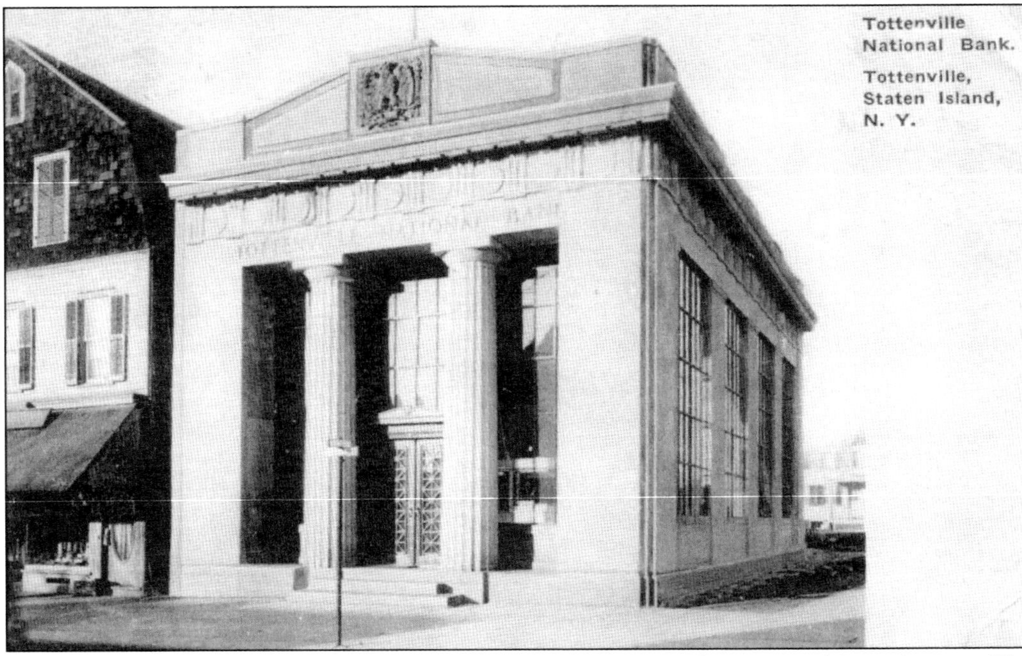

The Tottenville National Bank was located at 179 Main Street at the corner of Craig Avenue. The bank was built in 1915 with a limestone facade in the neoclassical style. It has been considered by many as the most impressive commercial building in Tottenville and boasts granite and marble floors.

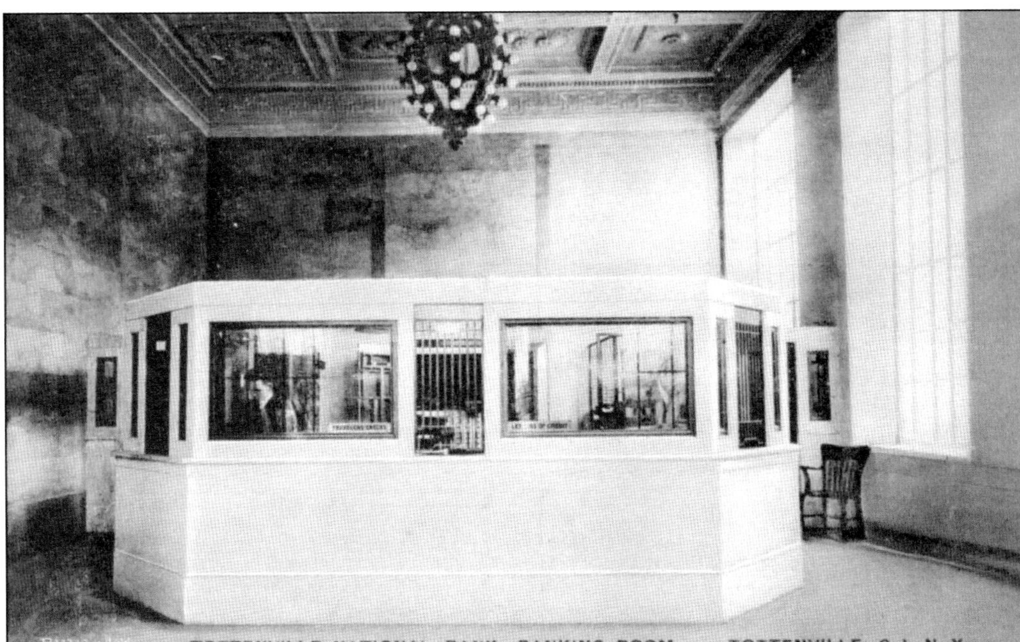

An interior view shows the bank's high molded ceiling and fanciful chandelier. Clerks conducted business from a freestanding booth with an iron grill window.

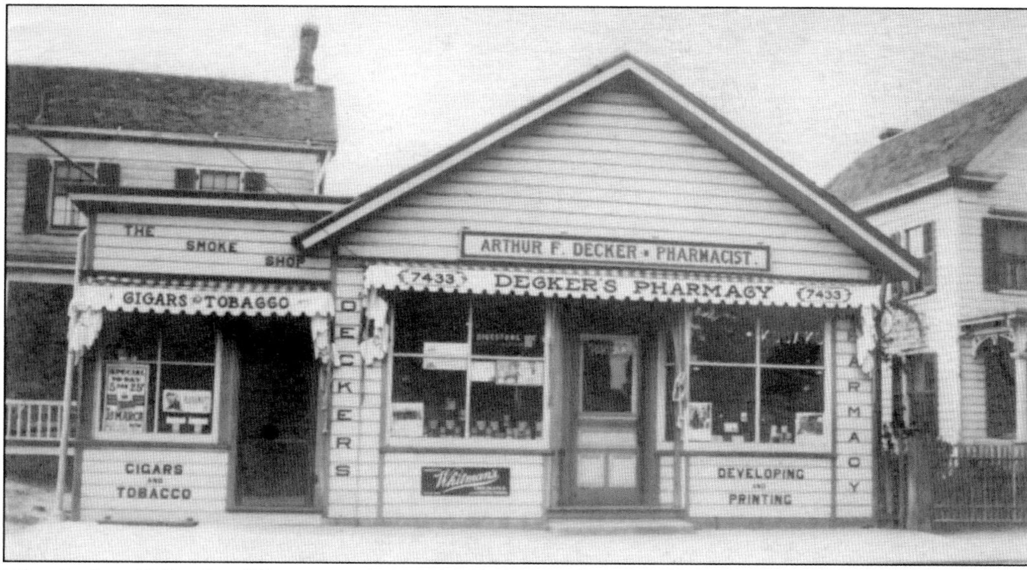

The Arthur F. Decker Pharmacy, located at 7433 Amboy Road, is pictured here in 1915. A small smoke shop offering cigars and tobacco adjoins it. The Deckers lived nearby on Johnson Avenue. Arthur's wife, Margaret, was a teacher at Public School 1 for 35 years. Dr. Alva Decker, Arthur's father, was a physician and pharmacist in the neighboring town of Pleasant Plains. In 1922, after Alva's retirement, father and son worked together at the Tottenville business. About 1945, a larger modern store with apartments above was erected on this site; the new address became 7437 Amboy Road. Today this building with embossed tin ceilings and walls houses Eggers Ice Cream store. (Courtesy of the Bedell Collection.)

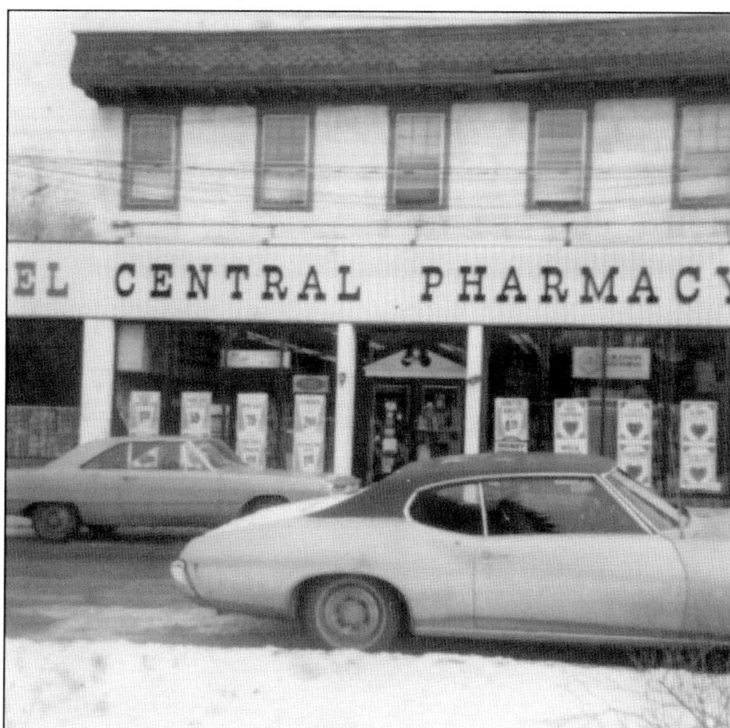

By the 1970s, Central Pharmacy moved into the former A&P building at 209 Main Street, after the supermarket relocated to a larger and more modern store on nearby Page Avenue. Today this structure houses a very modern laundromat. (Courtesy of the Janice and June Rose Collection.)

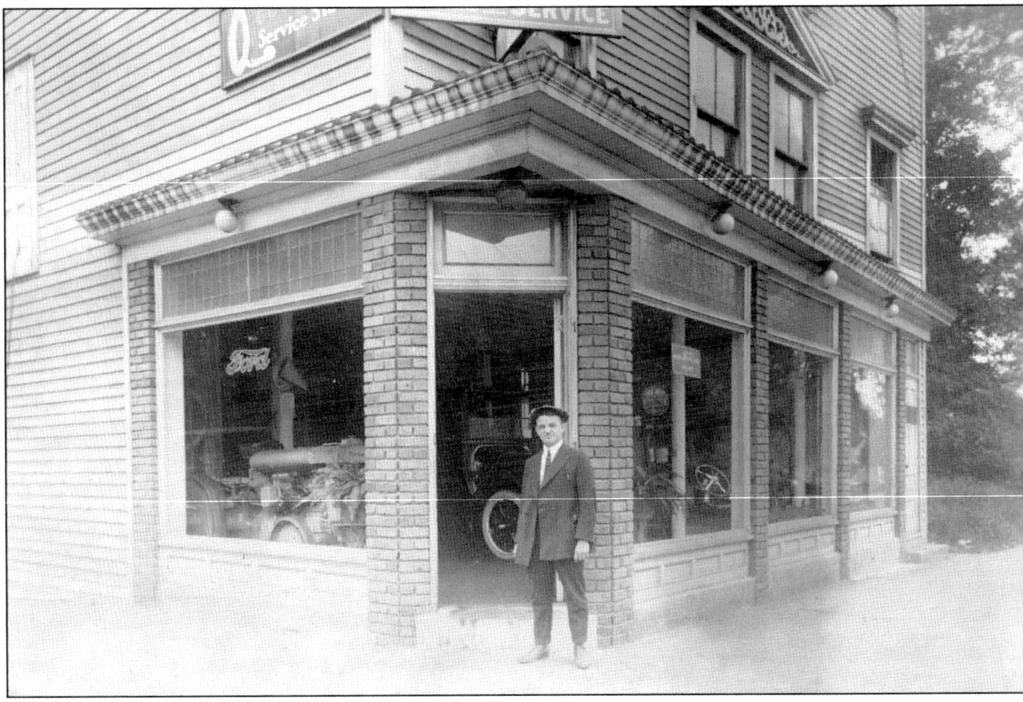

Owner George "Scotty" Carfoot stands proudly at the entrance to his Ford dealership, located at the corner of Amboy Road and Main Street. In the 1920s, the business occupied the ground floor of the Knights of Pythias Hall, which was built in 1888. (Courtesy of Judith Johnston Sarsten.)

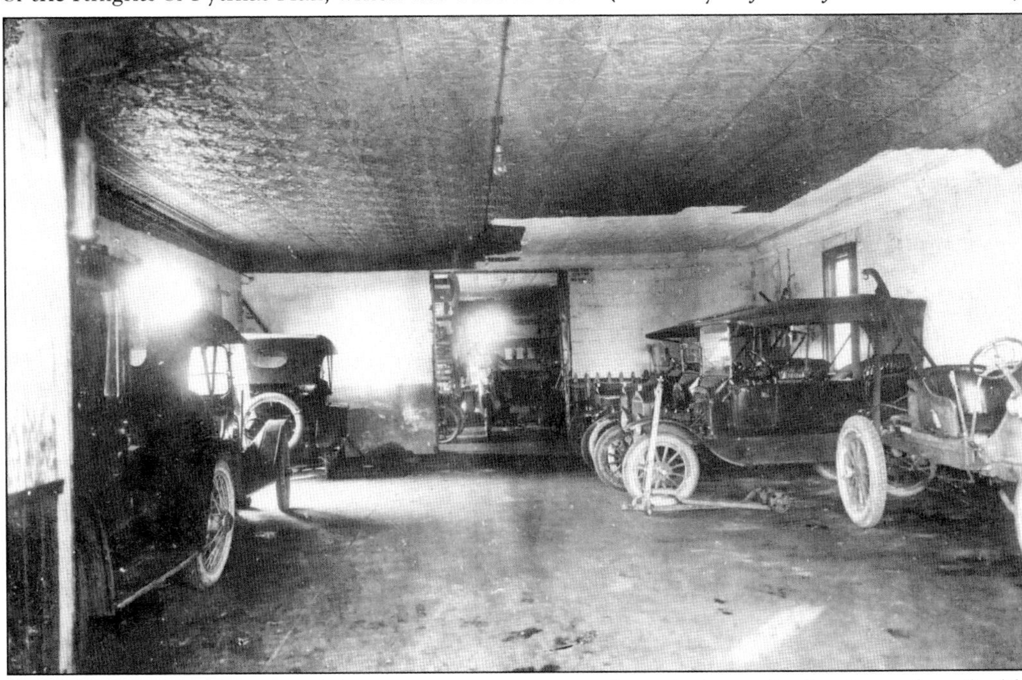

As early automobiles required frequent maintenance and repair, it was both wise and profitable for Carfoot to establish the repair garage seen in this rare interior image. (Courtesy of Judith Johnston Sarsten.)

The South Shore Chevrolet showroom was owned and operated by Harry Lebovitz and was located at 153 Main Street from 1927 to 1958. The brick building had two large glass showroom windows where prospective customers could view the automobiles from the street. In 1958, Harry established H&L Motors in New Dorp, at the corner of Hylan Boulevard and New Dorp Lane.

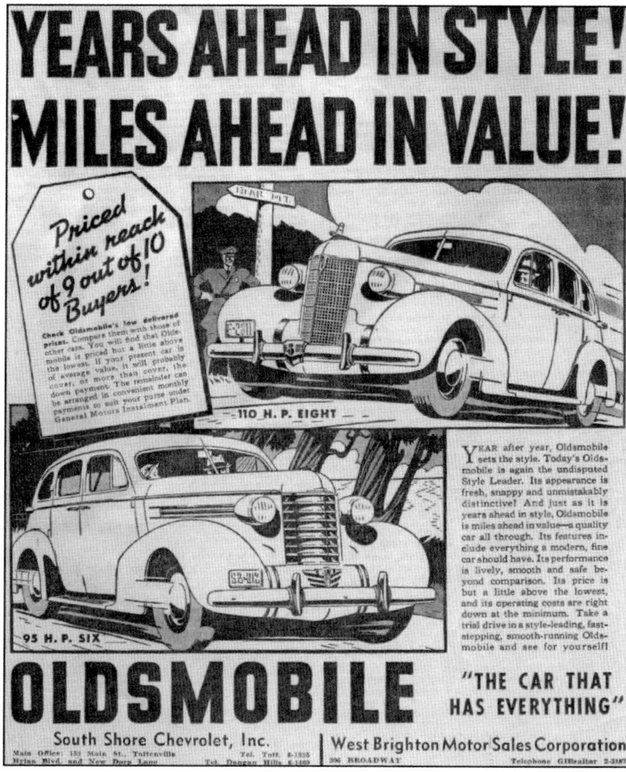

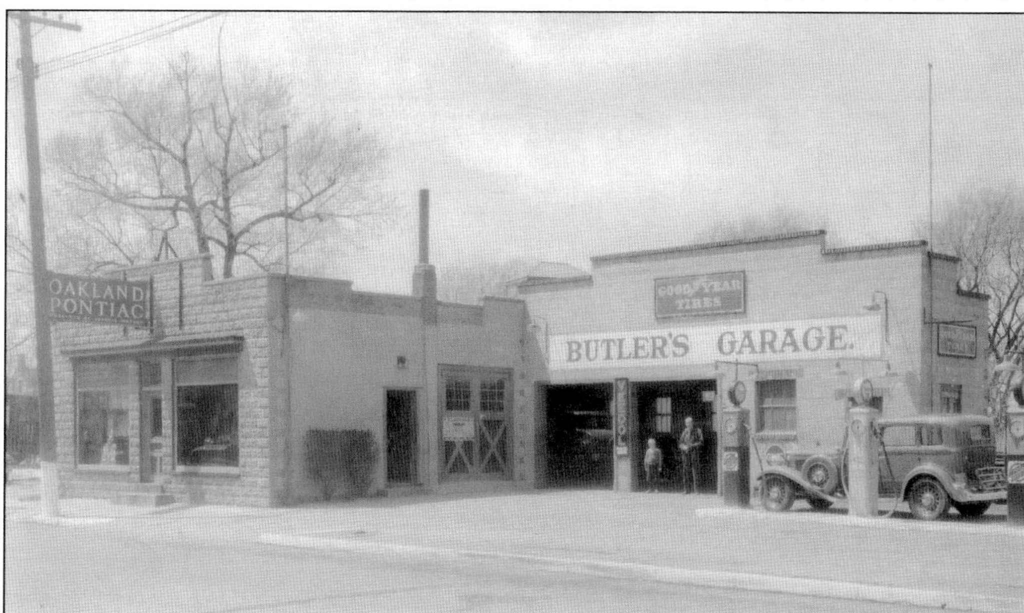

Butler's Garage, shown here in 1933, was located on Arthur Kill Road at Fisher Avenue. Raymond Butler started his business here in 1924 pumping gas and doing repairs. Butler was also a Pontiac car dealer and operated a showroom on the property. The young boy shown in the garage bay is Bill Butler, son of the owner; Charlie Warner, an employee, stands with him. (Courtesy of Bill Butler.)

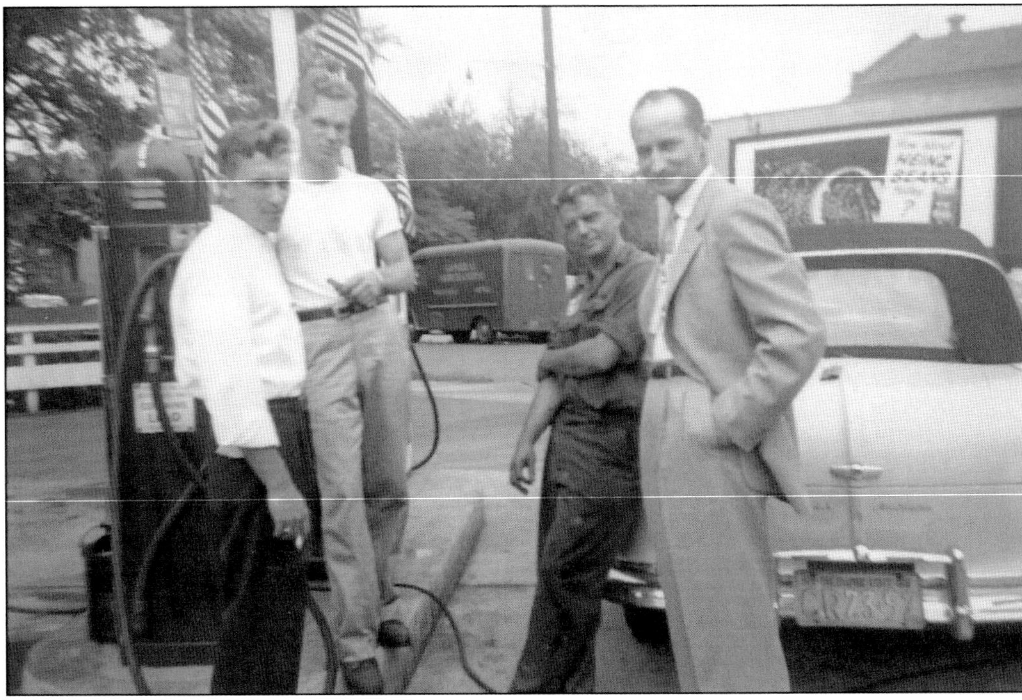

John Nelson operated his gas station from 1954 to 1961 at the busy corner of Main Street and Amboy Road. In this photograph are, from left to right, Henry "Spud" Wick, Tommy Buttermark, John Nelson, and Al Carfero. (Courtesy of Linda J. Noordzy.)

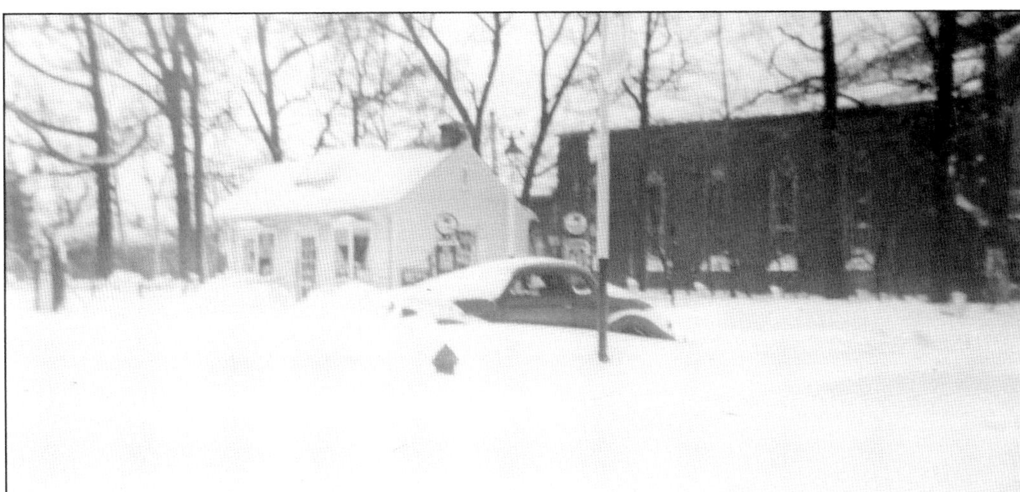

Snow blankets Nelson's filling station in this 1950s photograph. St. Paul's Methodist Church is in the background. (Courtesy of the Bedell Collection.)

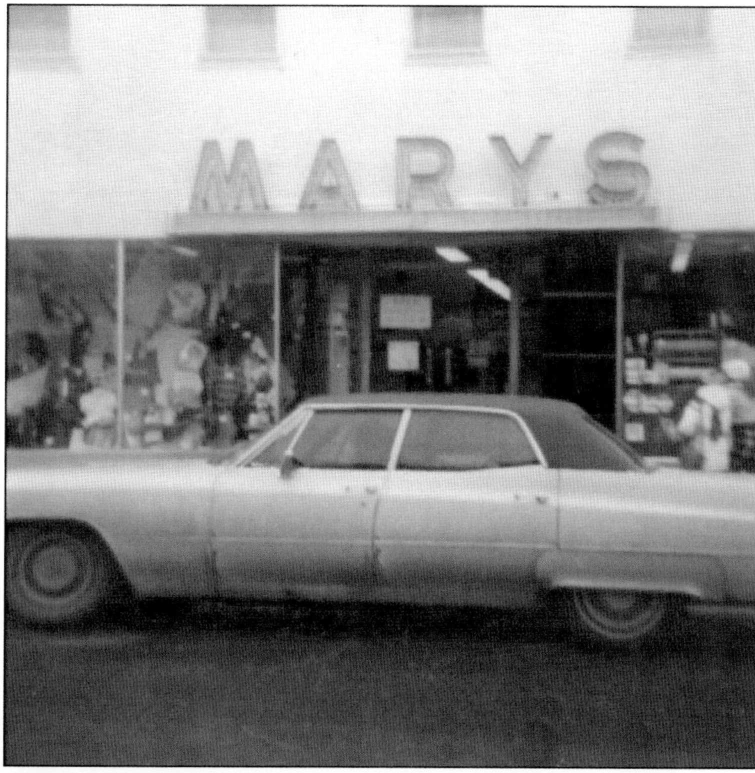

Mary's Department Store was first established about 1927 on Main Street. In 1938, it moved into the buildings at Amboy Road and Main Street. Large showroom windows displayed a huge assortment of items from lady's handkerchiefs to plastic toys and everything in between. Although the business closed in 1980, it has not been forgotten and remains a cherished memory of many South Shore residents. (Courtesy of the Janice and June Rose Collection.)

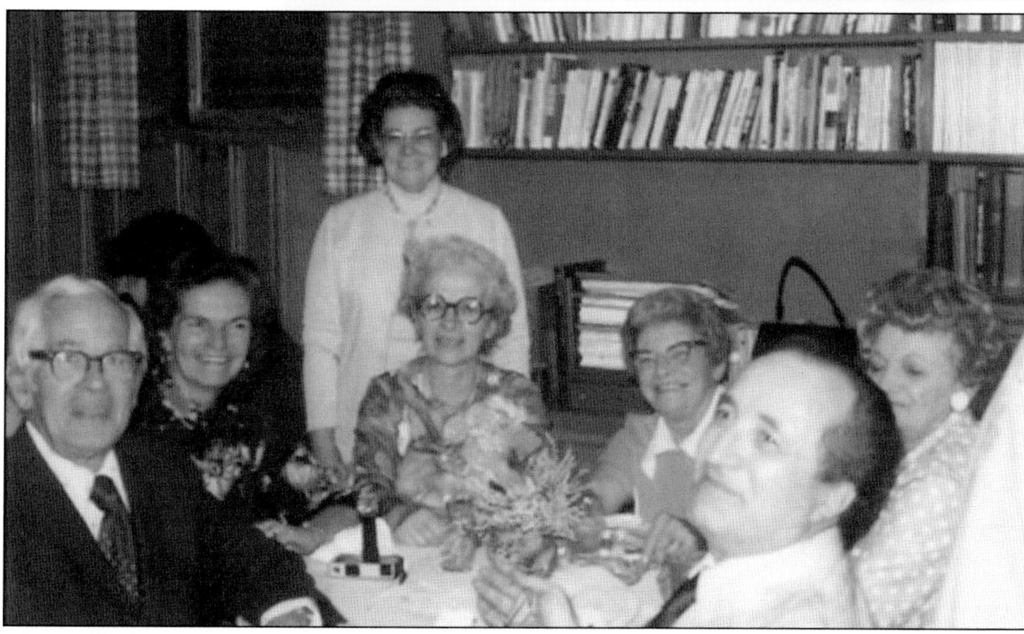

The staff of Mary's Department Store gathers for this photograph in 1975. Pictured are, from left to right, William Rapley, Ann Totten, Norma Friedman (standing), Helen Szuch, Jeanette Cote, Frances Rapley, and Irving Friedman. Norma is the daughter of the original owners, Louis and Miriam Grodzinsky. She and her husband, Irving, took over ownership of Mary's in 1946. (Courtesy of the Friedman family.)

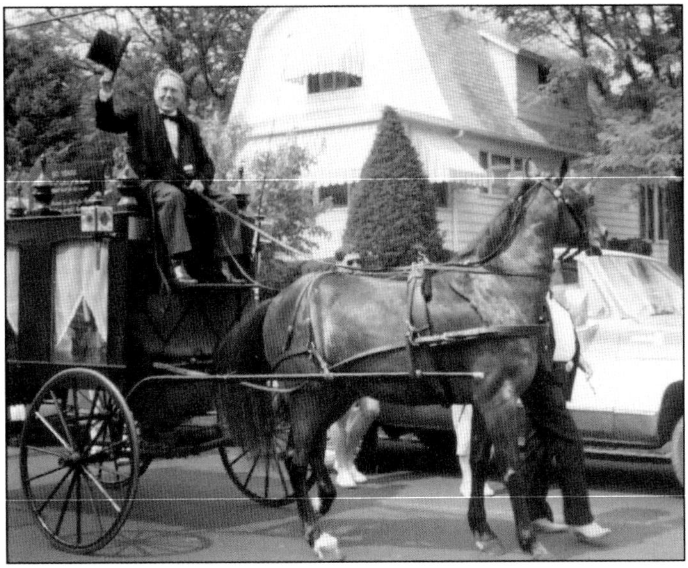

Joseph Bedell doffs his high hat to the crowds atop the horse-drawn recreation of his great-grandfather's hearse. The year 1991 marked the 150th anniversary of the Bedell Funeral Home, one of the oldest funeral homes in New York. The reproduction hearse was made by Louis and Joseph Pagliuco, and the town came out to celebrate the milestone with a small parade and loud applause. The frisky horse kept everyone alert that day. (Courtesy of the Jane M. Lutkenhouse Collection.)

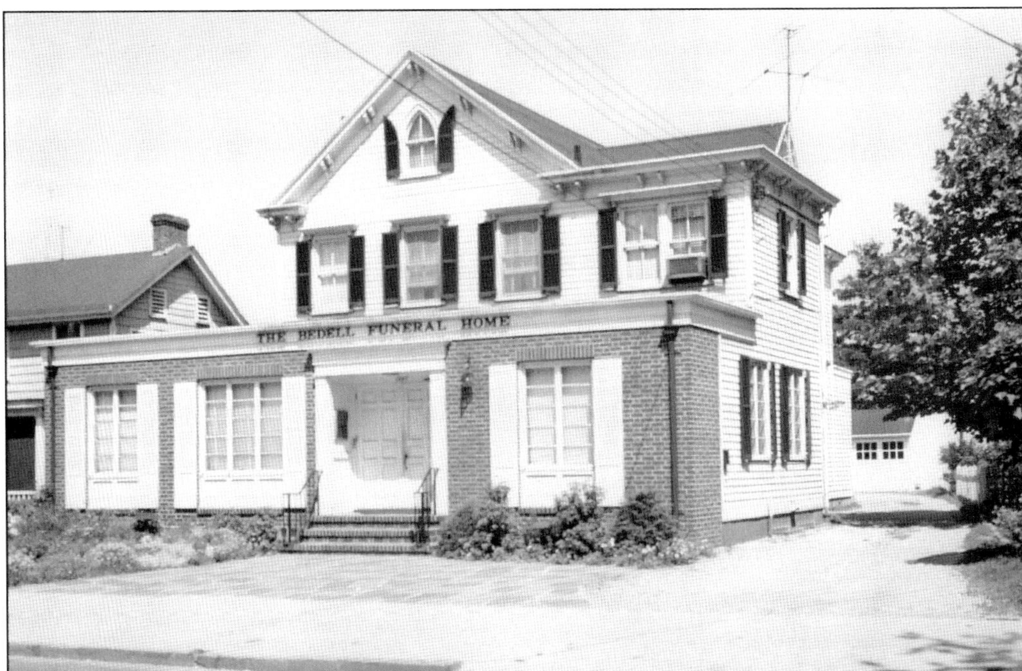

In 1909, following the death of Isaac P. Bedell, founder of the Bedell family undertaking business, James W. Bedell, Isaac's son, established the funeral home on the first floor of a house located at 7447 Amboy Road. The family lived upstairs. Following James's death in 1921, his four children carried on the business. Joseph E. Bedell, grandson of James, joined the business in 1937 and made alterations to the building, including this brick facade and a large addition to the left. Joseph had preserved the history of the family business by displaying items such as old Bibles, crosses, embalming equipment, coffins, and even a funeral bill dating to 1890, when the cost of typical services was $103.85. Almost 100 items were shown in a large room and open to the public. Joseph retired in 1989 as the last member of the Bedell family to run the business. (Courtesy of the Bedell Collection.)

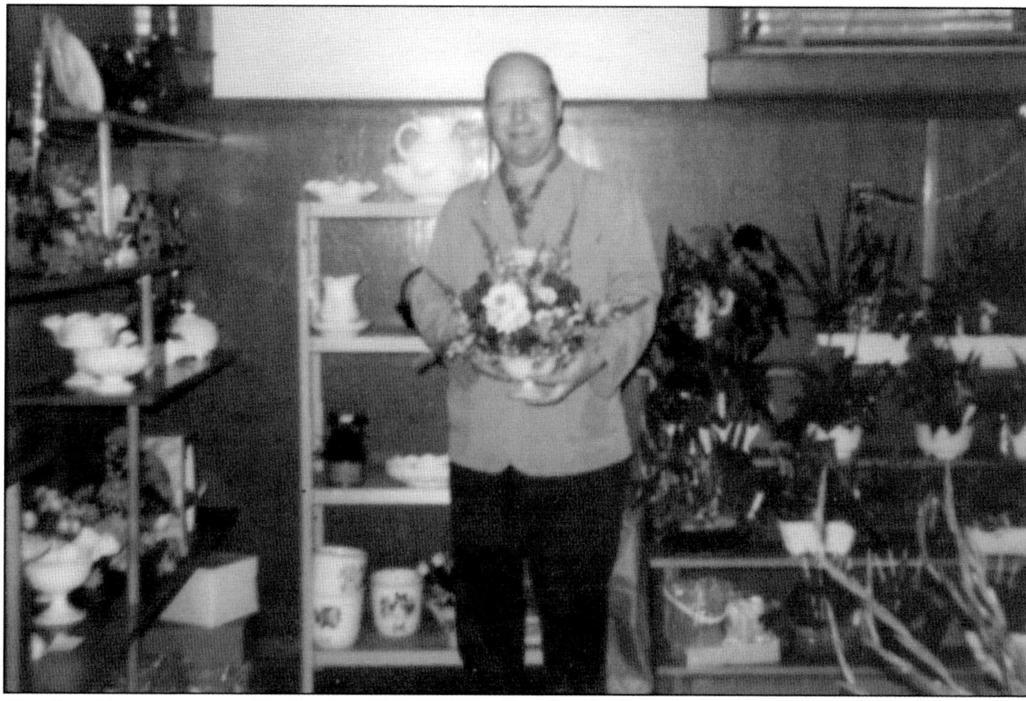

Gordon Ekstrand proudly shows off one of his floral arrangements inside his Amboy Road store. Gordon and his wife, Mildred, operated a florist shop at this location from June 1963 to November 1988. During busy holidays, the entire family would pitch in to help make corsages and arrange bouquets for customers. (Courtesy of the Janice and June Rose Collection.)

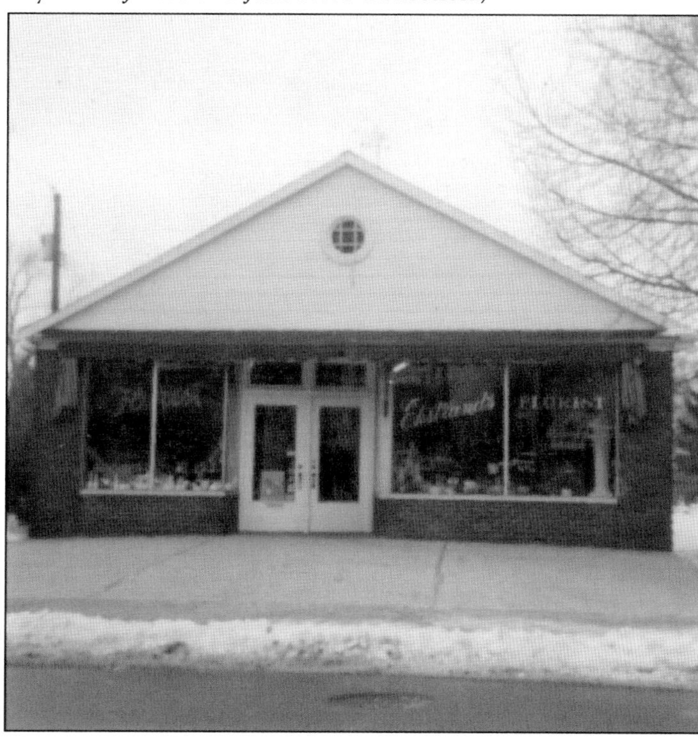

In 1963, Mildred and Gordon Ekstrand entered into the family floral business started by his parents. They moved into a building at 7407 Amboy Road, which had recently been a very popular luncheonette named the Hut that was a fun spot for high school students to have a Coke after school. On a Saturday evening in June 1963, the Ekstrands moved flowers, vases, ribbons, and everything else from his parents' shop to the new store across the street; they were open for business with an American flag proudly flying at 9:00 a.m. that Sunday morning. (Courtesy of the Janice and June Rose Collection.)

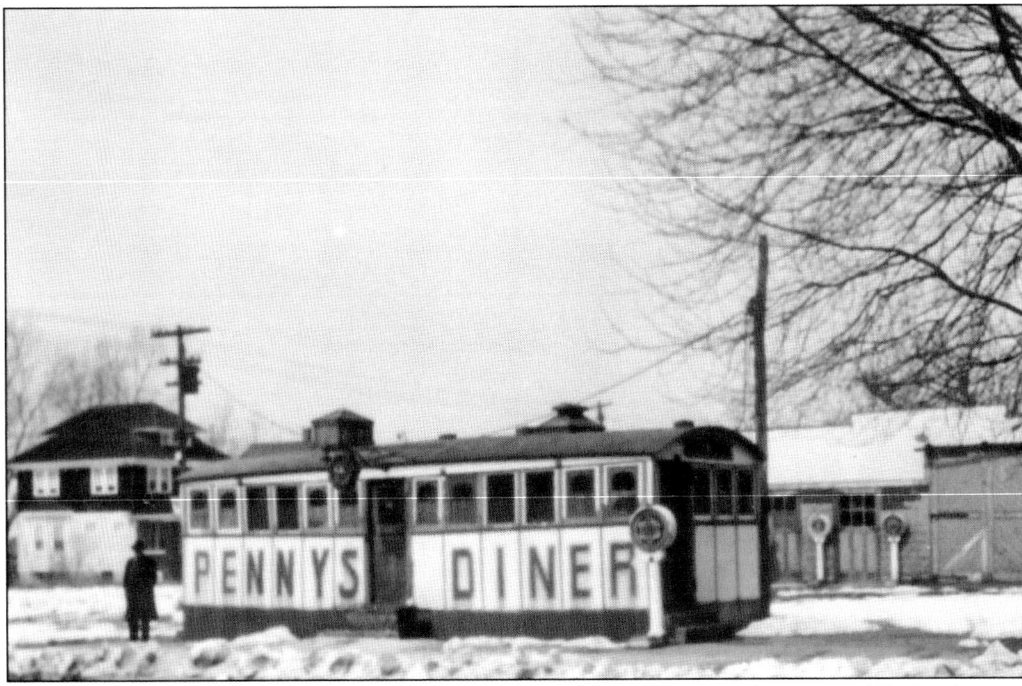

This 1939 photograph depicts Penny's Diner, which was located at Craig Avenue and Butler Avenue. The diner was owned by Walter Penny. Here customers could sit at the counter on a high stool and enjoy a good cup of coffee and a slice of pie along with some friendly conversation.

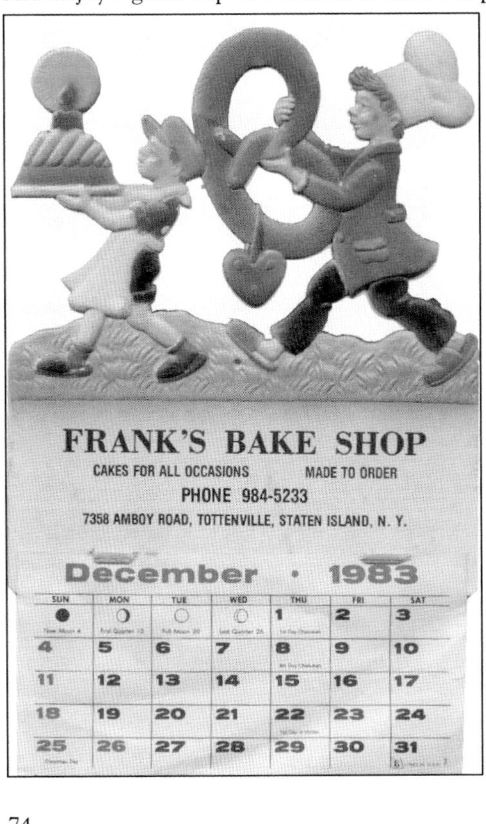

As far back as 1885, there has been a bakery at the corner of Amboy Road and Sleight Avenue. F. C. E. Petersen first operated his bakery at that early date. In 1963, Frank and Marleen Veraart opened Frank's Bake Shop, which quickly became a staple in the community. Frank was instrumental in founding the Tottenville Merchants Association, and when Frank and his family relocated, the local paper's headline read "Our Loss, Elsewhere's Gain."

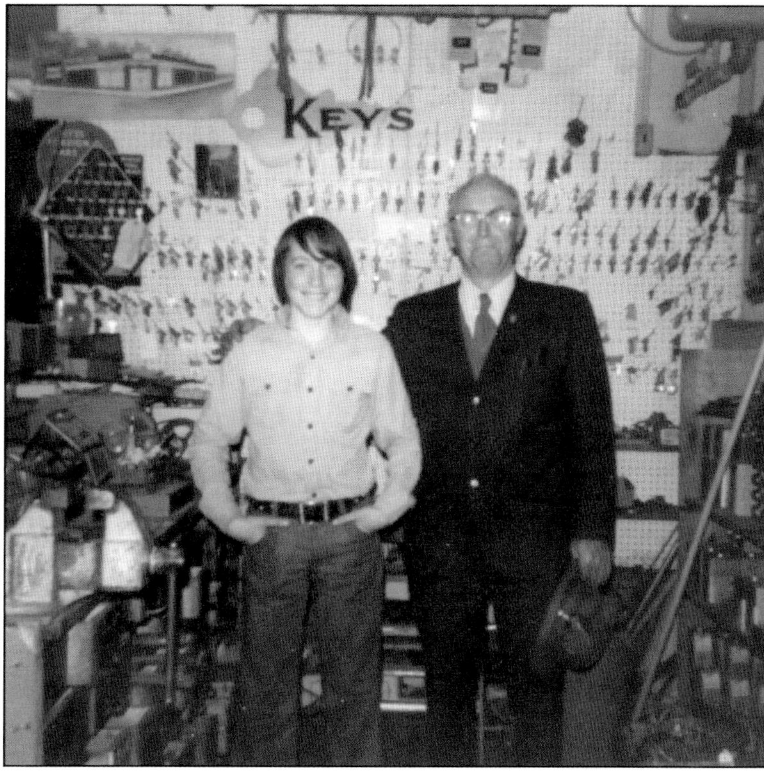

In the 1970s, long before the big box stores came to Tottenville, Lang's Hardware-Housewares, located at 7233 Amboy Road, served the community's needs. Owner John T. Lang stands proudly in front of a wall of keys in his store. (Courtesy of the Janice and June Rose Collection.)

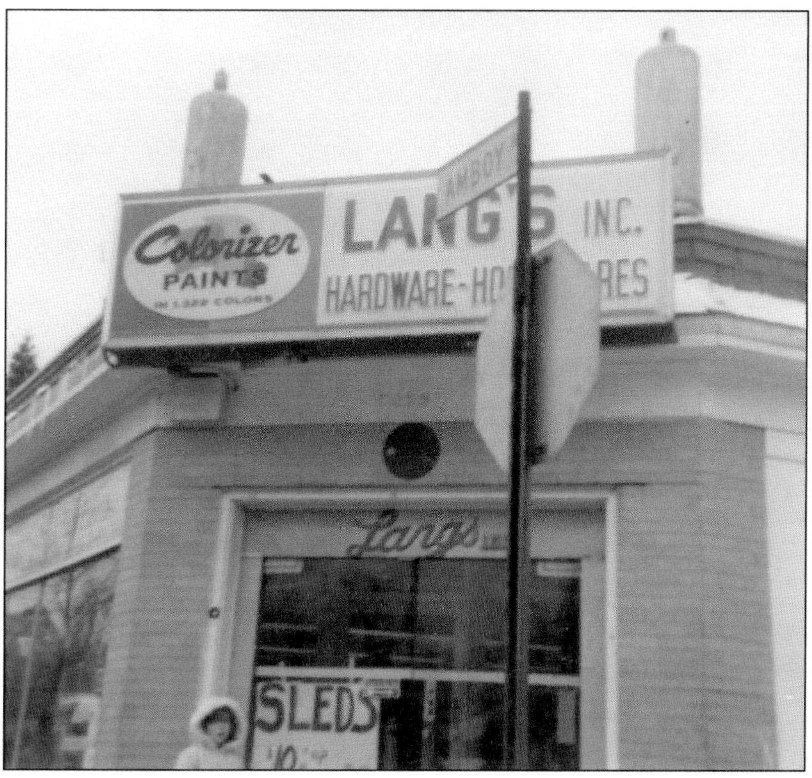

Two propane tanks stand atop the entrance to Lang's Hardware Store. Mom-and-pop stores provided all essentials within walking distance of home. Lang's even sold sleds on the snowy day this picture was taken. (Courtesy of the Janice and June Rose Collection.)

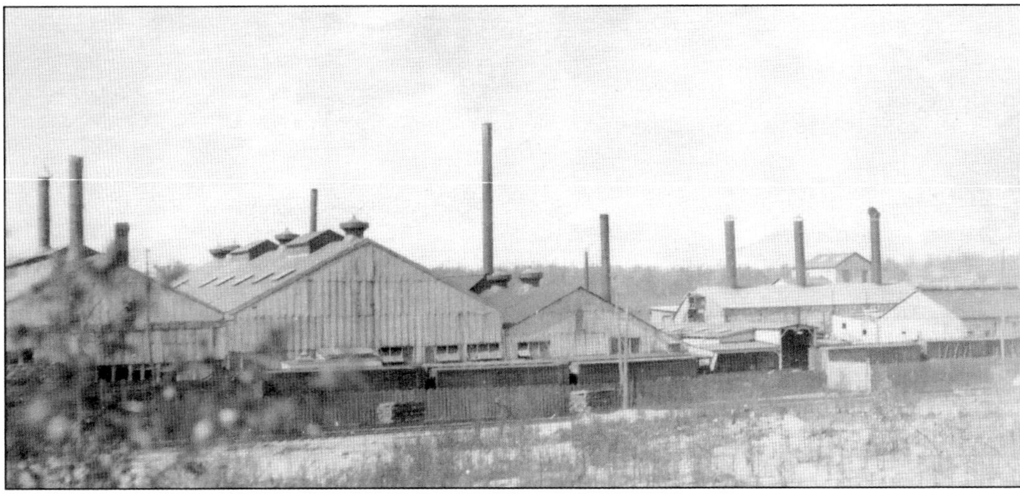

This 1926 image shows an overview of the Tottenville Copper Company, located at the edge of town along a railroad spur line and the Arthur Kill. Scrap metals, mostly lead and copper, were bought and melted down, refined, and then purified and resold at the plant. The company employed a good majority of the men of Tottenville and neighboring towns, and a train station was built nearby for the convenience of its workers. (Courtesy of the Wilkie-Farina family.)

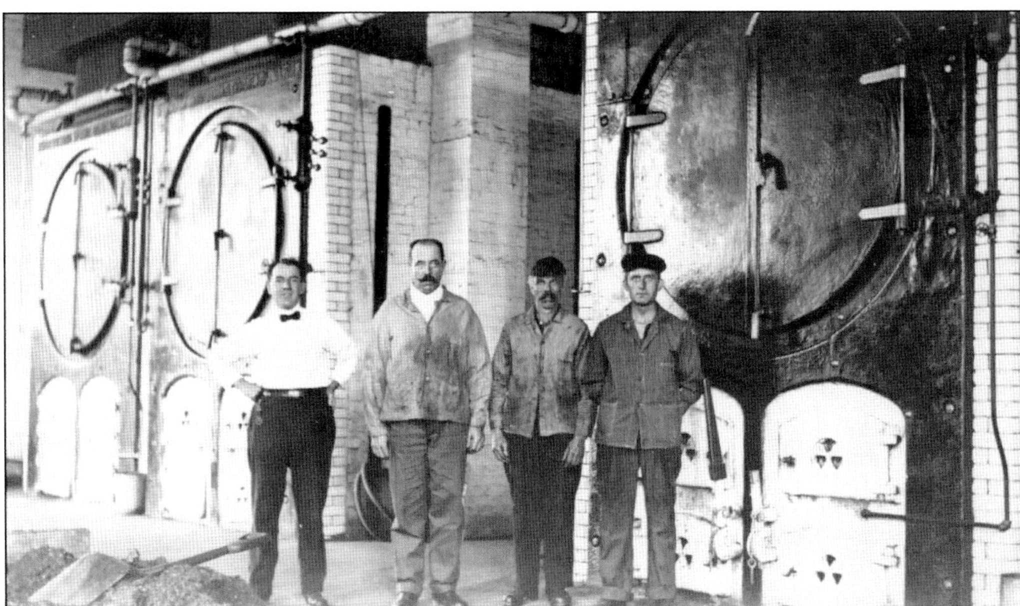

Management and workers pose for a rare 1920s interior photograph showing the huge boilers and furnaces at the copper works. Pictured are the firemen who shovel the coal, shown at the bottom left, into the furnaces. (Courtesy of the John Bieser Estate.)

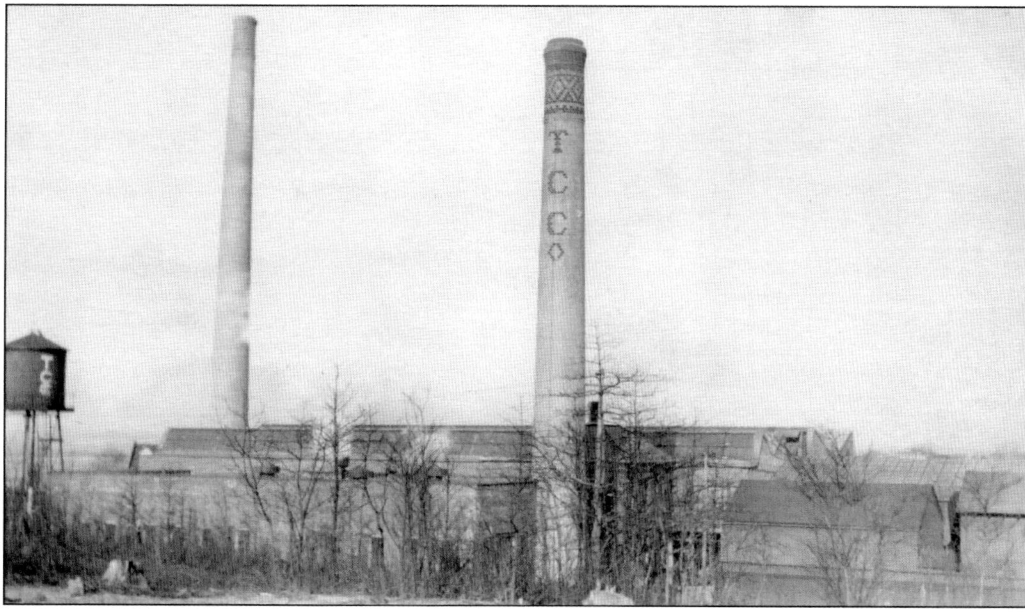

Tall smokestacks rise above the copper factory in this 1920s image. The smokestack shows an elaborate colored brick design at the top and also sports the company's initials. Established by Benjamin Lowenstein in 1900, the business was sold in 1931 to the Western Electric Company and renamed Nassau Smelting and Refining Company. (Courtesy of the John Bieser Estate.)

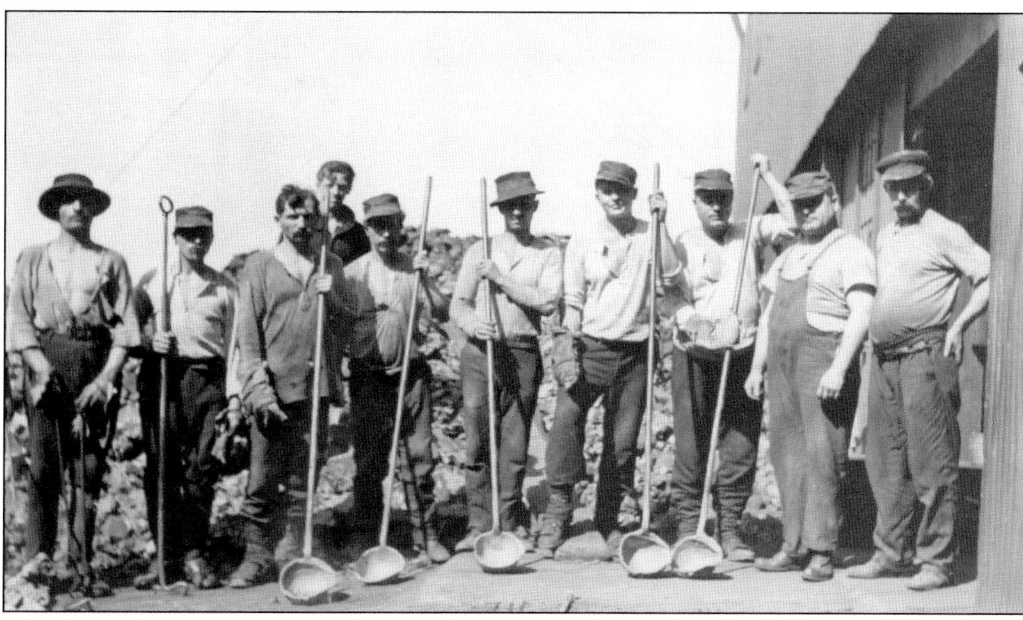

Another rare image shows a team of workers with their long-handled tools used in the process of melting iron ores and refining metals. (Courtesy of the John Bieser Estate.)

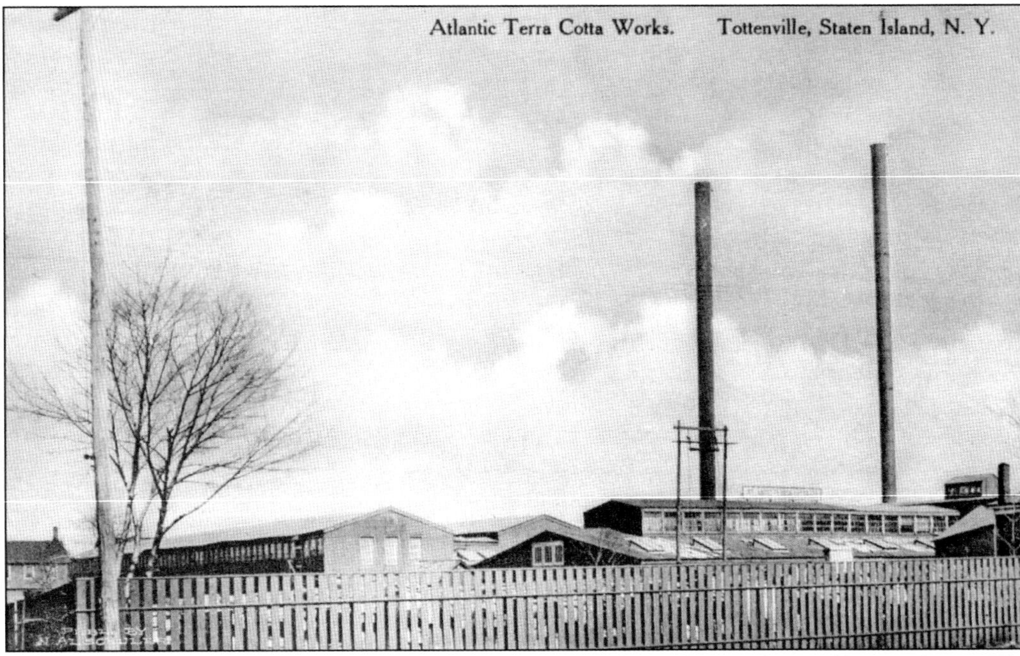

The Atlantic Terra Cotta Works was founded in 1897 along the Arthur Kill waterfront. The waterway provided a convenient means of shipping and receiving goods. Terra-cotta is basically fired clay that can be molded into a variety of building elements. The company made decorative and colorful clay products that were used on many important buildings, including the Woolworth Building, the original Madison Square Garden, and the elaborate pediment of the Philadelphia Museum of Art. This plant was one of the largest employers in the early 20th century.

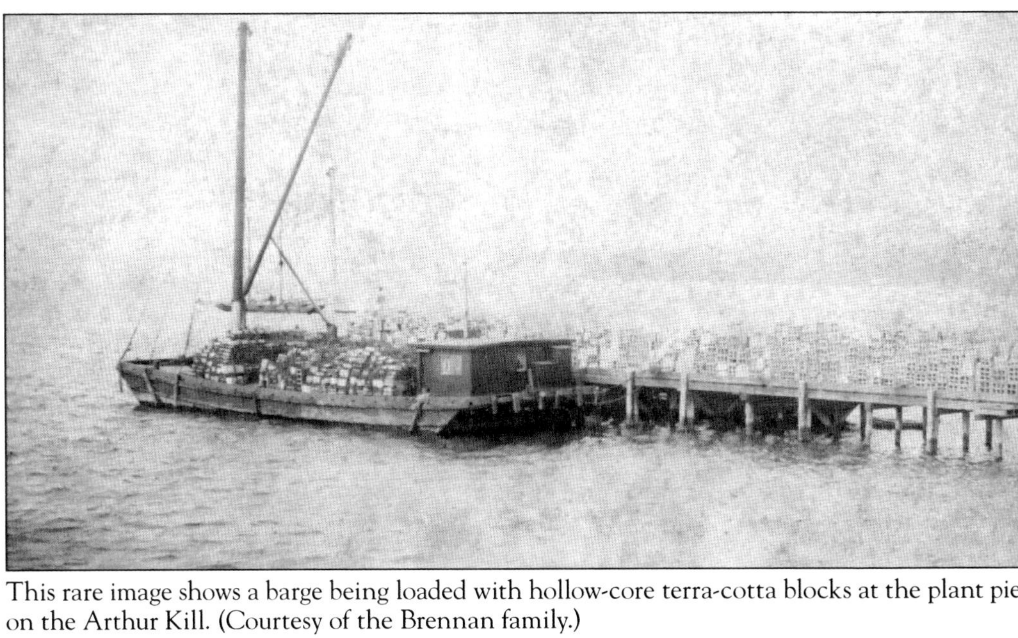

This rare image shows a barge being loaded with hollow-core terra-cotta blocks at the plant pier on the Arthur Kill. (Courtesy of the Brennan family.)

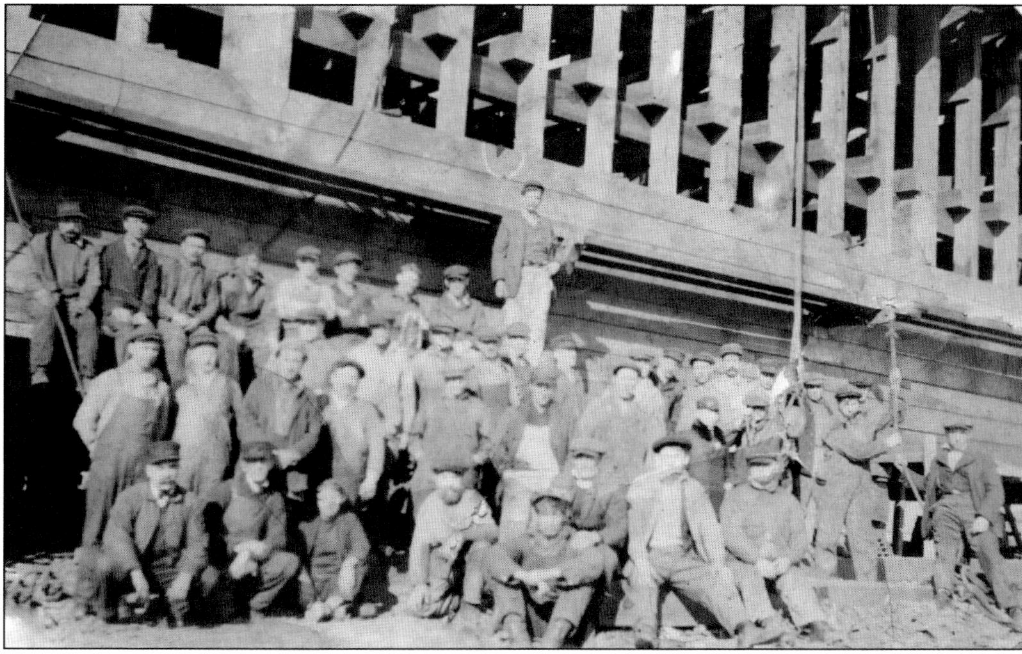

Workers at the Tottenville Shipyard pose in front of a massive dry dock in this *c.* 1920 photograph. The Tottenville waterfront had many successful shipyards, but little is known of this company other than that it was sold in 1958. (Courtesy of the Anna Papp Collection.)

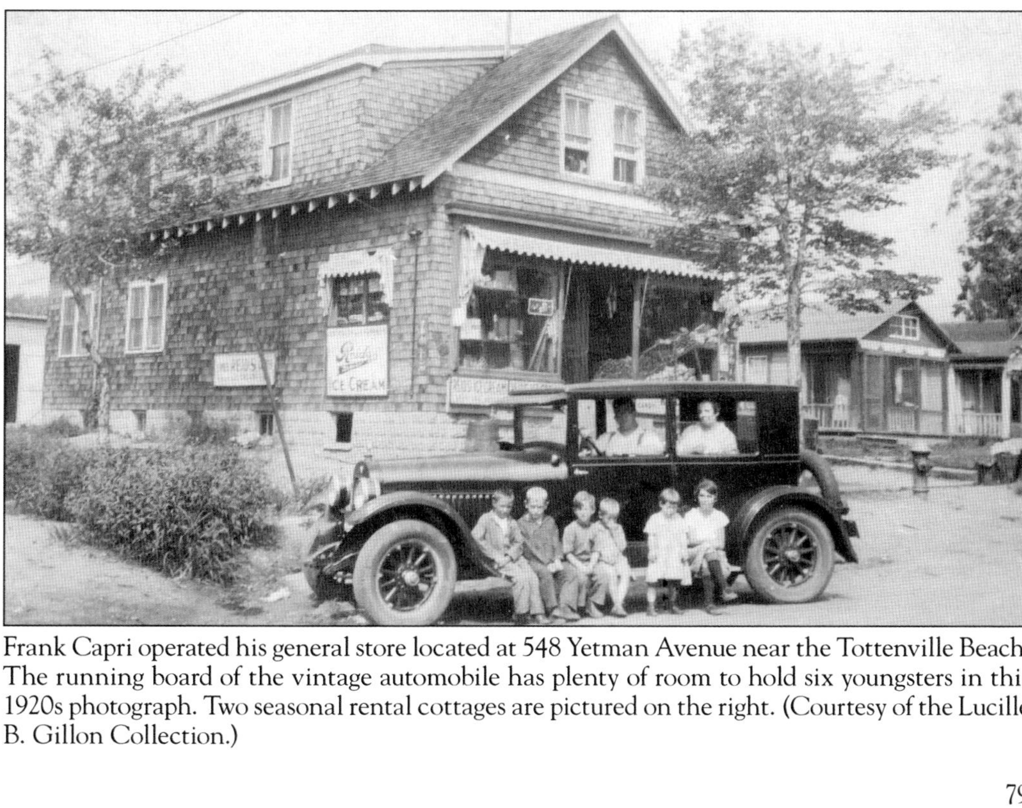

Frank Capri operated his general store located at 548 Yetman Avenue near the Tottenville Beach. The running board of the vintage automobile has plenty of room to hold six youngsters in this 1920s photograph. Two seasonal rental cottages are pictured on the right. (Courtesy of the Lucille B. Gillon Collection.)

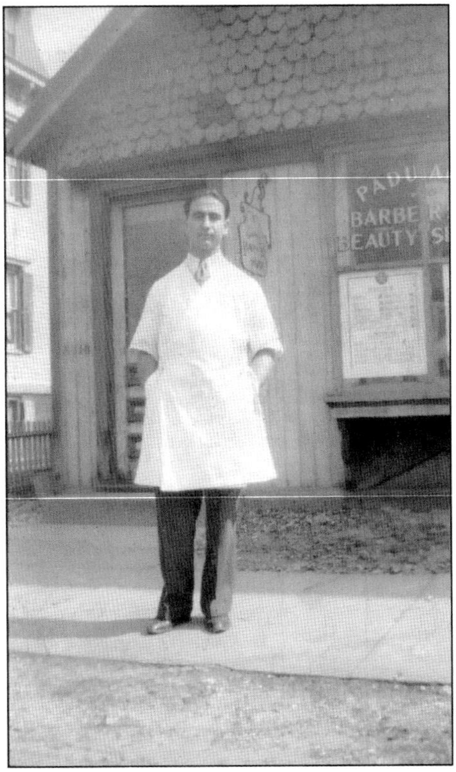

In 1934, at age 18, David Paduani poses for this photograph in front of his barbershop and beauty parlor. David took over the shop after his father's retirement. Located on Arthur Kill Road just off the corner of busy Main Street, the building had fanciful fish scale shingles on its gable. On the storefront window, haircut prices are posted. In the 1970s, George Burke, a talented local interior decorator and preservationist, remodeled the one-room, 14-foot-wide barbershop into a cozy cottage home. (Courtesy of the George Burke Collection.)

"Hi, neighbor!" was the cheery greeting given to all who walked through the door of Dave Walters's tavern at 83 Main Street. Better known as Pickles, the establishment was the best place to share a brew and a story. Dave was a member of the volunteer fire department and lined the walls of the tavern with fire memorabilia; a pool table took up the back area. Smiling Dave is pictured behind the tap in this 1978 photograph. (Courtesy of Judith Johnston Sarsten.)

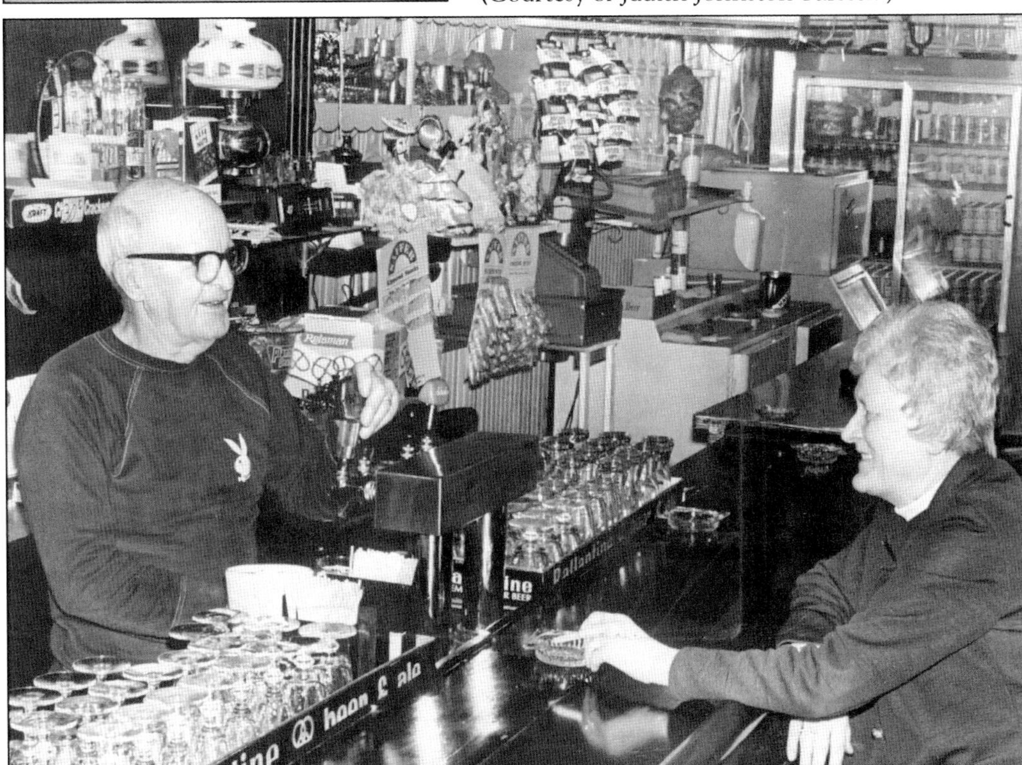

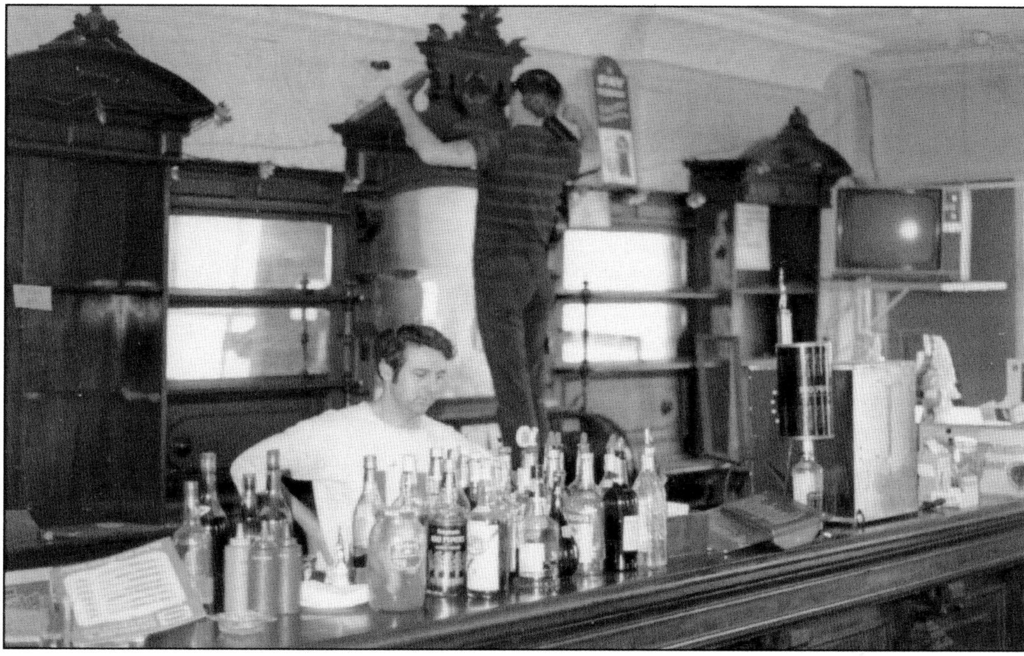

Preservationist and Tidewater Inn owner George Burke is pictured here in 1973 behind a newly installed bar. The bar and back bar were originally made in 1873 for the McAlpin Hotel in Manhattan. Burke restored several buildings in Tottenville using salvaged antique elements. (Courtesy of the George Burke Collection.)

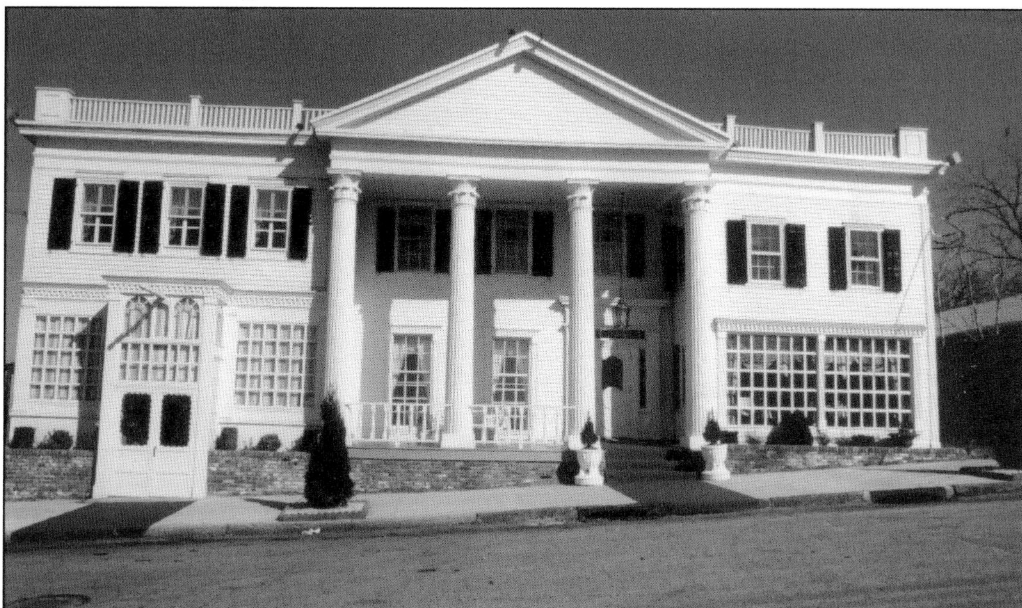

This beautiful 1853 Greek Revival house was moved in 1896 when the railroad was extended to Bentley Street. Its new location was next to the bustling railroad and ferry terminal at the foot of Bentley Street, and so it began a new existence as a successful commercial property. In 1973, George Burke bought the derelict building and began restoring it both inside and out. He opened it as the Tidewater Inn. (Courtesy of the George Burke Collection.)

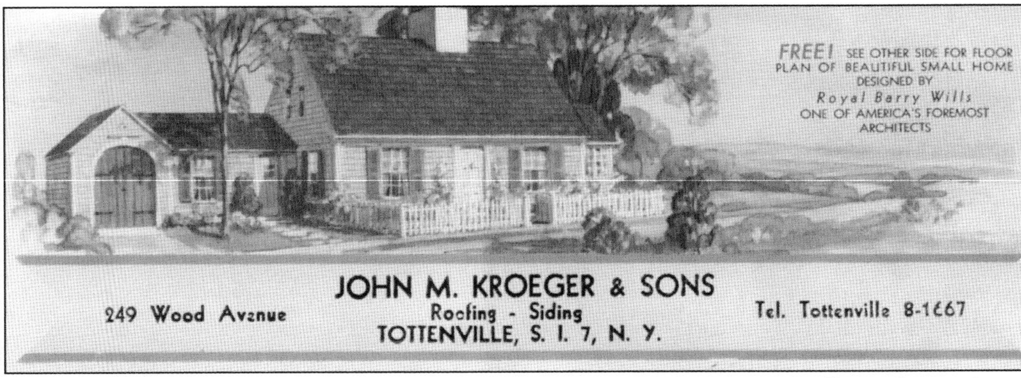

John M. Kroeger started his business in 1945 from a private house in Tottenville. Father and sons John and Arnold did roofing and siding and all types of general carpentry. Slate and tile roofs were a specialty of the company. In 1962, John M. Kroeger retired, and his sons continued the business from a commercial property on Yetman Avenue until their own retirement in 2005.

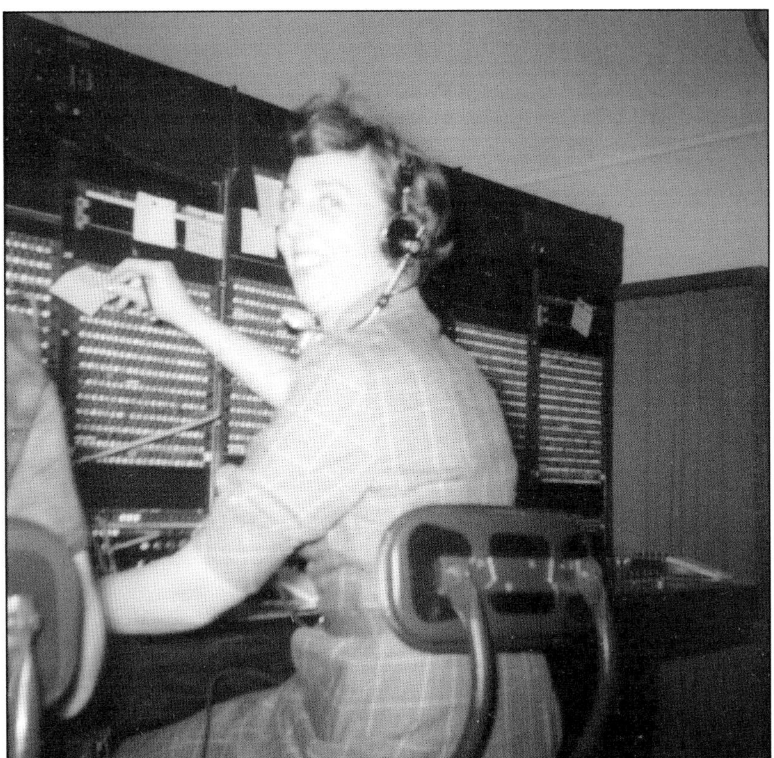

Chesta M. Dunigan is shown here working a manually operated switchboard directing telephone calls for the Tottenville 8 exchange. The phone exchange was located in a private house at 7255 Amboy Road from 1921 until 1958. (Courtesy of Chesta M. Dunigan.)

The Homestead Luncheonette in this 1945 image was owned by Chesta E. Dunigan and was located at 7222 Amboy Road. A fancy tile floor leads to the screen door and past the large display window. (Courtesy of Chesta M. Dunigan.)

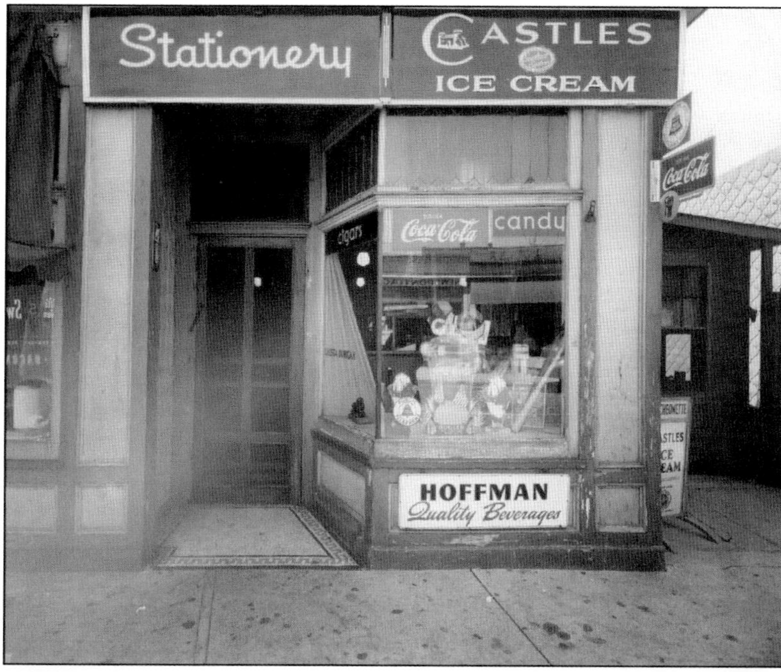

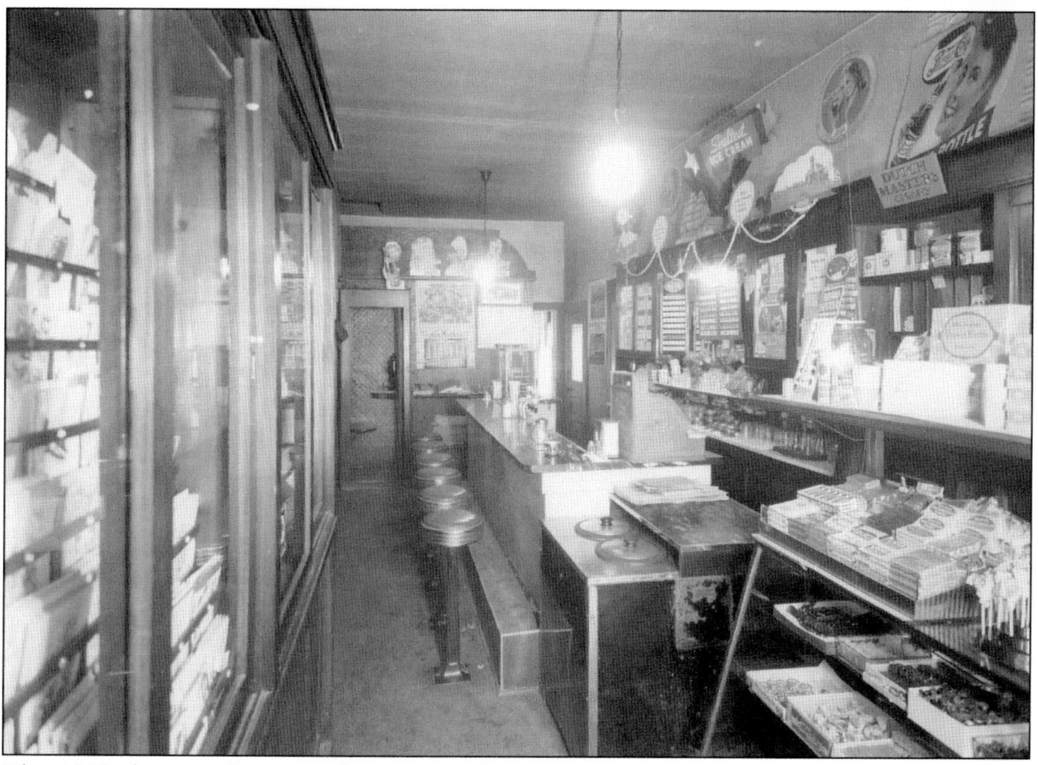

This 1945 photograph gives a glimpse into the interior of the store. The glass doors on the left hold magazines, while candies and treats are displayed on the right. High stools are lined up at the counter, and a refrigerated icebox with two lids contains Castles ice cream. (Courtesy of Chesta M. Dunigan.)

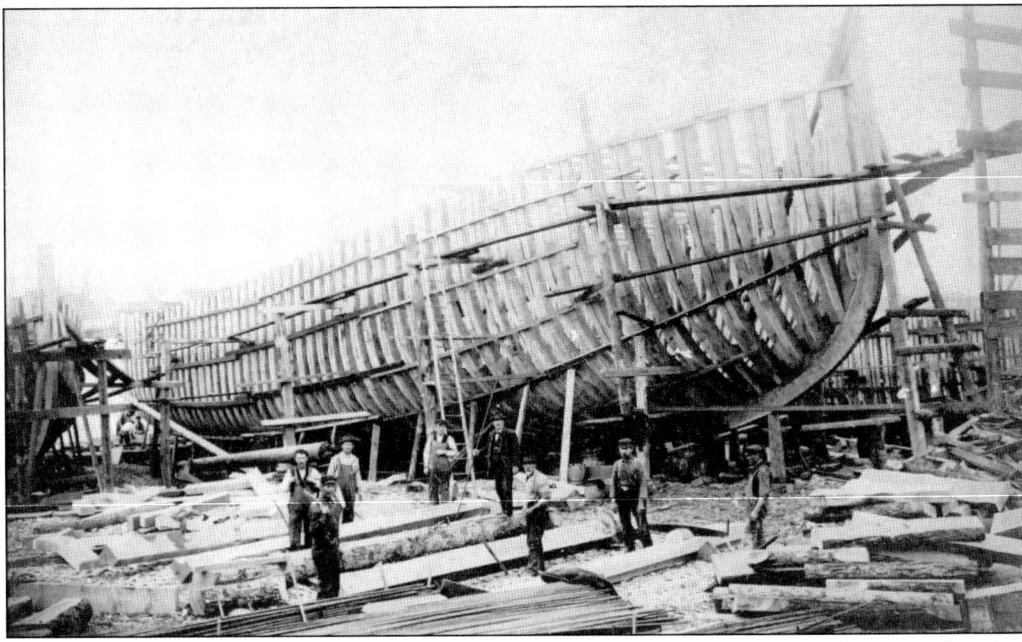

The giant ribbed hull of a tugboat takes shape at the A. C. Brown Shipyard at the foot of Amboy Road. Brown's was well known for building tugs and had a contract to build them for the government during the First World War. (Courtesy of the Charles Munroe Collection.)

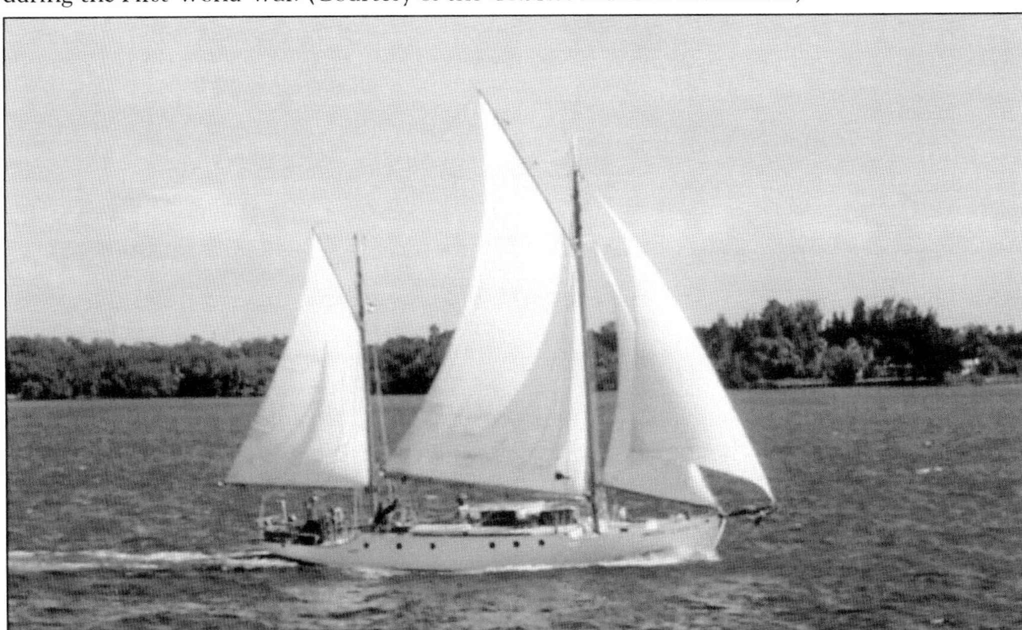

One of the last surviving yachts built by A. C. Brown Shipyard came back to its place of construction in August 2007. The ketch *Carib II*, owned by David Soule, stopped on its way to Maine for restoration work. During its stay in Tottenville, the *Carib II*, built in 1924, was moored at the Bentley Yacht Club in the very same waters from which it was launched over 80 years ago. The owner was gracious enough to allow the Tottenville Historical Society to host an "open boat" reception, and many people came out to board this grand vessel. (Courtesy of David Soule.)

Six

Around the Town

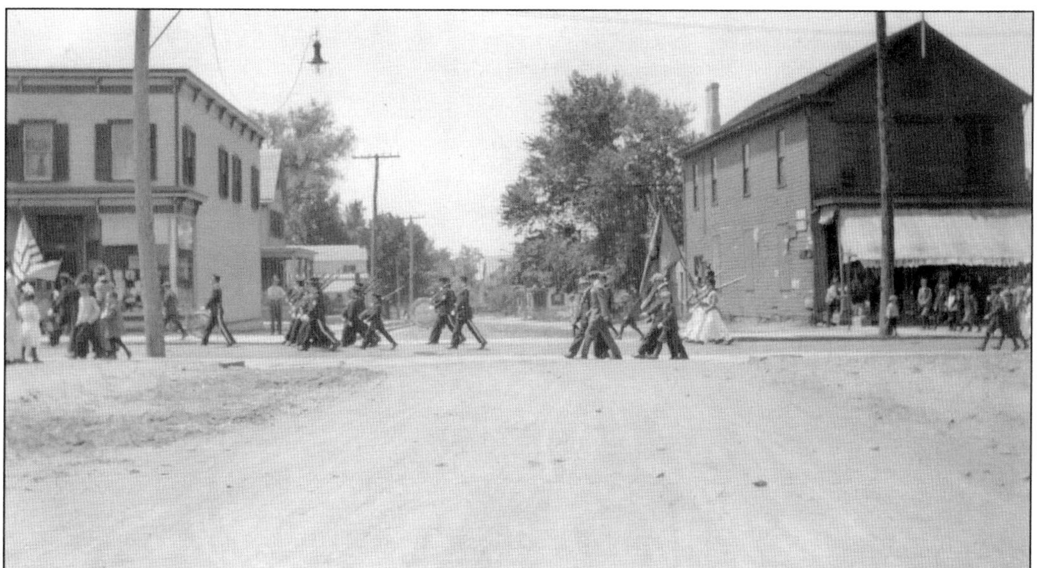

A parade is marching south on Main Street towards Amboy Road in this rare 1907 photograph. The building on the right was constructed as the Pepper and Joline General Store in the 1870s and continues today as the Cracker Barrel delicatessen. In 1917, the Richmond County Federal Savings and Loan Association replaced the frame building pictured on the left with a new bank. (Courtesy of the John Bieser Estate.)

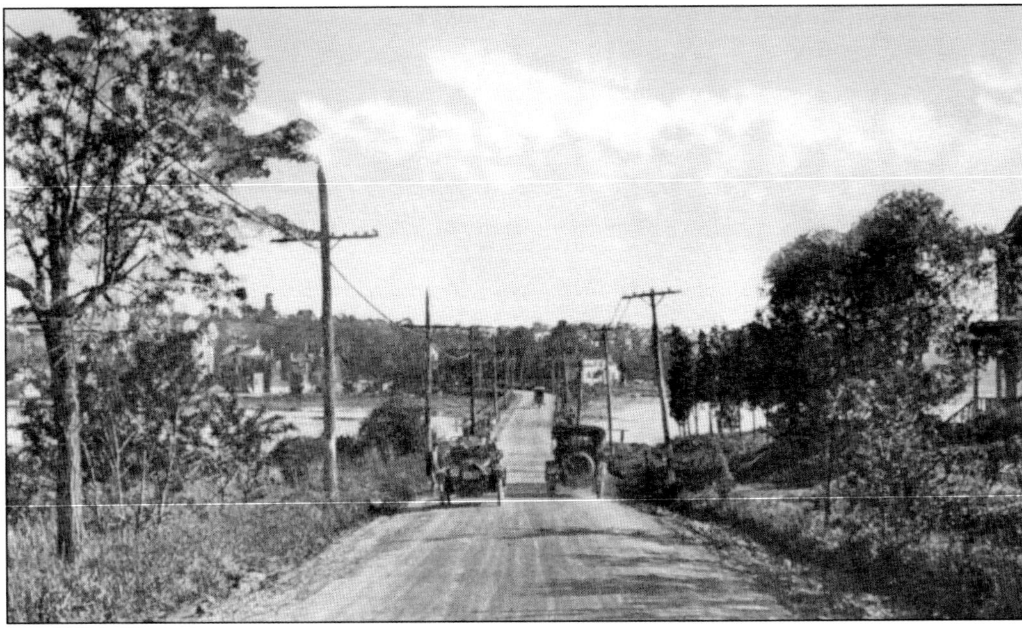

The view of Fresh Kills Road, now Arthur Kill Road, looking towards Tottenville is very different today. Part of the creek on the left was filled in for the expansion of the Tottenville Copper Company. The road was reconfigured in the 1930s when the railroad grade crossings were eliminated.

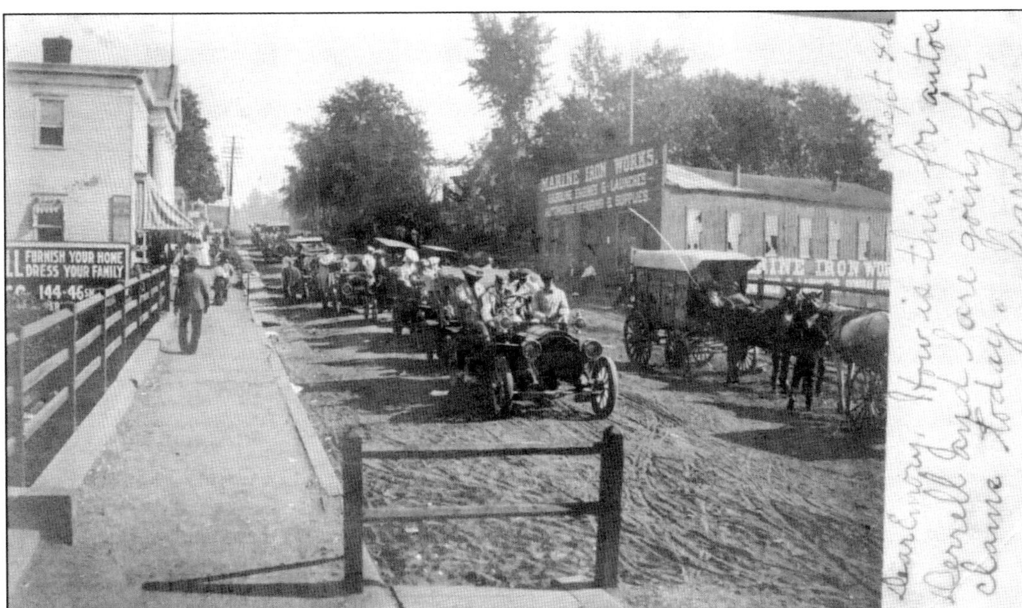

A long line of automobiles and horse-drawn carriages awaits the arrival of the Perth Amboy–Tottenville ferry in this rare 1906 postcard. The Marine Iron Works on the right repaired boat and automobile engines. The Ferry Hotel on the left served travelers on the New York-to-Philadelphia route.

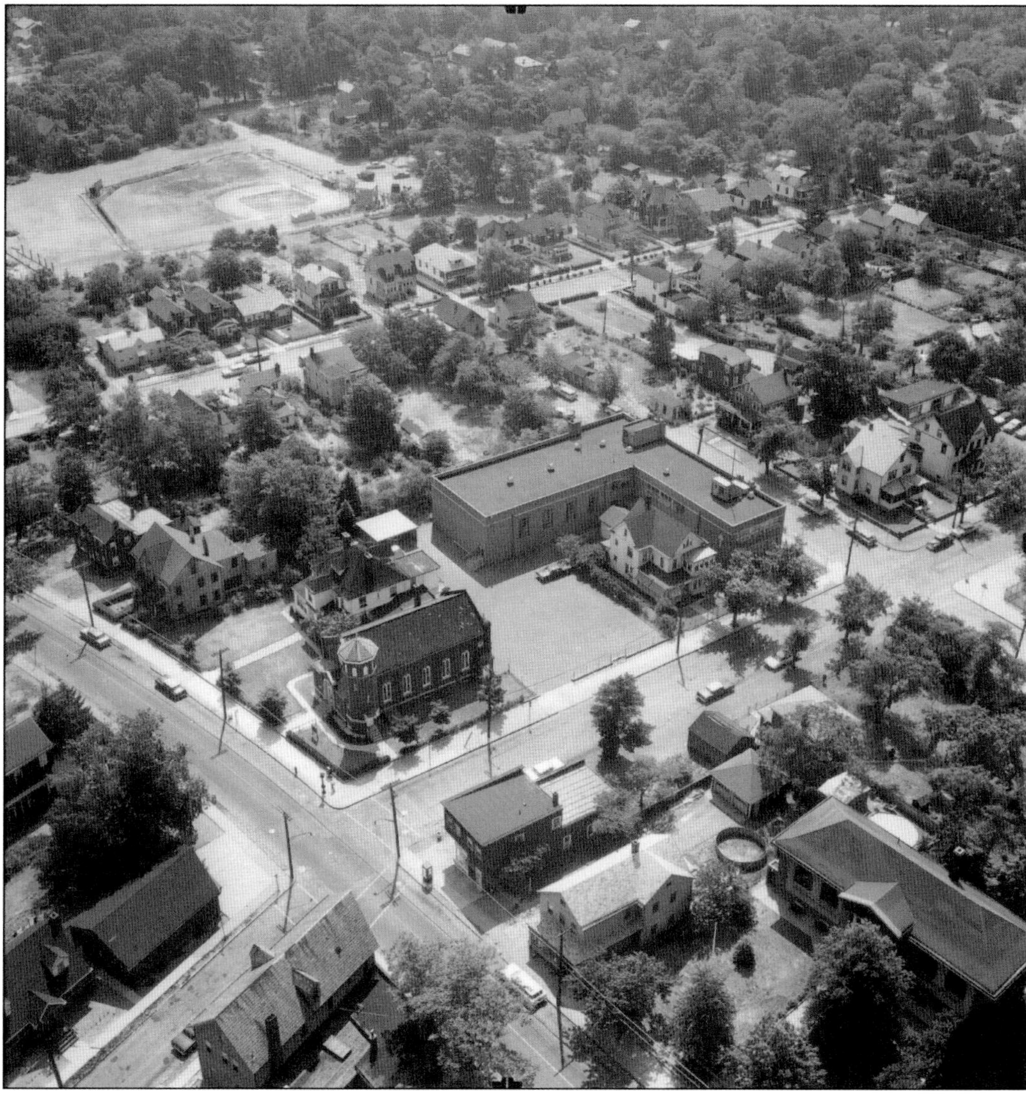

In the center of this 1960s photograph is Our Lady Help of Christians Church and School, located on Yetman Avenue and Amboy Road. The Aquehonga baseball field can be seen in the upper left. The large building in the lower right-hand corner is the Tottenville Library, located on Amboy Road. (Courtesy of the Eckel family.)

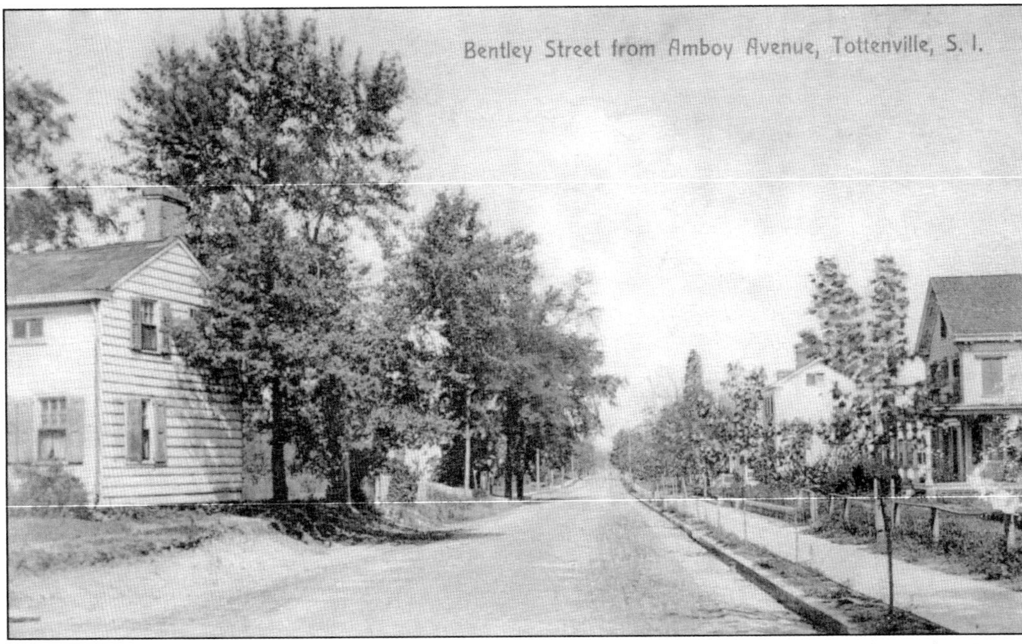

For unknown reasons, the 19th-century house on the corner of Amboy Road and Bentley Street seen in this 1915 postcard was moved to face Bentley Street. Moving houses was not an uncommon practice into the 20th century.

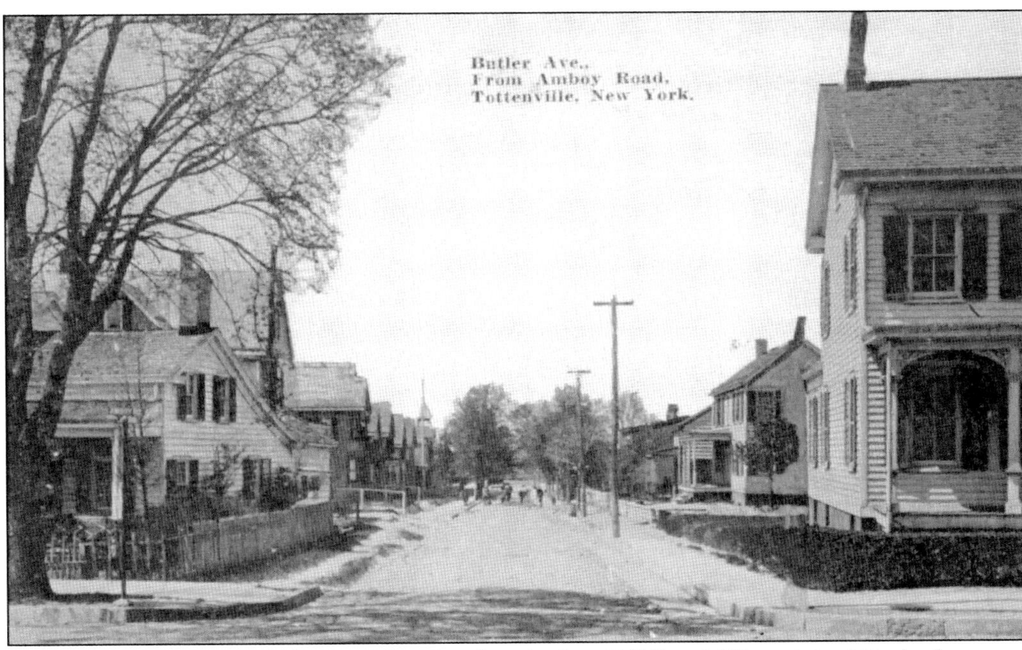

Butler Avenue runs north from Amboy Road to Arthur Kill Road. The original Butler house on the left, 7583 Amboy Road, was built for Daniel Butler, an oysterman, on several acres of land. The house on the right was built in 1875 for oysterman and developer Charles Drake.

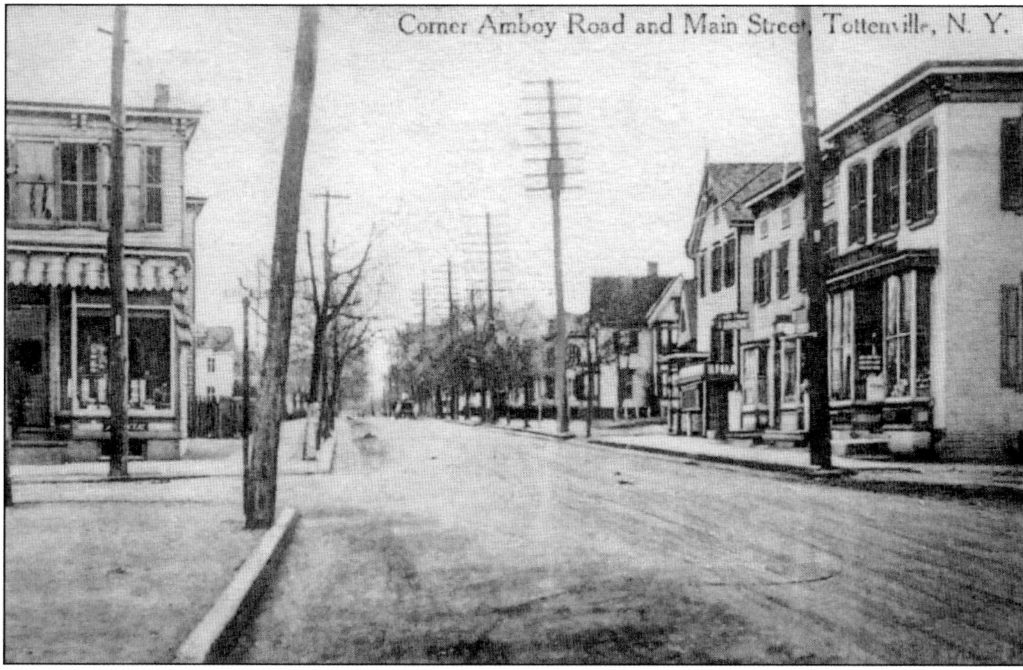

The corner building on the right housed the first local A&P and later became Mary's Five and Ten. Across Amboy Road is H. E. Sprague's Confectionery at 249 Main Street. Since 1870, this building has been almost continually occupied by a food service business.

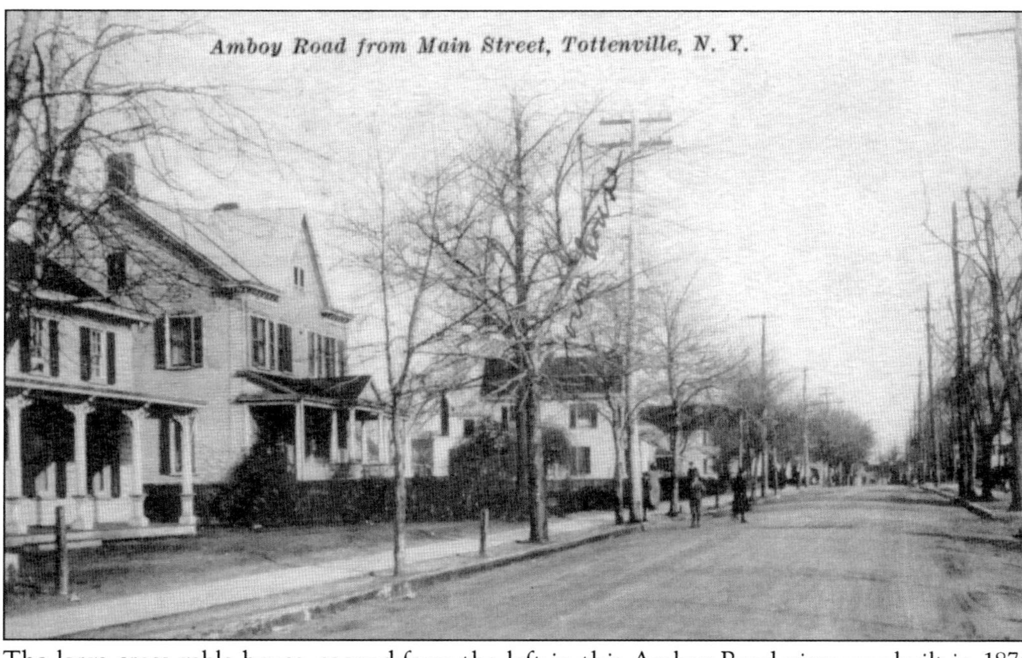

The large cross-gable house, second from the left in this Amboy Road view, was built in 1874 for oyster dealer Abraham Latourette. From 1890, Dr. David Coleman, a longtime Tottenville physician, maintained his office and residence here for almost 50 years. The home on the far left was demolished; a row of stores occupies the site today.

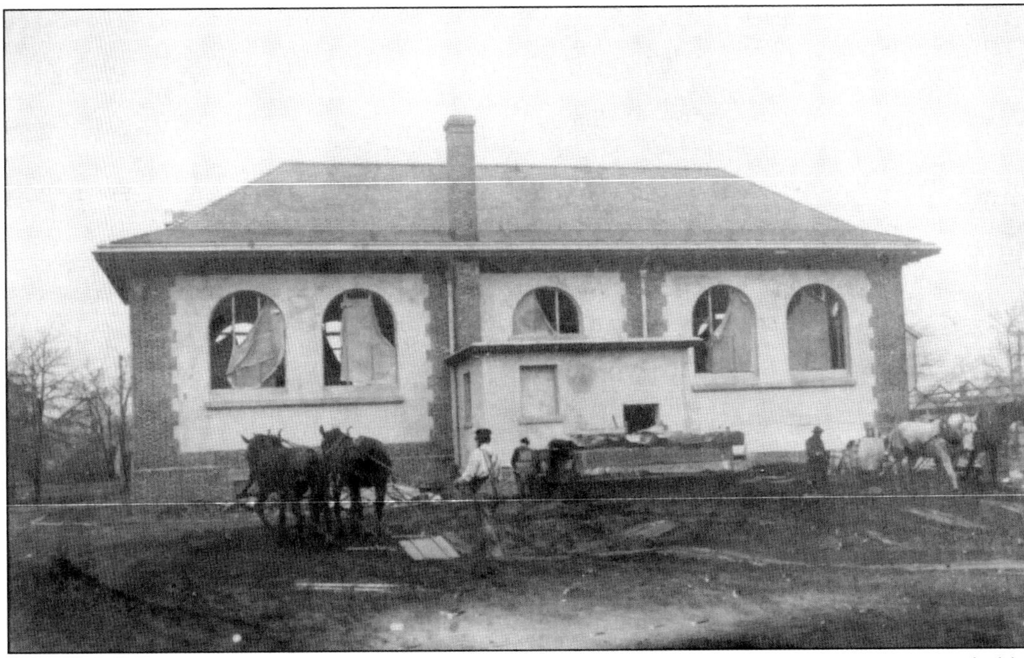

Construction of the Tottenville Branch Library at 7430 Amboy Road began in 1903. Funded by philanthropist Andrew Carnegie, it was the first public library built on Staten Island. Horses provide power during construction in this 1904 view of the building's rear facade. The elongated, round-arched window glass had not yet been installed. Designed by architects Carrere and Hastings, the building was designated a New York City landmark in 1995. (Courtesy of the New York Public Library.)

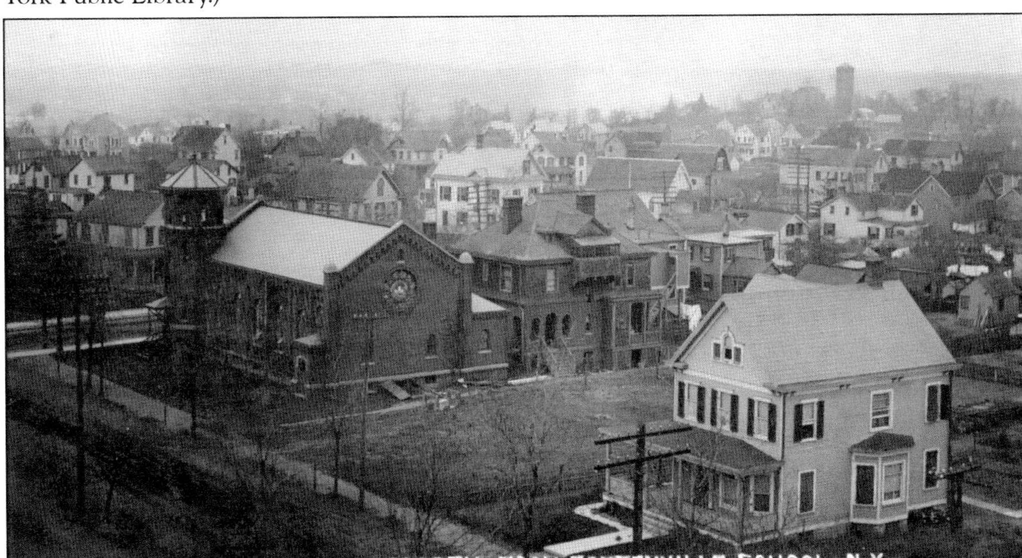

This 1906 bird's-eye view looking north was taken from the elementary school. A rear view of Our Lady Help of Christians Church shows its large stained-glass rose window. This Romanesque-style brick church was heavily damaged by fire in 1985 and replaced with a modern structure in 1990. The building in the foreground was the convent. (Courtesy of the Nancy Ryan Williams Collection.)

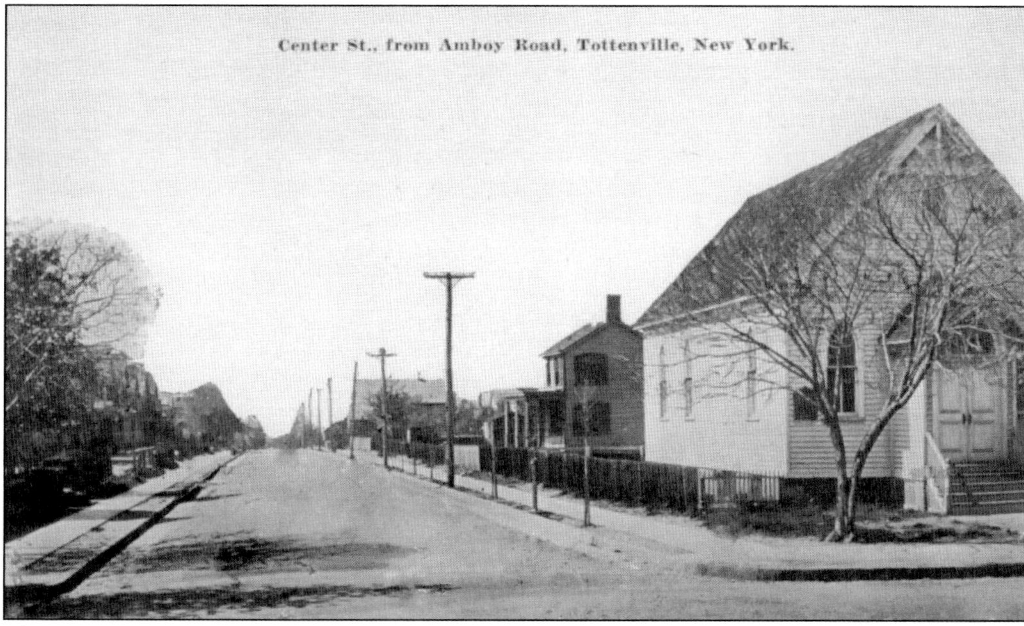

This 1915 postcard image shows Center Street, now Lee Avenue, from Amboy Road. The house behind the church had been moved from Amboy Road around 1906. In 1926, the church, known as the Wells Memorial Church, underwent extensive renovations.

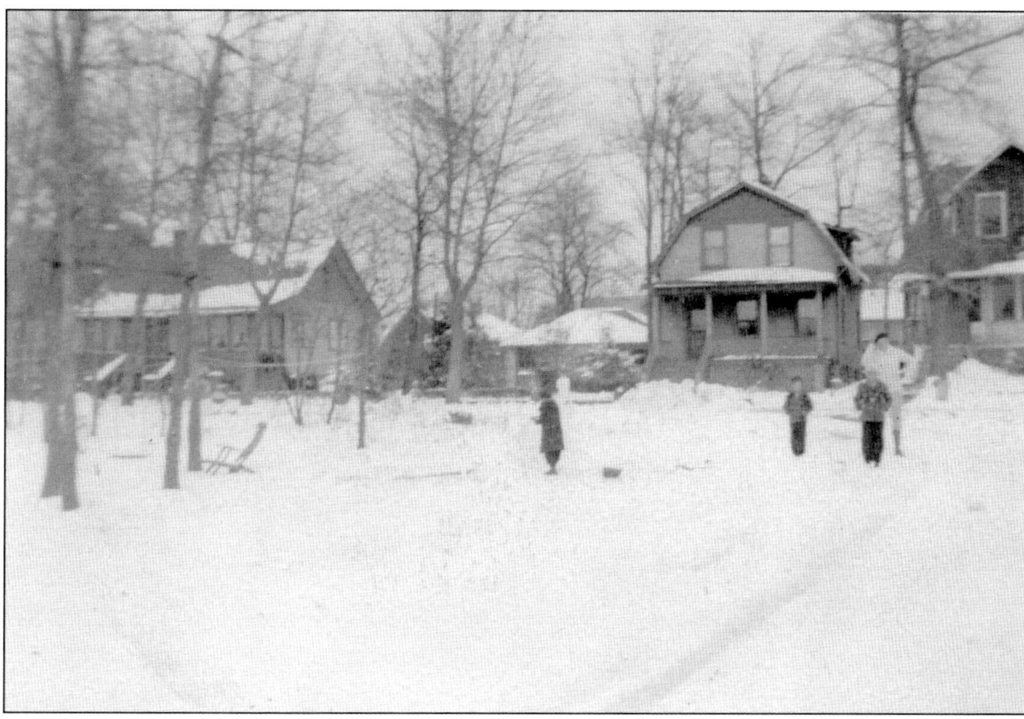

These children are playing in the snow on Summit Road near Aspinwall Street in this 1945 photograph. The empty lot on the corner was a favorite playground for the neighborhood children. (Courtesy of the Linda Cutler Hauck Collection.)

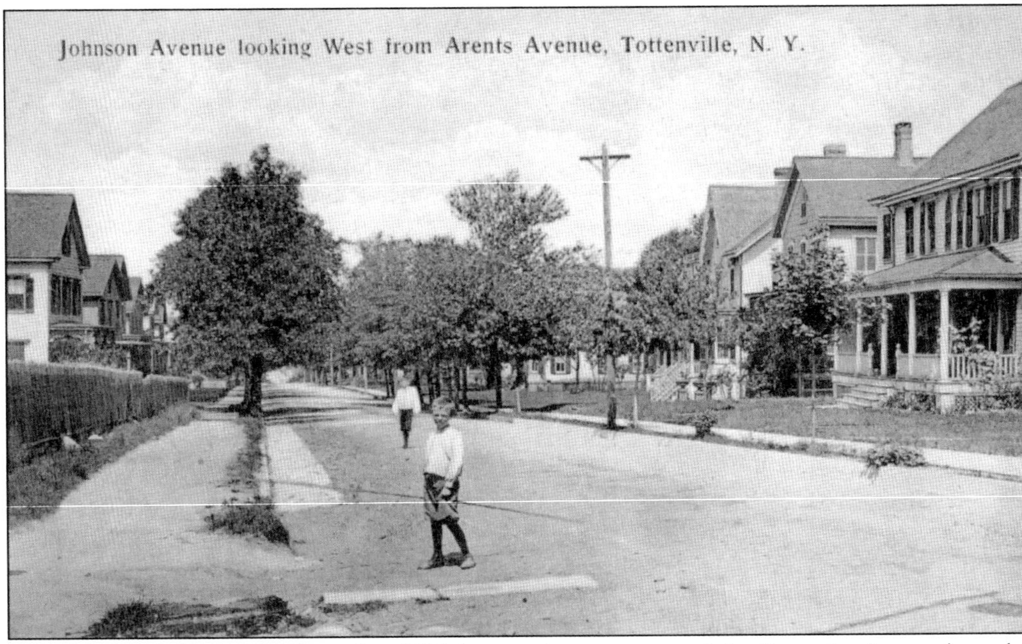

The two-family house on the right, 175 Johnson Avenue, was originally set back on a large lot owned by the Arents family and later was moved closer to the street. This 1910 view is from Arents Avenue, now named Craig Avenue.

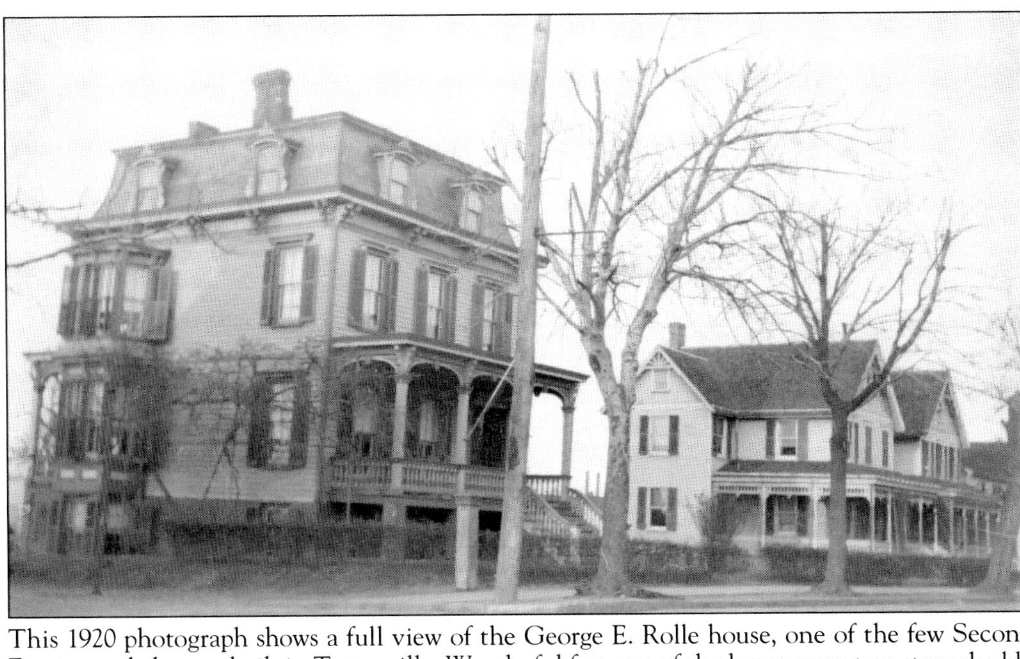

This 1920 photograph shows a full view of the George E. Rolle house, one of the few Second Empire–style houses built in Tottenville. Wonderful features of the house were two-story double bay windows, a porch with teardrop fretwork, and a mansard roof. The home was demolished in the 1930s. In the early 1930s, the *Staten Island Transcript* newspaper moved its printing offices from Amboy Road and built a new facility on this site at the corner of Amboy Road and Johnson Avenue. (Courtesy of the John Bieser Estate.)

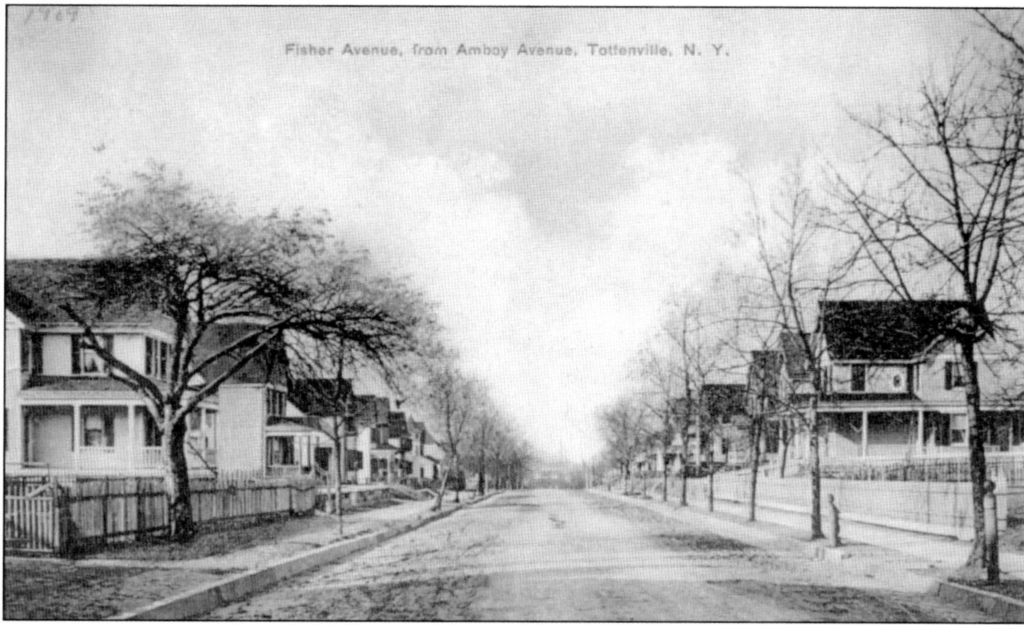

Young trees line Fisher Avenue, formerly called Fisher's Lane. The hitching posts in this 1909 postcard help date the image. The Victorian house on the right was built in 1906 for Eugene LaForge, a dental works technician.

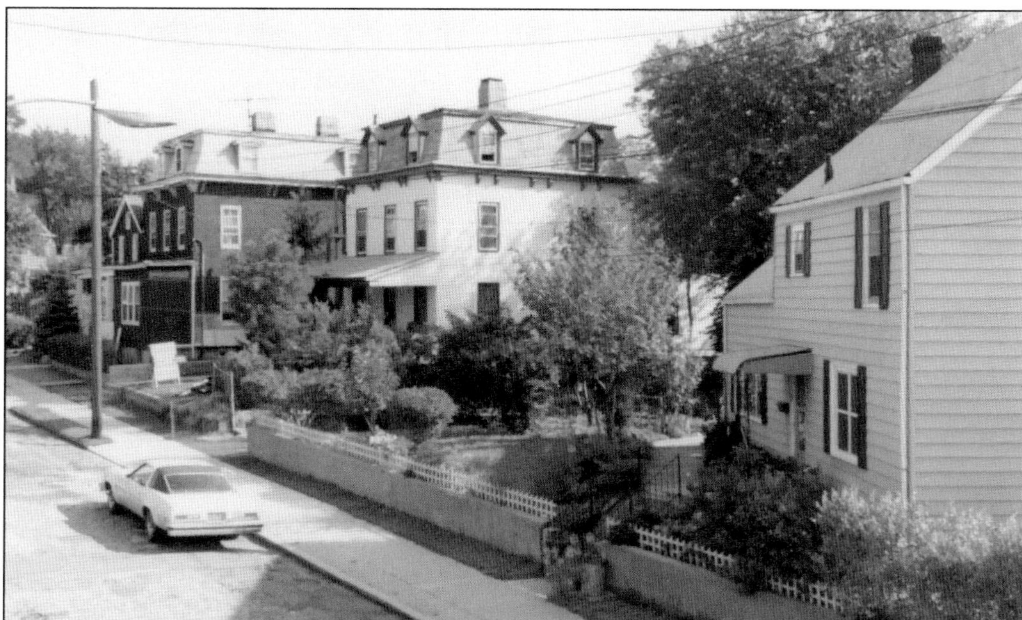

This 1981 view of lower Main Street was taken from the Tottenville train pedestrian overpass. The house on the right, 62 Main Street, is the oldest surviving home in the former village of Tottenville, occupied by John Totten Jr. and his wife, Elizabeth Butler Totten. Built around 1834 or earlier, this residence is called the Compass House because of its exact orientation. The two mansard-roof houses to its left were built for Totten's daughters, Mary and Anna Louise. (Courtesy of the Schaming family.)

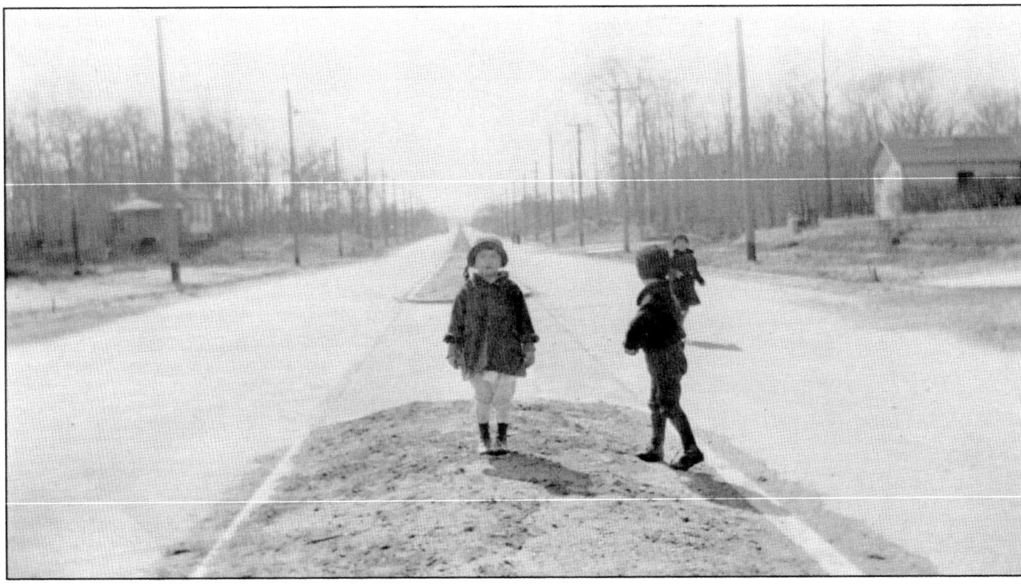

Chesta M. Dunigan (left) and friends play on the median near Manhattan Street on the newly constructed Hylan Boulevard in 1927. (Courtesy of Chesta M. Dunigan.)

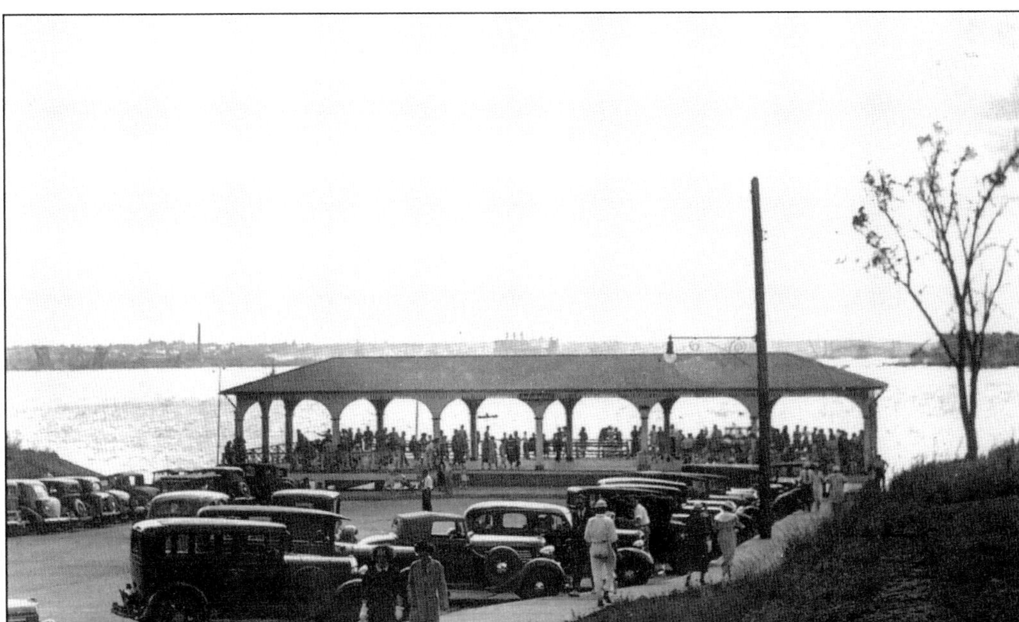

The original Russell Pavilion at the foot of Hylan Boulevard, shown here in this 1930s photograph, was a great gathering place to listen to concerts or catch a cool breeze. It was erected in 1934 to honor local resident Almer G. Russell, who was killed in action during World War I. (Courtesy of the Biller family.)

Seven

TRANSPORTATION

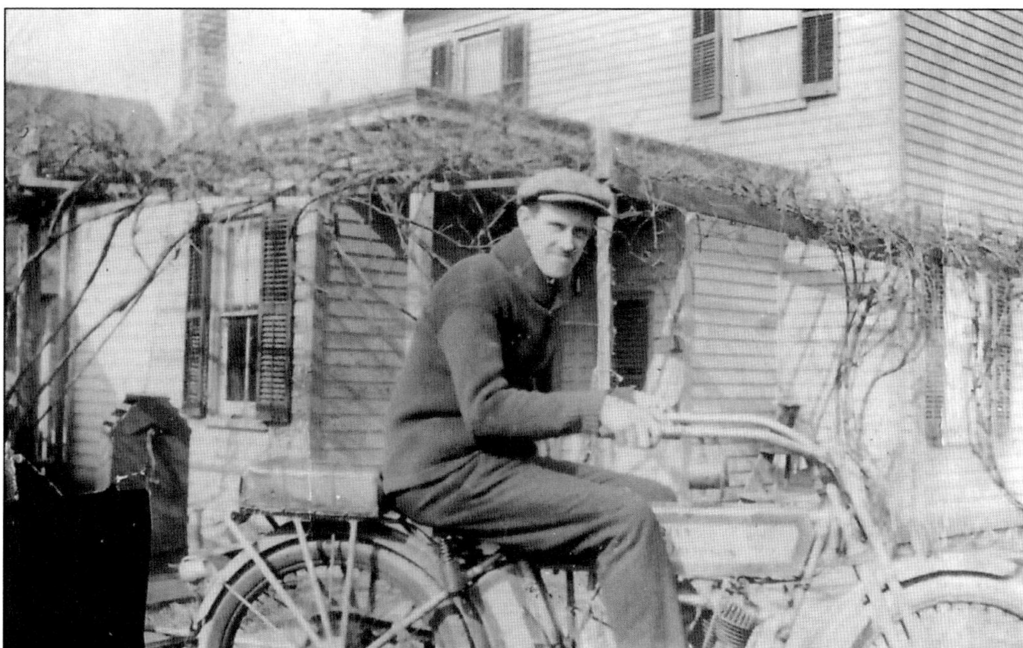

Nils Joseph Peterson is pictured in this *c.* 1918 image aboard his beloved Harley Davidson motorbike. Early motorcycles were basically motorized bicycles and very simple in style, as this photograph shows. (Courtesy of Ingrid Peterson.)

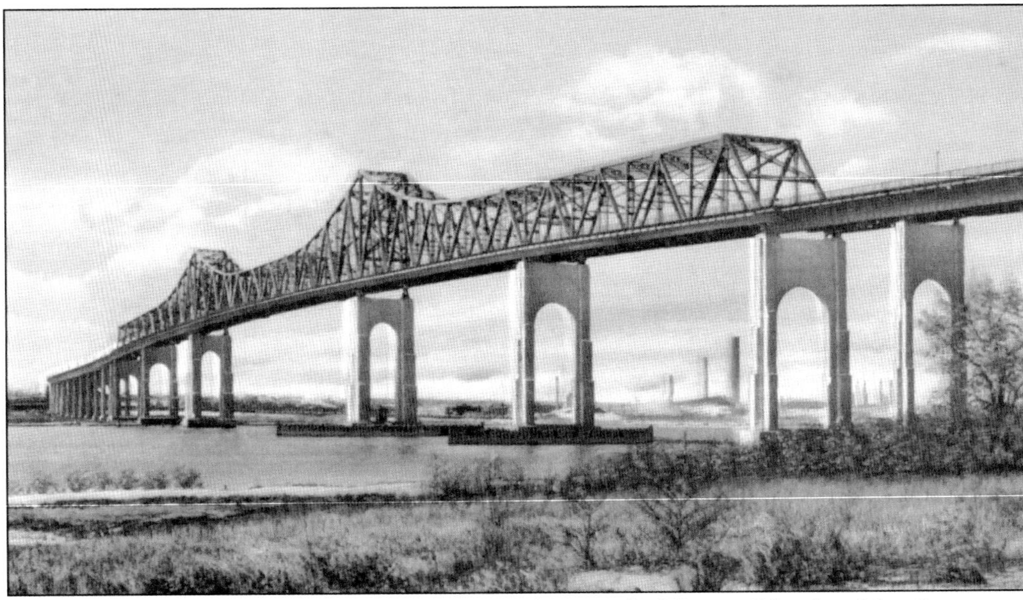

The Outerbridge Crossing, connecting the southern end of Staten Island to New Jersey, was opened in 1928. Tottenville and Perth Amboy, New Jersey, had long been linked economically, as many residents from Tottenville worked in Perth Amboy and vice versa. Tottenville residents were also attracted to Perth Amboy's large shopping district, which was within walking distance of the ferry. Despite the advantage of a modern bridge and road system, the Tottenville–Perth Amboy ferry operated for another 35 years.

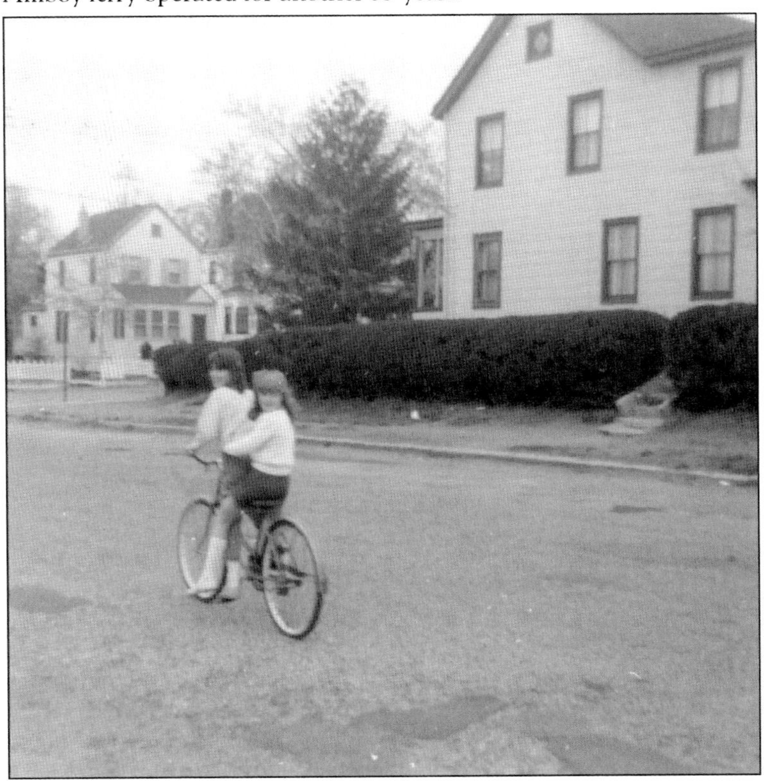

With fewer cars on the roads in 1967, Tottenville pals Kathy Beach (left) and Lisa Hohmann are riding double along Craig Avenue near Wood Avenue. (Courtesy of Linda Cutler Hauck.)

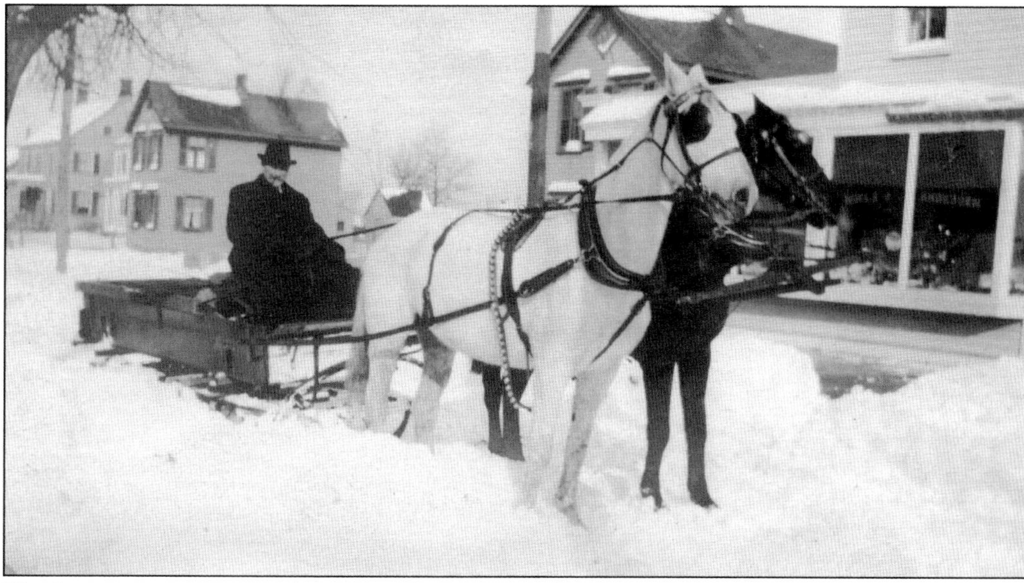

The best way to get around town in the snow was by a horse-drawn sled. An unidentified well-dressed gentleman guides his team of horses down Yetman Avenue past house builder Nils Andersen's storefront at 195 Yetman Avenue in this early 1920s photograph. (Courtesy of the John Bieser Estate.)

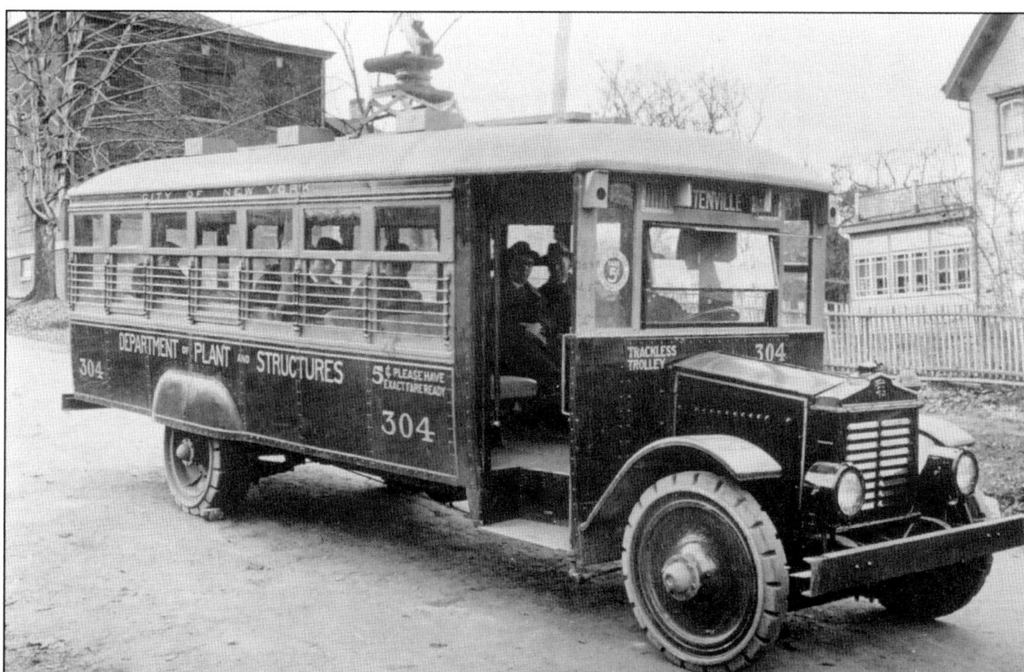

From 1922 to 1927, the trackless trolley ran along Arthur Kill Road from Richmond to Tottenville. The fare was 5¢. The trolley lasted only five years and ended in October 1927, when it was replaced by bus service with a 10¢ fare.

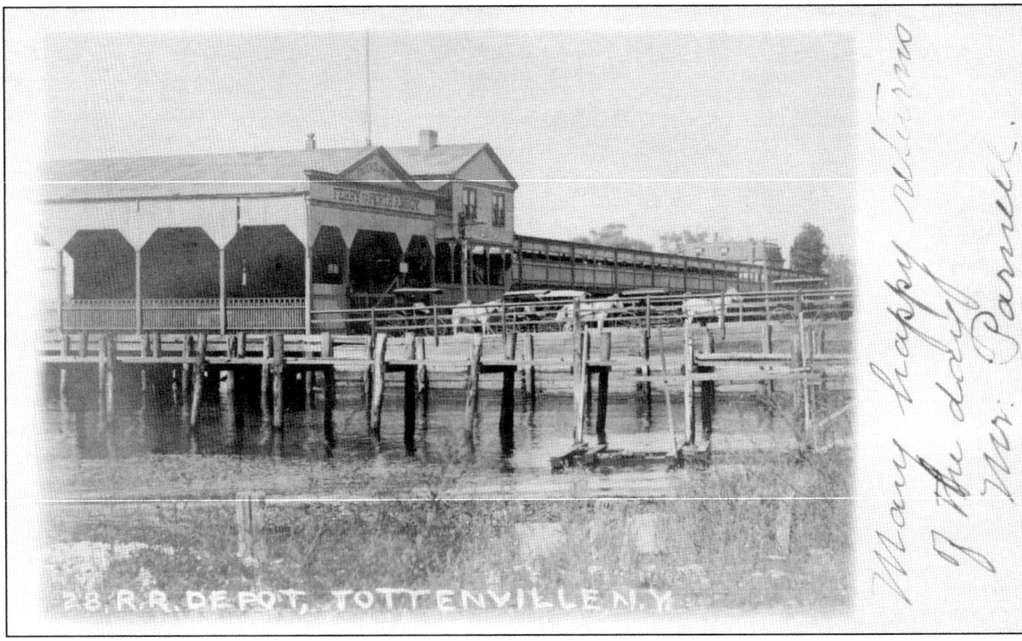

In 1896, the railroad was extended from Main Street two blocks west to Bentley Street. At that time, a new dock and terminal were built for the large, steam-powered side-wheelers that plied the waters to Perth Amboy. Pictured in this 1905 postcard are horses and carriages lined up and awaiting disembarking passengers from New Jersey. A long covered walkway extends from Main Street to the train yard. On the north side of the terminal were a waiting room and ticket and telegraph office, while the south side had a small freight house. By the 1940s, smaller diesel-powered boats were shuttling passengers to Perth Amboy, which offered jobs, shopping, and entertainment. The last ferry ran in 1963.

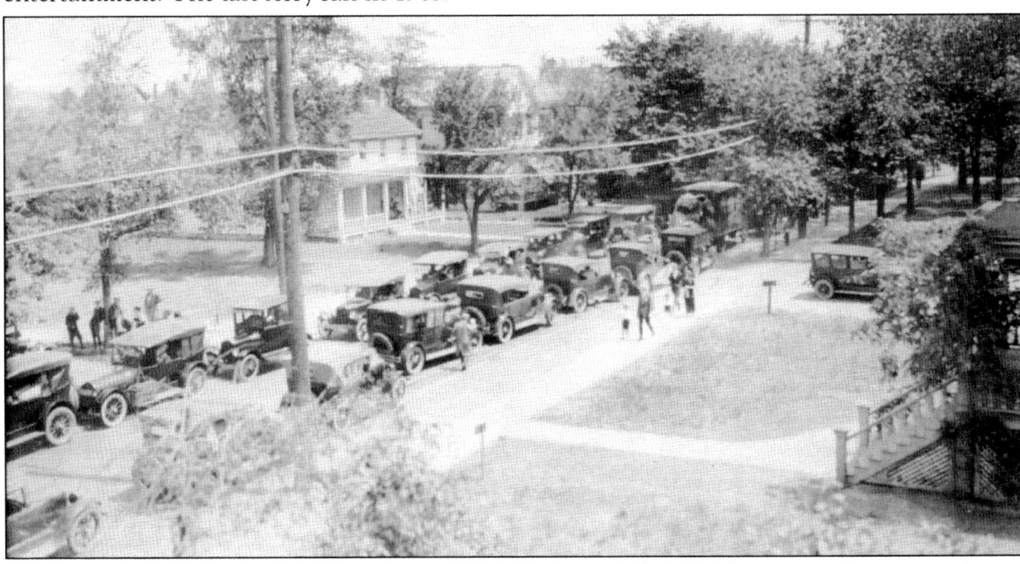

This 1920s photograph depicts a line of cars on Amboy Road at Brighton Street waiting to board the Perth Amboy Ferry, approximately 1 mile away. Ferry transportation was the only means of leaving or entering Staten Island by car until 1928, when the Goethals Bridge and Outerbridge Crossing were built. (Courtesy of the Bedell Collection.)

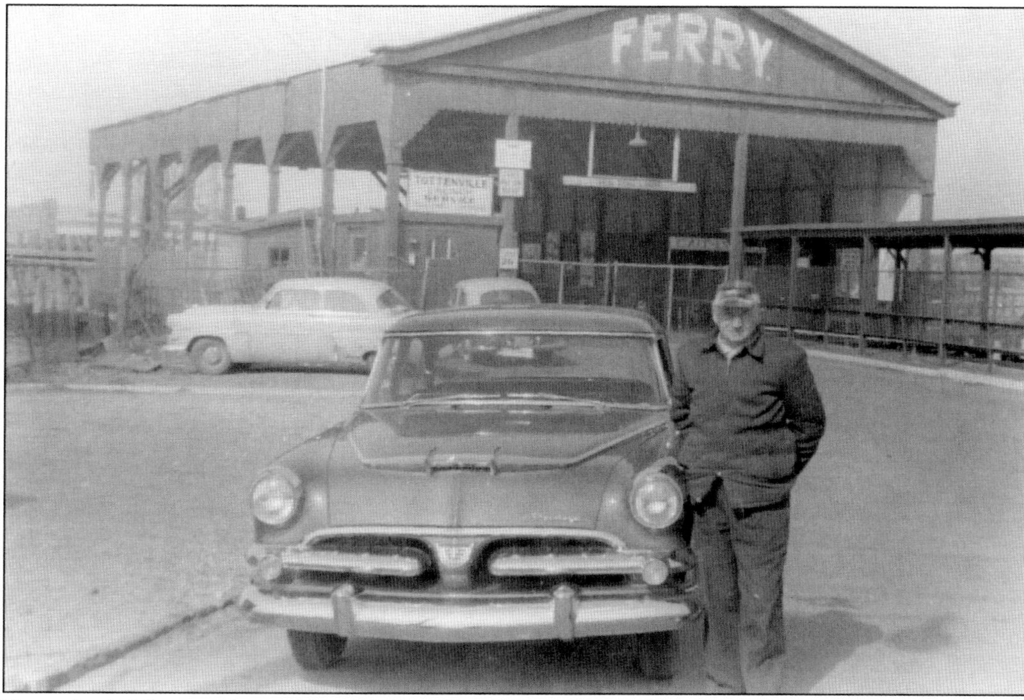

From the 1920s to early in 1970, Adolf M. Bundesen, pictured here in 1950, owned and operated a taxi at the end of Bentley Street at the Tottenville train station and ferry terminal. Within those years, Richard Powers and William Jahns also ran a taxi service from the same location. Each man owned and operated his own business but shared the hours of operation. Harry Schneider was another independent owner/operator just across the street from the other three men. Much of their clientele came from the commuters going to work in Manhattan and the people who were going to shop in Perth Amboy. (Courtesy of the Pagliuco family.)

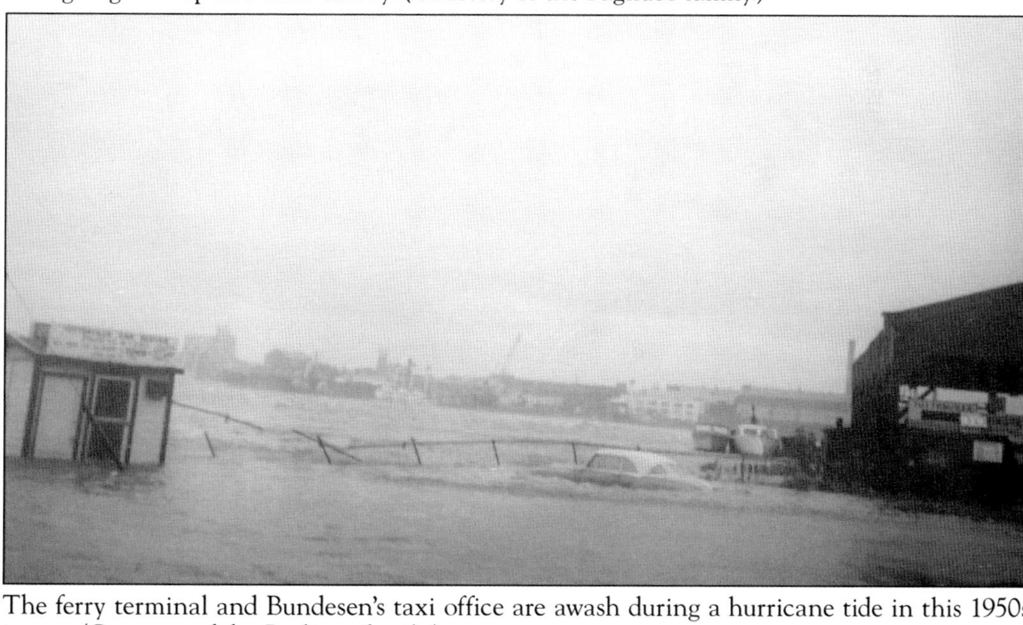

The ferry terminal and Bundesen's taxi office are awash during a hurricane tide in this 1950s image. (Courtesy of the Pagliuco family.)

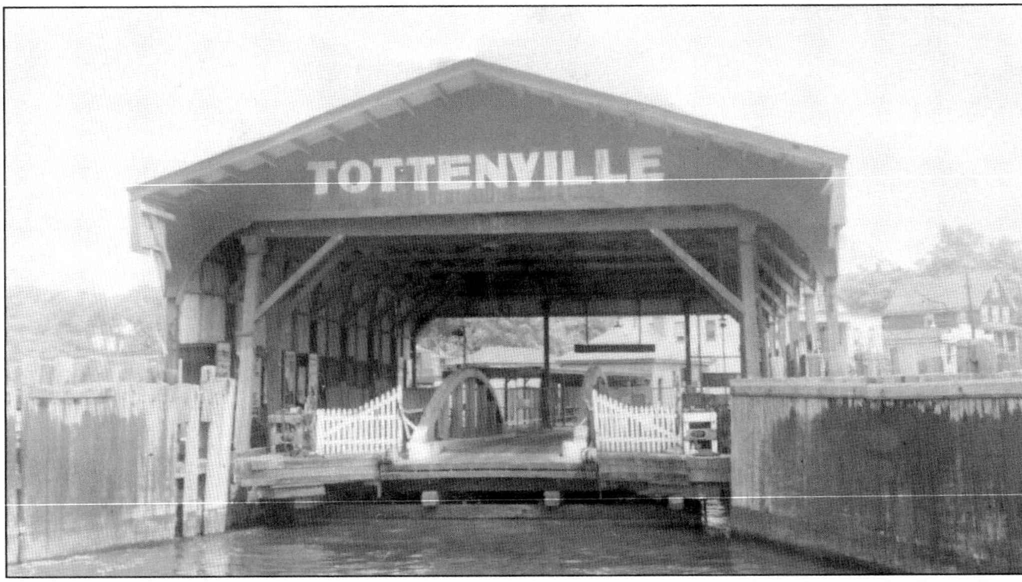

This 1940 photograph of the Tottenville ferry slip is a rare view taken from a docking ferry. (Courtesy of Tina Kaasmann-Dunn.)

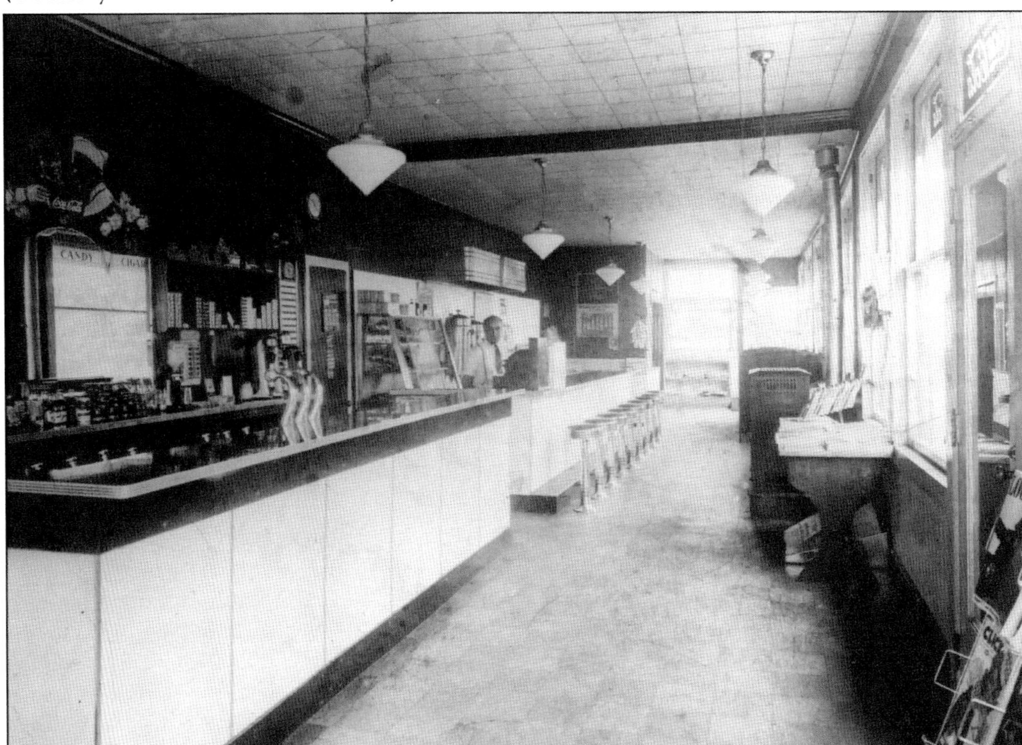

The coffee shop pictured here, known as Pete's, was operated by the Kusulas family from about 1940 to 1959. The shop was located at the foot of Bentley Street, next to the Tottenville train station and the ferry terminal to Perth Amboy. It was a popular stop for ferry and train travelers and sold coffee, soda, shakes, ice cream, pie, hot dogs, and sandwiches plus comic books, newspapers, and magazines. (Courtesy of the Elias Kusulas Collection.)

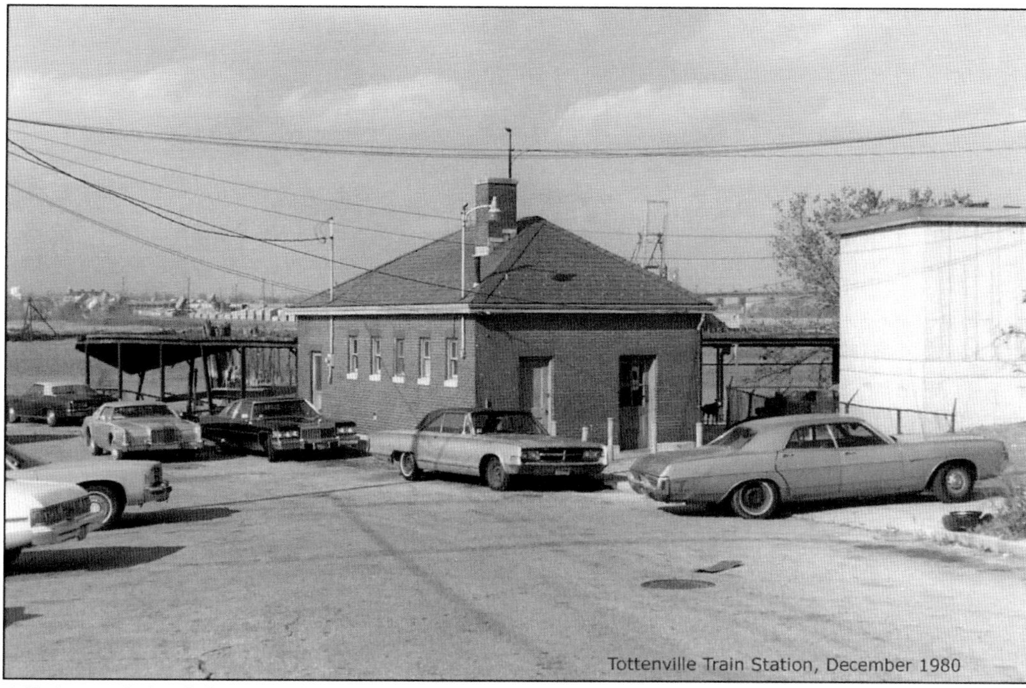

All that is left of the once bustling Bentley Street transportation hub is the small brick ticket office and waiting room shown in this 1980 photograph. Pilings denote the site of the long-gone ferry slip, and today barriers separate land from water. (Courtesy of Cliff Lavelle.)

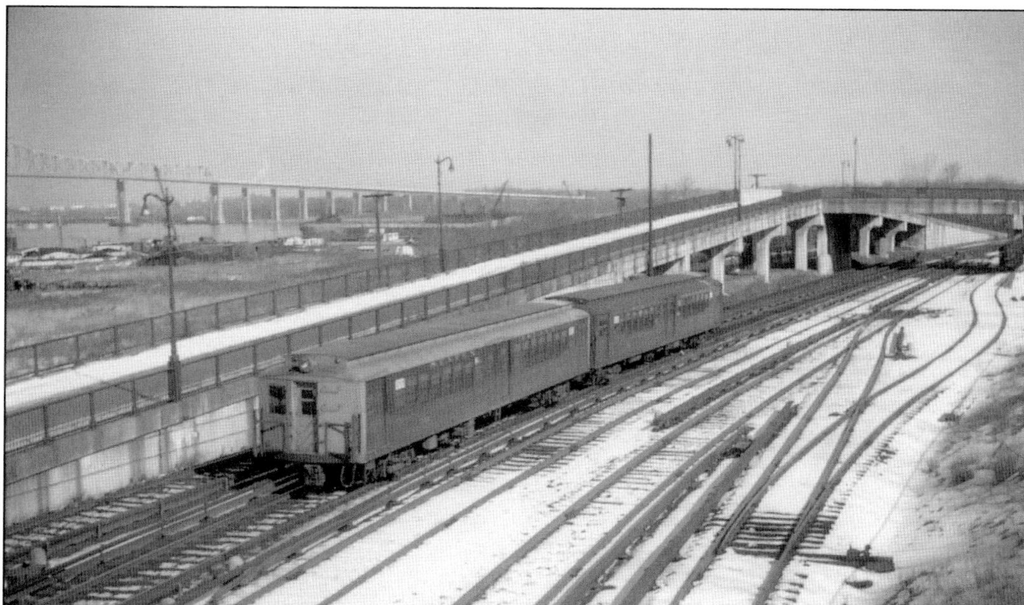

The Johnson Avenue T bridge, in the top right of this image, was built to provide access to Ellis Street from Arthur Kill Road. The bridge was a favorite spot for sleigh riding in the wintertime. Due to its deteriorating condition, it was removed in the 1990s. Pictured in this 1965 photograph is the Staten Island Rapid Transit Railway Company car 55, built in 1925. (Courtesy of the Douglas N. Grotjahn Collection.)

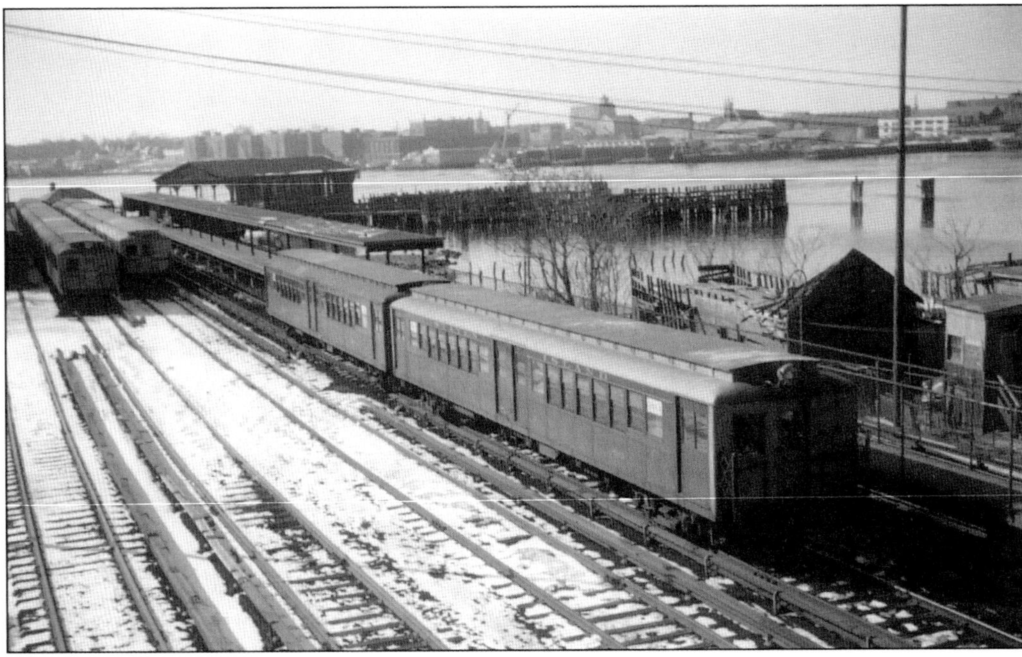

This 1965 photograph shows the Tottenville train station and yard and the recently abandoned ferry slip. Train 366, seen in this photograph and built in 1925, is preserved at the Seashore Trolley Museum in Kennebunkport, Maine. The city of Perth Amboy, New Jersey, is in the background. (Courtesy of the Douglas N. Grotjahn Collection.)

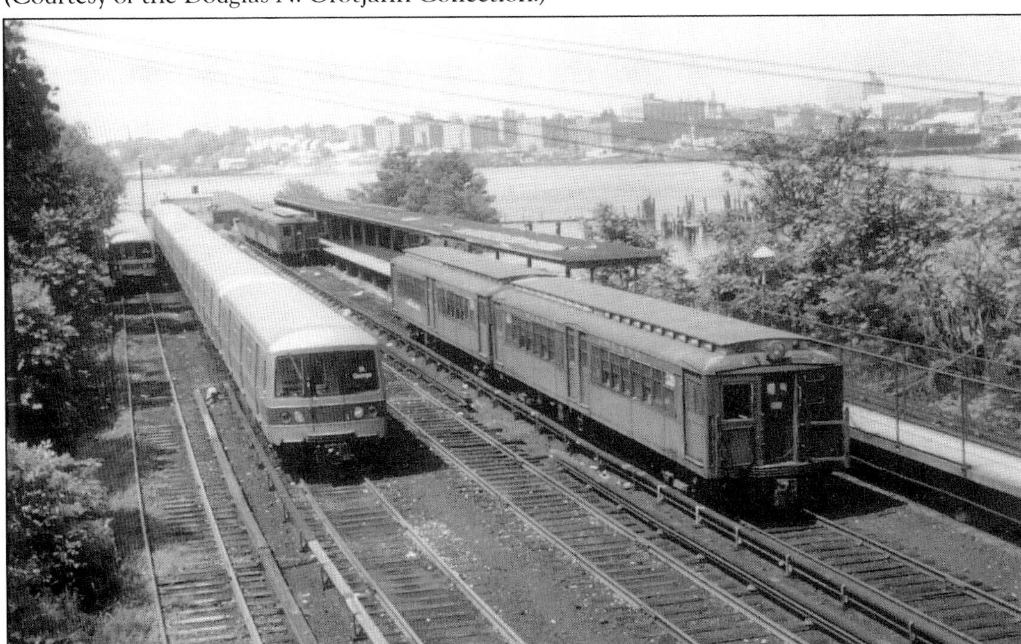

By 1973, the former ferry terminal and dock pilings had all but disappeared. Today only a handful of pilings are visible. This 1973 photograph also provides a side-by-side view of the earlier trains (1925) that were replaced by the new R-44 cars in 1973. (Courtesy of the Douglas N. Grotjahn Collection.)

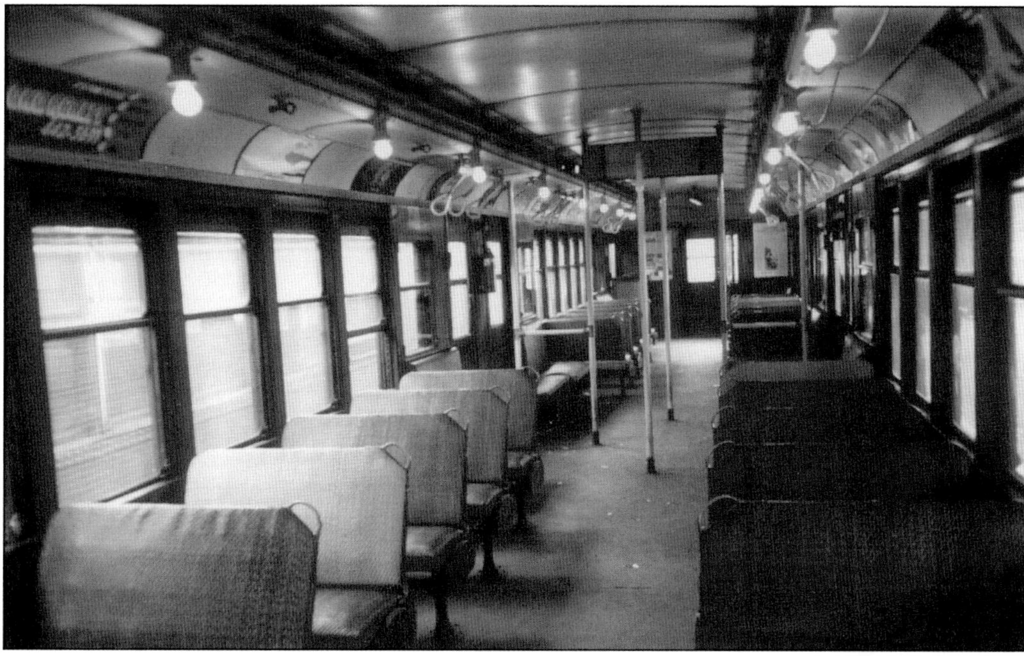

The interior of this 1925 train shows the reed-covered seats, which could be flipped to face the direction of travel. High school girls and women traveling to work were careful not to snag their nylon stockings on the broken strands of wicker. These trains remained in service through the 1970s. (Courtesy of the Douglas N. Grotjahn Collection.)

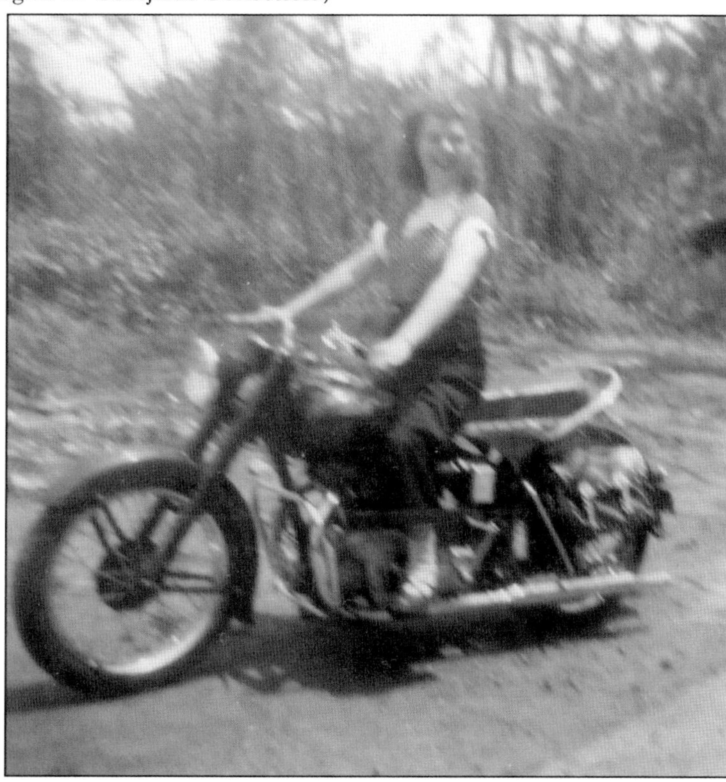

Free spirit Alice Williams is all smiles posing on her Indian Scout motorcycle. Women riders were indeed a rare breed in the 1950s, when this picture was snapped. Alice dearly loved to ride around town, and she still owns this bike! (Courtesy of Alice Williams.)

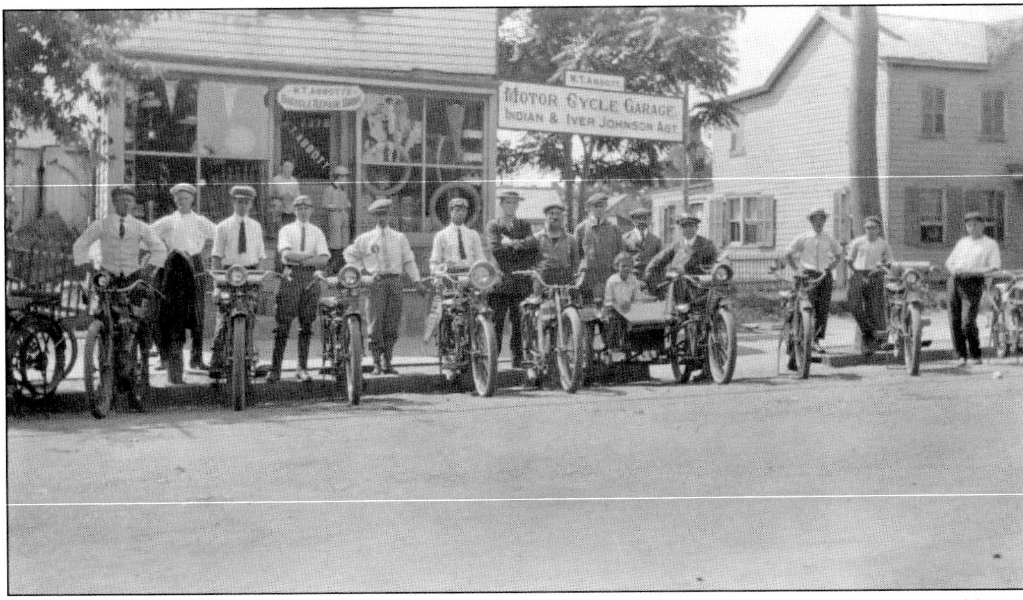

The popularity of the motorcycle is clearly evident in this early 1920s photograph. W. T. Abbott's Motor Cycle Garage was located at 7378 Amboy Road. Among the members of the motorcycle club pictured here is Michael Filimon. There is a sidecar on the right, and the men are wearing ties and hats. (Courtesy of the John Bieser Estate.)

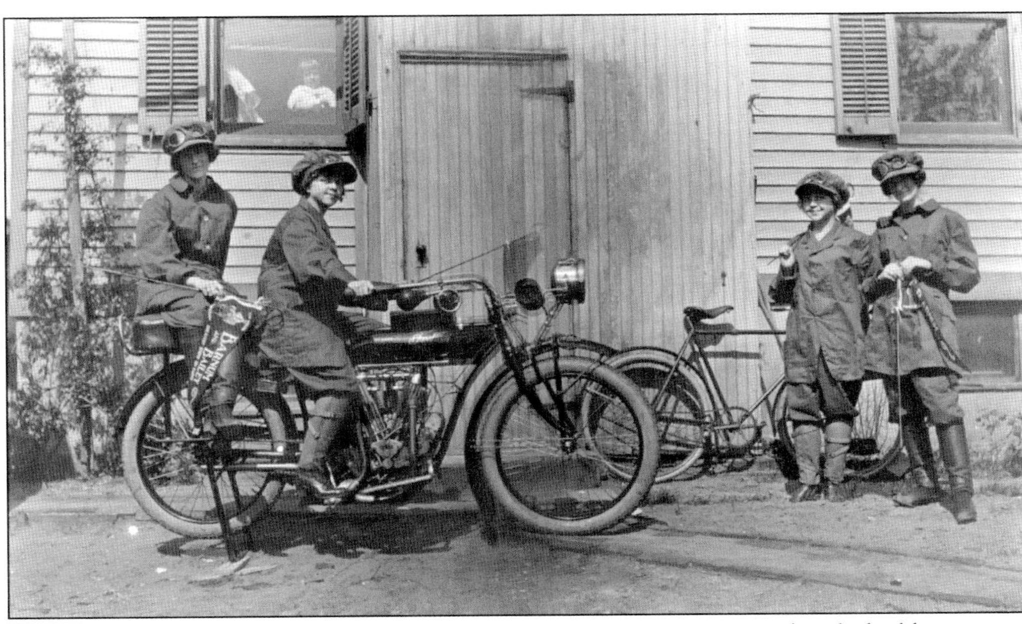

The year was 1918 when talented photographer John Bieser experimented with double exposure photography in capturing Lillian Covell and her friend Nellie Preacher. (Courtesy of the John Bieser Estate.)

Eight

Community and Social Groups

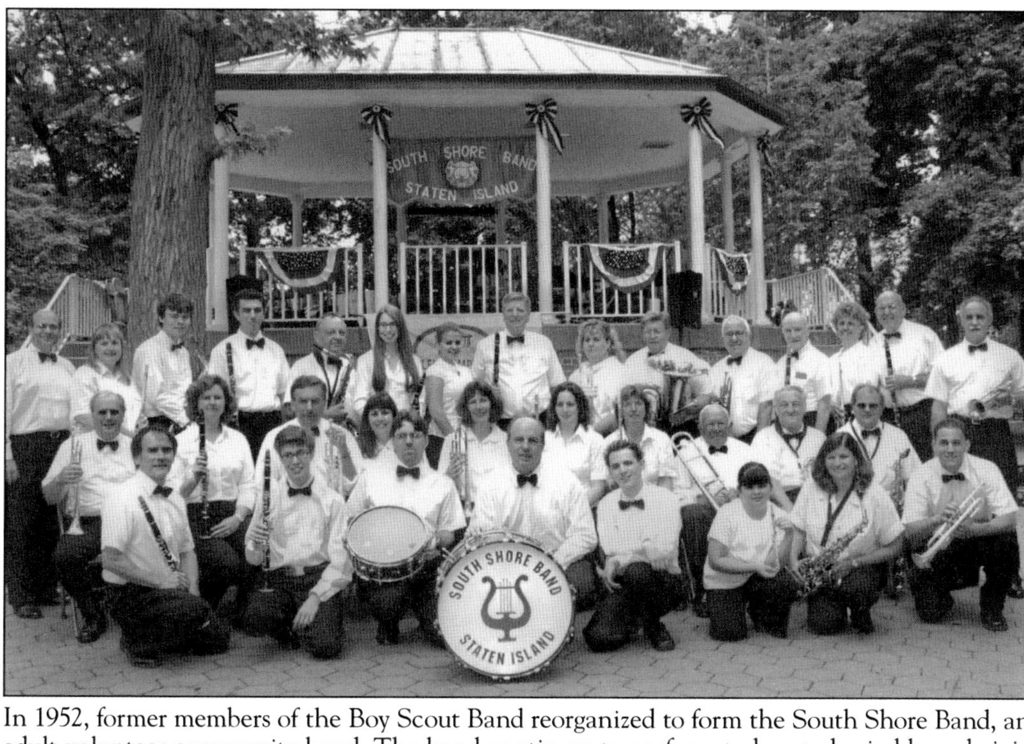

In 1952, former members of the Boy Scout Band reorganized to form the South Shore Band, an adult volunteer community band. The band continues to perform today at charitable and civic events in the tri-state area, including the St. Patrick's Day Parade in Manhattan. An open-air concert in Westerleigh Park, Staten Island, has been part of their concert season for many years. The band consists of 50 members ranging from high school to retirement age. (Courtesy of Tom Doty.)

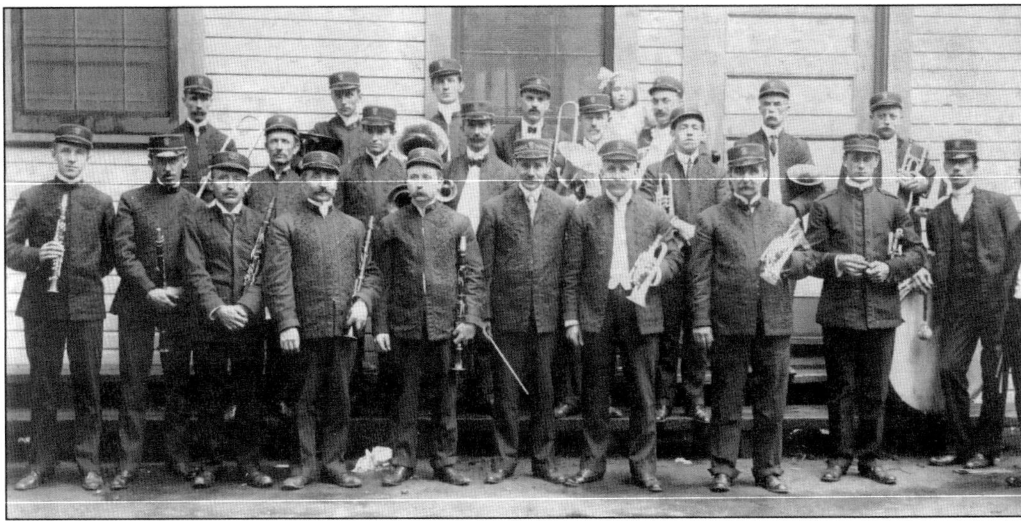

Tottenville's first adult community band was organized in 1870 with 13 members. It lasted for three years. In 1878, the Tottenville Cornet Band was formed. Regarded as one of the best amateur bands in New York State, the group played for churches, civic groups, and political rallies, and was often invited to parades in Manhattan, Boston, Philadelphia, and Washington, D.C. For many years, it gave weekly open-air concerts, adding much pleasure to hot summer evenings. Among the members of the 1904 Cornet Band pictured here are Charles U. Thrall, Frank L. Hadkins, David J. Pepper, Andrew M. Sprague, and James W. Bedell. (Courtesy of the Bedell Collection.)

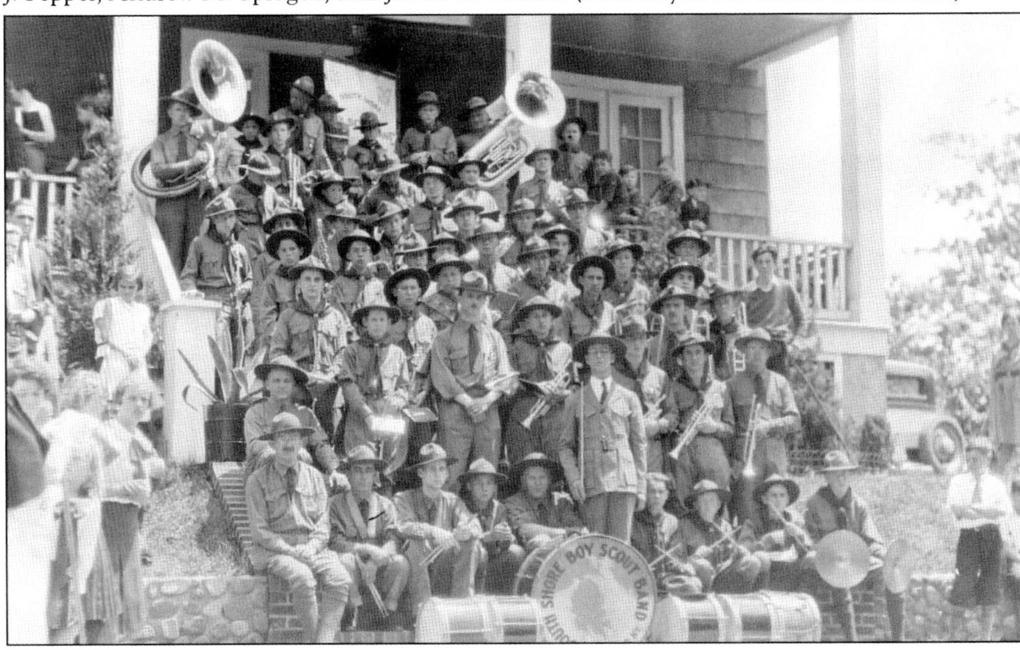

The South Shore Boy Scout Band was organized in 1932. It practiced weekly in the Guthrie Scout Shack, located on the grounds of Bethel Church on Amboy Road. Many of the instruments in this photograph are still used by the South Shore Band today. The Boy Scout Band disbanded in 1943, when too many members went into the armed services. This photograph was taken on the steps of the American Legion Beauvais Post on Main Street following the 1934 Memorial Day parade. (Courtesy of the John Bieser Estate.)

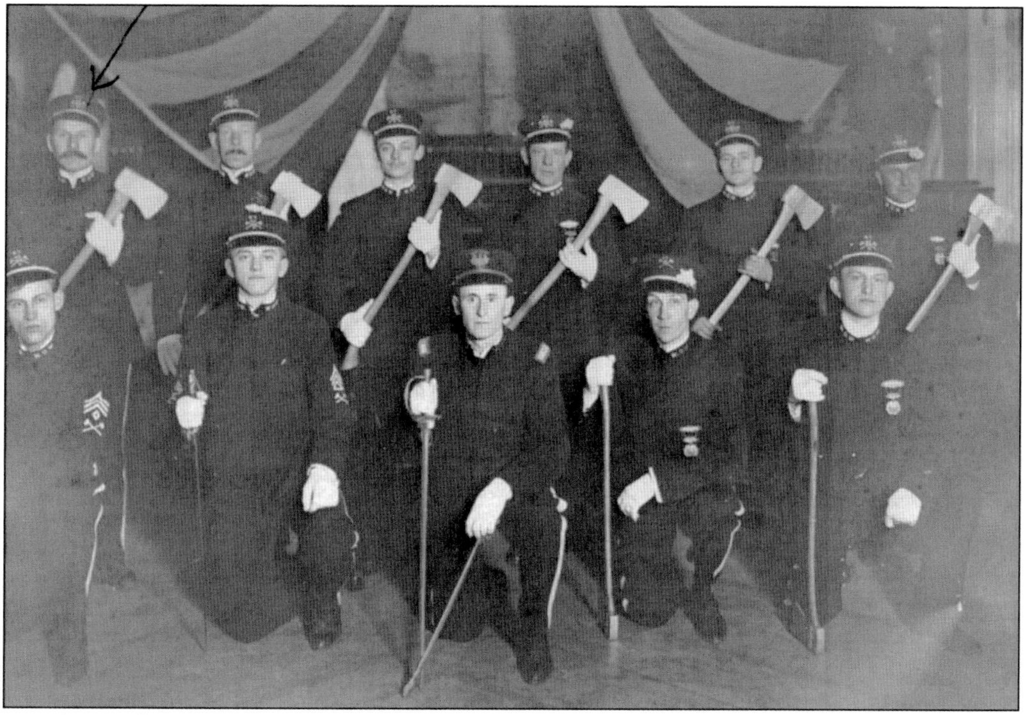

Woodmen of the World (W.O.W.) is a fraternal benefit society organized in Nebraska in 1890. It is not known when Tottenville's local chapter, Richmond Camp No. 85, was organized. The members identified in this *c.* 1904 photograph are Frank W. Schult (second row, far left) and Charles W. Hamilton (first row, center). (Courtesy of the Anita Schult Collection.)

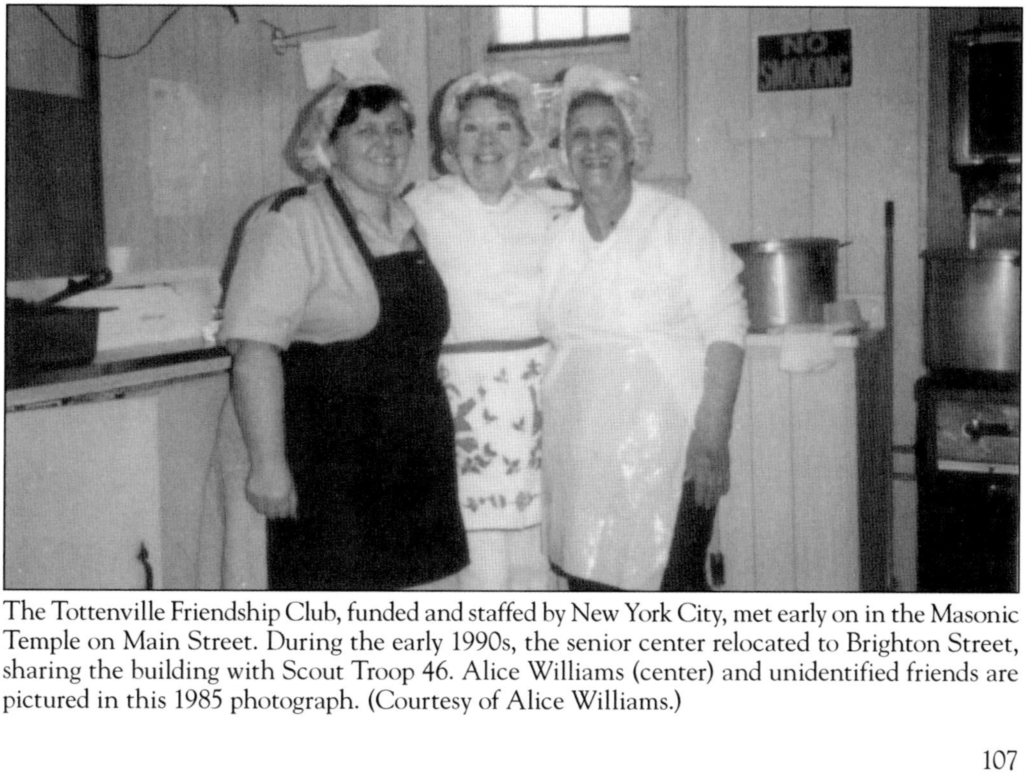

The Tottenville Friendship Club, funded and staffed by New York City, met early on in the Masonic Temple on Main Street. During the early 1990s, the senior center relocated to Brighton Street, sharing the building with Scout Troop 46. Alice Williams (center) and unidentified friends are pictured in this 1985 photograph. (Courtesy of Alice Williams.)

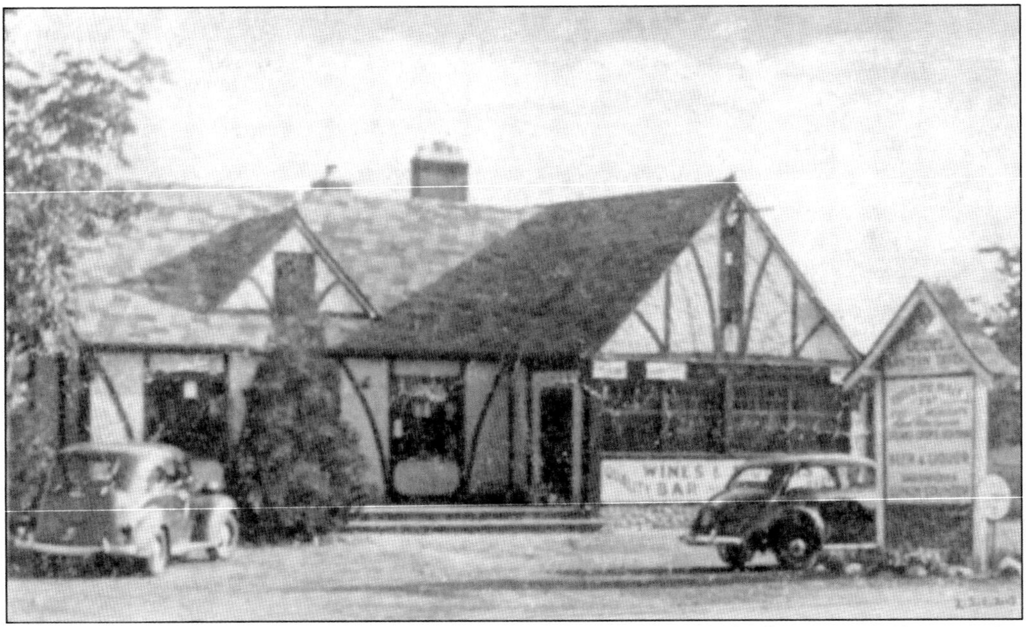

Geidel's Lantern Tavern advertised "Good Food-Wines-Liquors" in the late 1930s. This popular gathering place was located at the southeast corner of Hylan Boulevard and Page Avenue. The restaurant later became a nightclub, the Totten Villa, where an impressive list of jazz legends including Herbie Mann, Freddie Hubbard, and Stan Getz played in the 1950s and 1960s. Al Halliday was the proprietor in 1951. (Courtesy of the Wilkie-Farina family.)

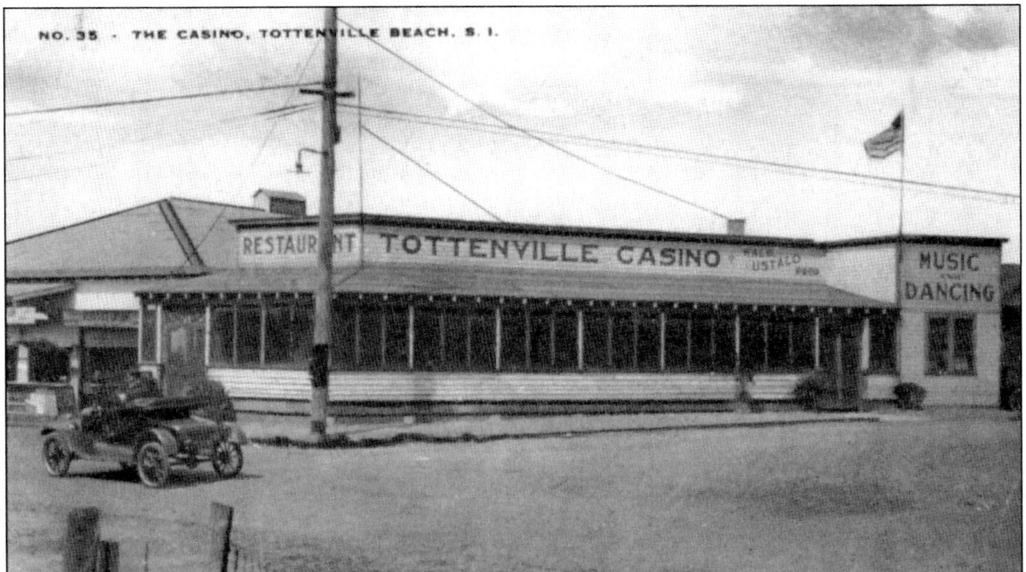

In 1939, due to the repeated demands of South Shore jitterbugs, Joseph "Nipper" Bedell and his orchestra returned to the Tottenville Casino, a popular summer dance hall and restaurant on Surf Avenue along the Raritan Bay waterfront. In the 1930s, with Nipper Bedell on drums, Johnny MacEvoy at piano, and Dorothy Schaaff's melodic voice, patrons were entertained with swing tunes by Glenn Miller, Benny Goodman, Rosemary Clooney, Tommy and Jimmy Dorsey, and others. The building burned down in 1940. (Courtesy of Evelyn H. Bedell.)

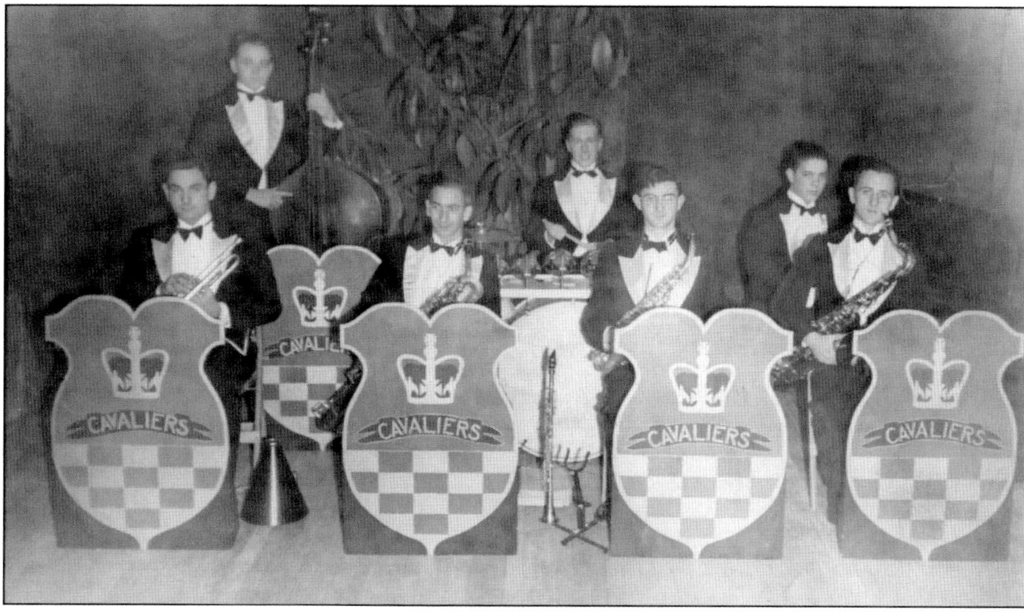

Joseph Bedell, who later owned and operated the family business, the Bedell Funeral Home, was a talented musician and band leader. His orchestra entertained at a variety of venues beginning in the early 1930s. Joseph Bedell is the drummer for the Cavaliers in this undated photograph. (Courtesy of Evelyn H. Bedell.)

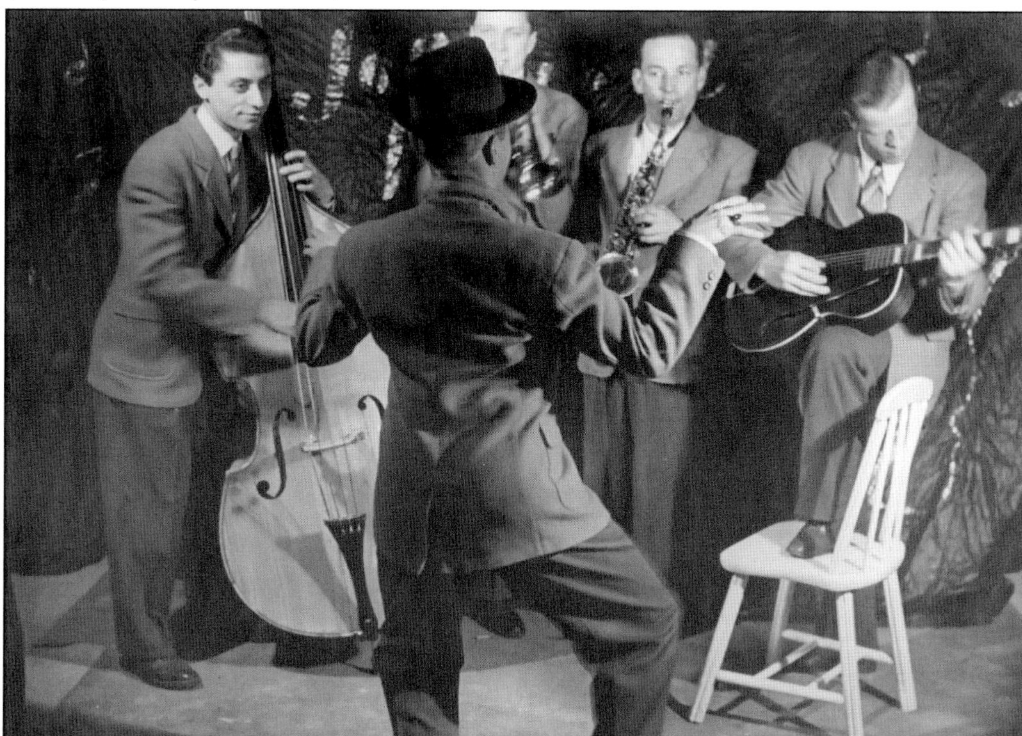

Cool cat Joseph Bedell, the well-dressed bandleader wearing a fedora, does the shimmy-shake while leading his band in this late 1930s photograph. (Courtesy of Evelyn H. Bedell.)

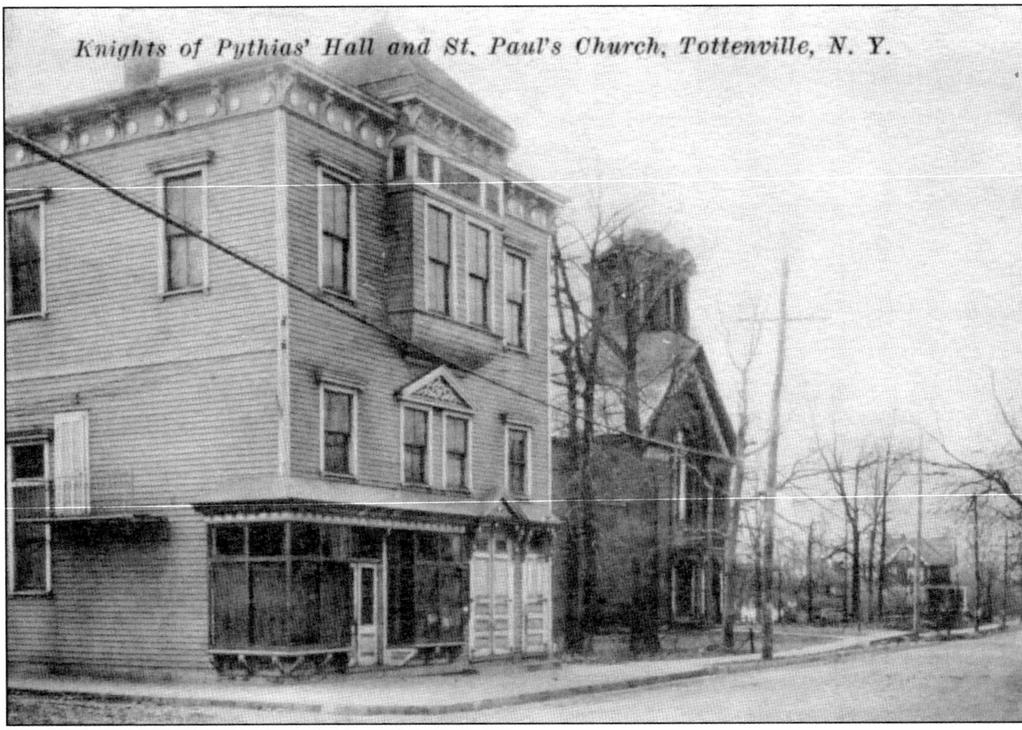

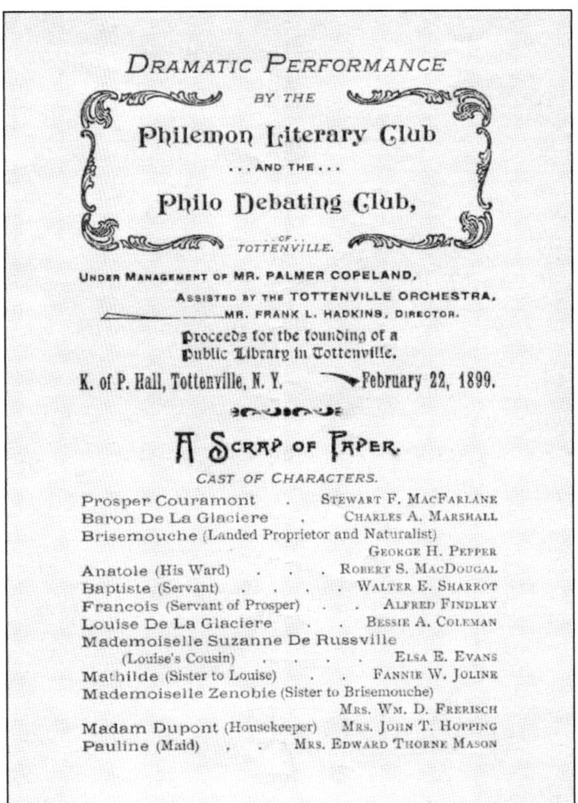

DRAMATIC PERFORMANCE

BY THE

Philemon Literary Club

... AND THE ...

Philo Debating Club,

OF TOTTENVILLE.

UNDER MANAGEMENT OF MR. PALMER COPELAND,

ASSISTED BY THE TOTTENVILLE ORCHESTRA,

MR. FRANK L. HADKINS, DIRECTOR.

Proceeds for the founding of a Public Library in Tottenville.

K. of P. Hall, Tottenville, N. Y. February 22, 1899.

A SCRAP OF PAPER.

CAST OF CHARACTERS.

Prosper Couramont . STEWART F. MACFARLANE
Baron De La Glaciere . CHARLES A. MARSHALL
Brisemouche (Landed Proprietor and Naturalist) GEORGE H. PEPPER
Anatole (His Ward) . . . . ROBERT S. MACDOUGAL
Baptiste (Servant) . . . . . WALTER E. SHARROT
Francois (Servant of Prosper) . . ALFRED FINDLEY
Louise De La Glaciere . . BESSIE A. COLEMAN
Mademoiselle Suzanne De Russville (Louise's Cousin) . . . . . ELSA E. EVANS
Mathilde (Sister to Louise) . . . FANNIE W. JOLINE
Mademoiselle Zenobie (Sister to Brisemouche) MRS. WM. D. FRERISCH
Madam Dupont (Housekeeper) MRS. JOHN T. HOPPING
Pauline (Maid) . . MRS. EDWARD THORNE MASON

The largest fraternal organization in the former village of Tottenville was Richmond Lodge No. 80, Knights of Pythias, which organized in 1878. In 1890, the Pythians built a handsome hall and clubhouse, seen here in this *c.* 1910 postcard, on the southwest corner of Amboy Road and Main Street. K. of P. Hall provided rental space for businesses on the ground floor and rooms for public entertainment and meetings above. The building was used as a dance hall, gymnasium, lecture hall, motion picture theater, civic center, and religious meeting place. The actors, musicians, and organizers of this 1899 production of *A Scrap of Paper*, a three-act comedy, were members of two local organizations—the Philemon Literary Club and the Philo Debating Club. (Left: courtesy of Robert P. Ford.)

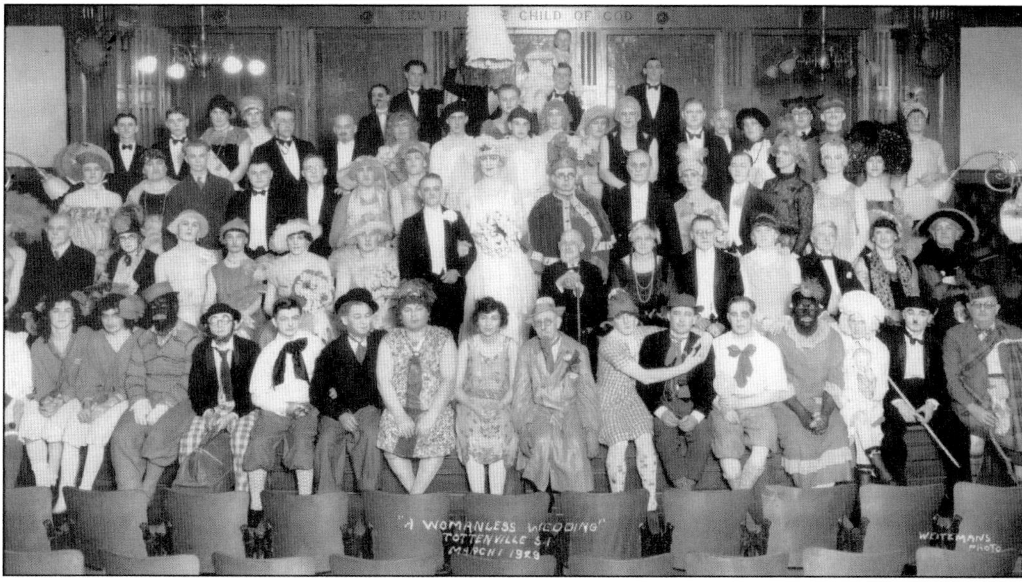

In 1929, a womanless wedding, a popular farce featuring an all-male cast, was produced by the Philemon Society in the elementary school auditorium. The full cast poses onstage for this photograph. Proceeds from this fund-raising event, totaling $438, benefited the recently restored Conference House and the Richmond Memorial Hospital Building fund. (Courtesy of the Alva E. Schulz Collection.)

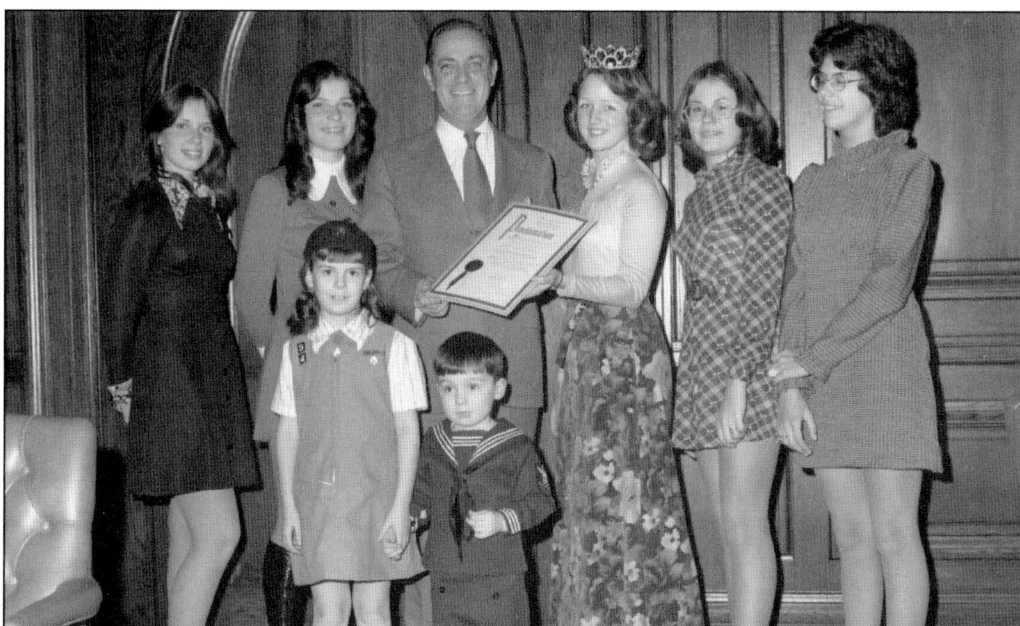

Borough president Robert T. Connor proclaimed January 15, 1974, as Miss Tottenville Day during a visit by Tara O'Shea, Miss Tottenville 1973, and her court. Pictured here, from left to right, are (first row) Nancy Okeson and Peter Okeson; (second row) Tracy DePaul, Nancy Fox, Robert O'Connor, Tara O'Shea, Lorraine McLaren, and Cheri Elfenbein. Tara was the first to wear the Miss Tottenville crown. Fran Okeson (not pictured), Nancy and Peter's mother, served as pageant coordinator. (Courtesy of the Janice and June Rose Collection.)

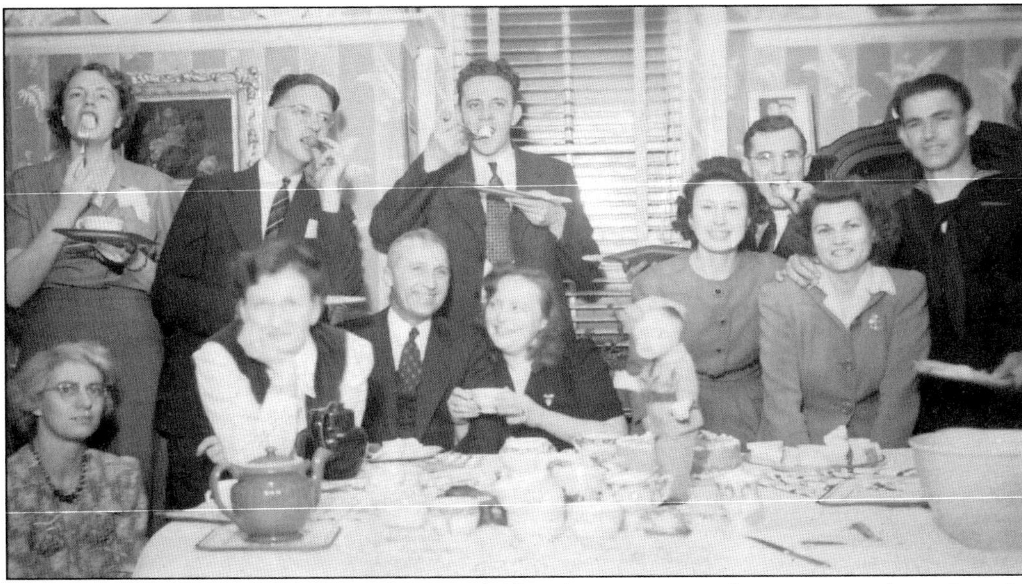

The Parish Players of St. Stephen's Episcopal Church, an amateur theater group, formed in the late 1930s and continued intermittently through the early 1990s as a social organization dedicated to staging challenging plays for public entertainment and for their own enjoyment. Some of the original players who pose for a group picture in the early 1940s include Mabel Miller, Harmon Hunt, Lou Hasselbach, Doris Edwards, and Muriel Rössel. Carl Rössel is the photographer. (Courtesy of Dorri L. Aspinwall.)

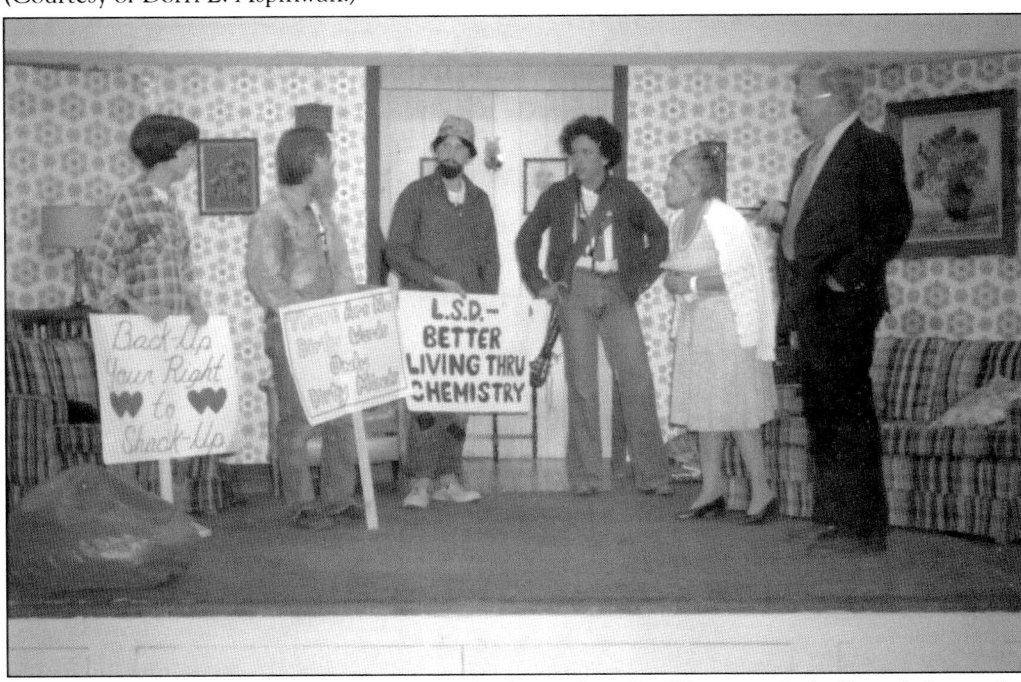

The parish players in the 1977 production of *What Did We Do Wrong?* include (from left to right) Carol Fraser, Bobby Gundacker, two unidentified, Janet Nilsen, and Eddie Chapman. The play was directed by William Eisengrein and performed at St. Stephen's Church. (Courtesy of Dorri L. Aspinwall.)

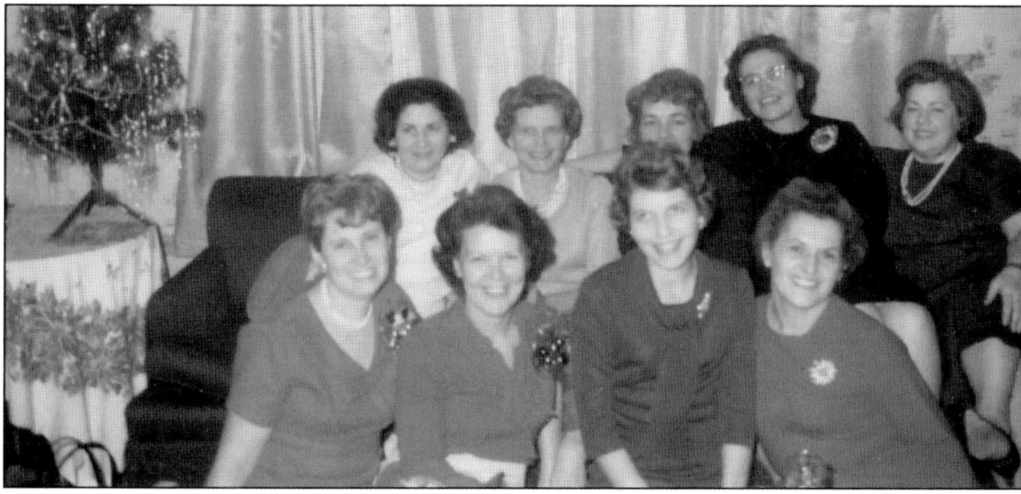

Like many small towns, Tottenville had its girls' clubs. In 1948, ten women, nine married with families and one single woman, formed the Tuesday Nite Girls Club. They partied and picnicked together, laughed and cried together, and formed lifelong friendships. Three original "girls" still live in Tottenville and get together for lunch and visits after more than 60 years. Original members pictured in this 1963 photograph are, from left to right, (first row) Irene Wuethrich, Juanita Grimes, Margaret Kelly, and Johanna Leschke; (second row) Evelyn Rebeck, Evelyn Erickson, Muriel Buickerood, Dot Fithian, and Lucinda Conine. Pauline Carstenson took the picture. (Courtesy of the Wuethrich family.)

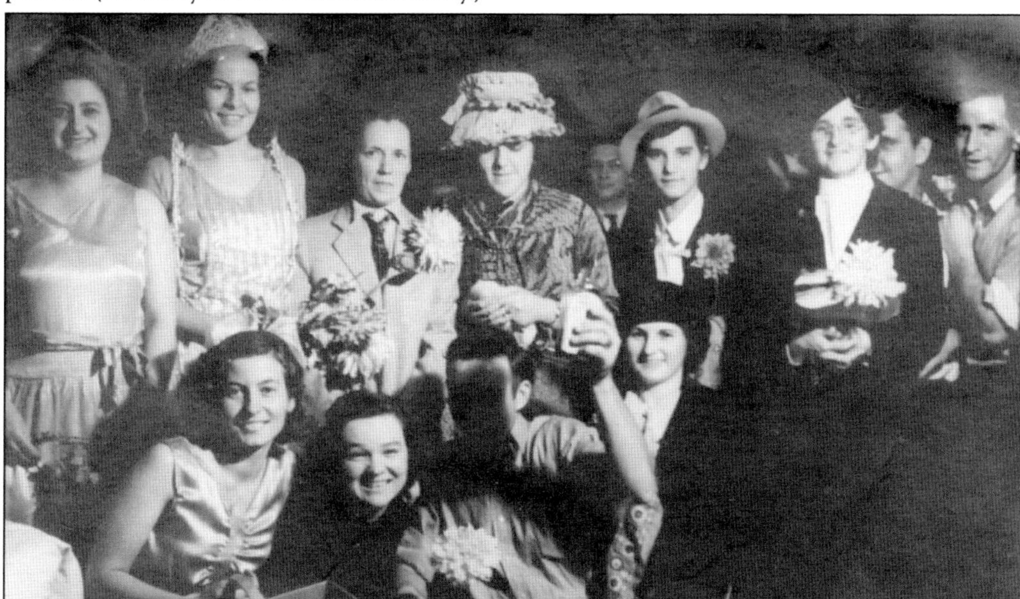

Women's social clubs were organized as early as the 19th century and continue today. Little is known about the Women of the World Ladies Club of the 1930s. This late 1930s image was taken following their production of a mock wedding play. The costumes reveal the parts they played, and their smiles tell that they enjoyed the event. Some of the club members pictured here include (first row) Betty Zboray and Ann Wilkos Ciepierski; (second row) Helen Wilkos Gaul, Casimira Cerkanowicz Nowicki, and Donathy Nowicki Grzeskowiak. (Courtesy of the Grzeskowiak family.)

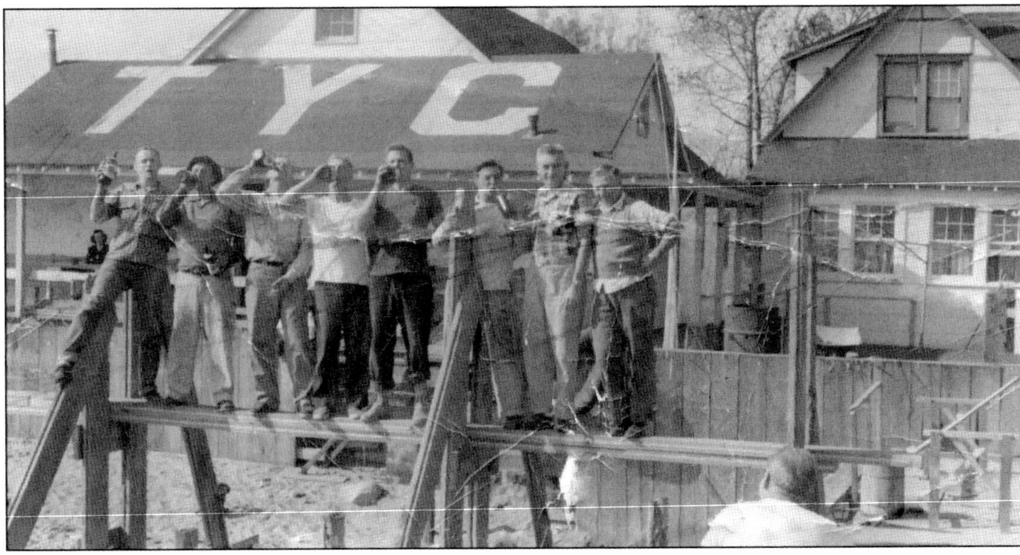

The Tottenville Yacht Club was formed in 1940 on property owned by Schmidt's Boat House. It was incorporated in 1945 to "encourage the sport of boating" and to "provide and maintain a suitable clubhouse and anchorage for the use and recreation of its members." In November 1950, hurricane winds and flood tides destroyed the clubhouse on Surf Avenue and Manhattan Street. Four years and 1,200 man hours later, a new clubhouse, a white frame building with large yellow letters on its roof, was erected on the same site under the supervision of builder Hans Hansen. (Courtesy of the Leyes family.)

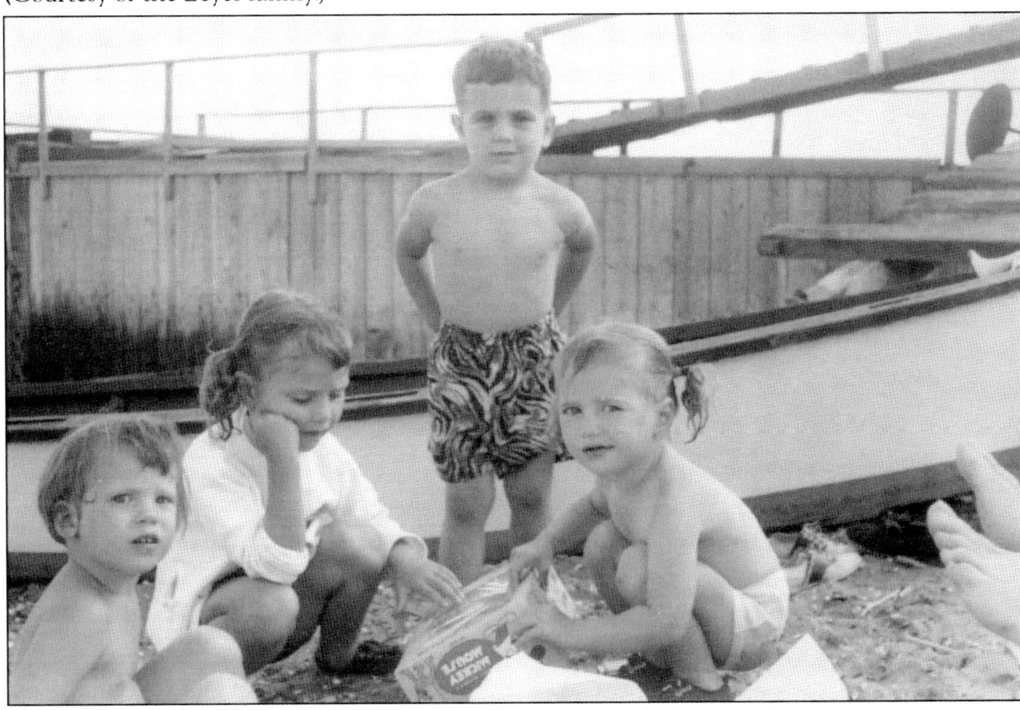

The Tottenville Beach provided hours of fun for adults and kids alike. From left to right, Donna Leyes, Kathy Wilson, Robert Lombardi, and Janet Wilson are playing in the sand in this 1956 photograph. (Courtesy of the Leyes family.)

A 3-mile community walk for charity, organized by the Tottenville Improvement Council (T.I.C.) in 1974, raised funds for several local organizations. Rita McDonough (center) sits at the Tottenville Pool checkpoint. Rita was the first female president of T.I.C. and the organizer of the Tottenville Unity Group (T.U.G.), a senior citizens social group providing community service. (Courtesy of the Janice and June Rose Collection.)

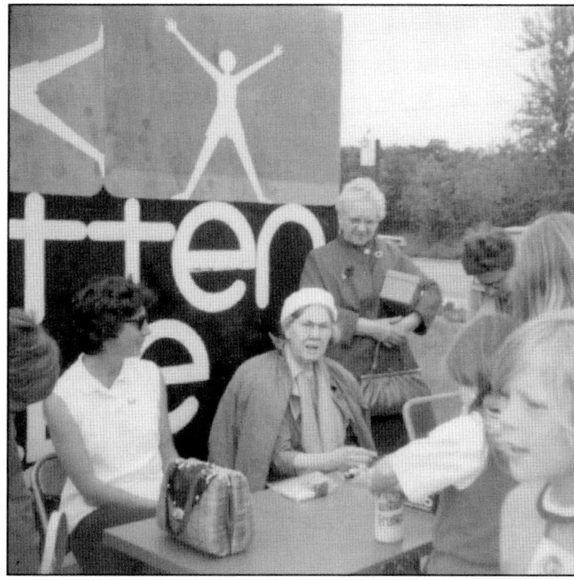

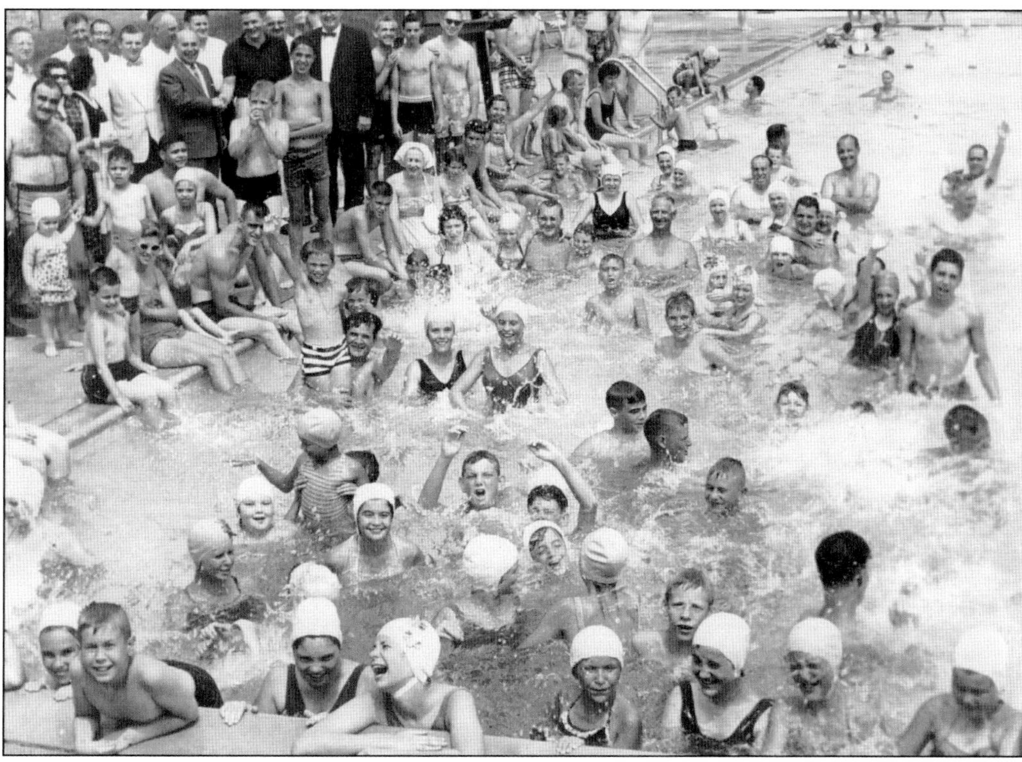

The South Shore Swimming Club, at 6736 Hylan Boulevard, has a long and illustrious history. The hard work and dedication of its members and the friendships and memories it fostered for so many families have helped sustain the club for more than 50 years. On August 28, 1958, the first meeting of the original incorporators took place at the home of Gene and Walter Drill, and on July 23, 1961, just three years later, the pool and bathhouse were opened. Later on, the 5-acre complex would include a clubhouse, picnic area, and tennis, badminton, and horseshoe courts. (Courtesy of Margaret Meehan.)

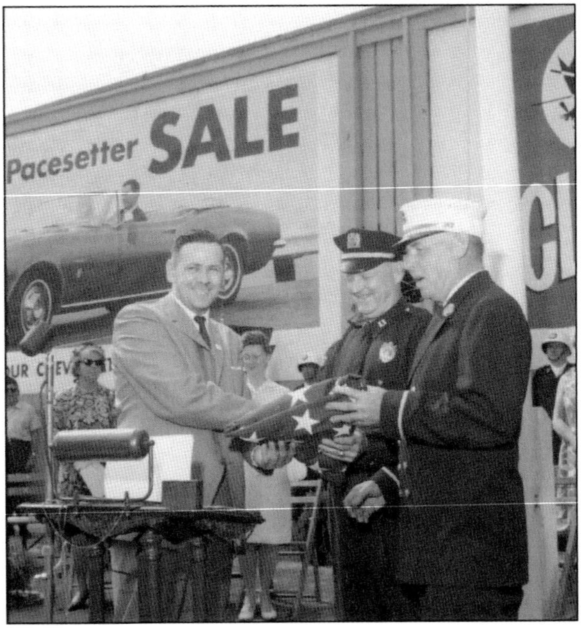

Frank Veraart (1933–2009), owner of Frank's Bake Shop on Amboy Road, was instrumental in founding the Tottenville Merchants Association in the 1960s. On June 11, 1967, a parade with more than 60 organizations preceded the flag-raising ceremony and dedication of Tottenville Memorial Park at the corner of Amboy Road and Main Street. The park honors the memory of those members of the New York City Fire and Police Departments who died in the line of duty. In this photograph, representatives from the police and fire departments present Frank Veraart, as president of the Tottenville Merchants Association, with the first American flag to fly over the park. (Courtesy of the Eckel family.)

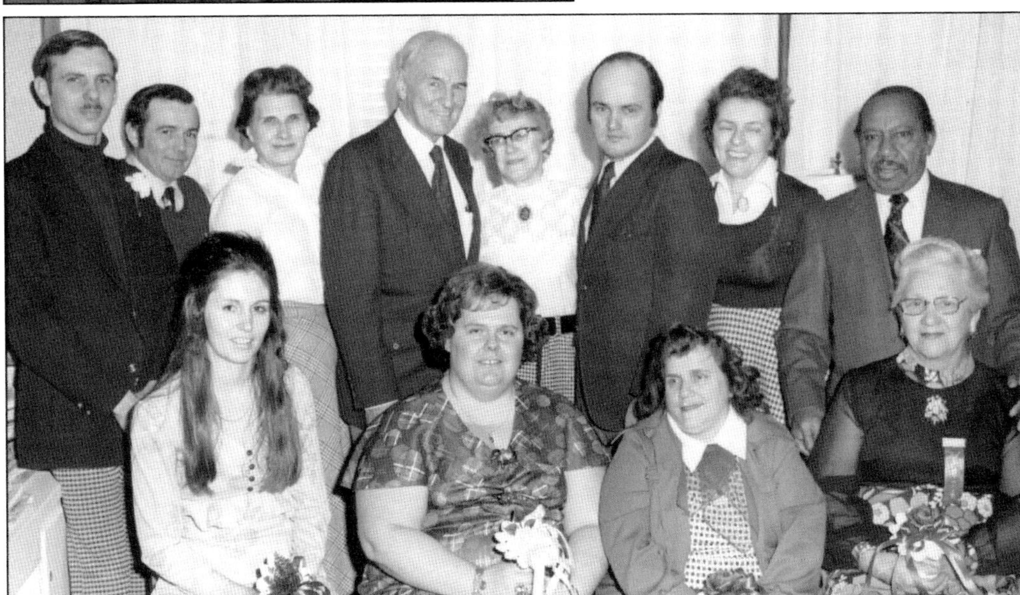

The Tottenville Improvement Council (T.I.C.) was organized in 1967 as a civic organization dedicated to the preservation and improvement of Tottenville. The council organized and sponsored numerous community activities and events, including the Miss Tottenville and Little Miss Tottenville Pageants, an annual outdoor Yule festival, community walks and cleanups, bike-a-thons, and summer youth recreation programs. The council also served in an advisory capacity on land use and zoning issues. Newly elected officers of the Tottenville Improvement Council gather for a group portrait in February 1976. Shown are, from left to right, (first row) Mrs. John Peters, president Fran Okeson, Janice G. Rose, and Ruth Lund; (second row) Ronald Biller, Arnold Kroeger, Eleanor Holt, Raymond and Lee Kirchmeyer, Joseph Fisler, Patricia Mullin, and James L. Josey. (Courtesy of the Janice and June Rose Collection.)

Nine

PROTECT AND SERVE

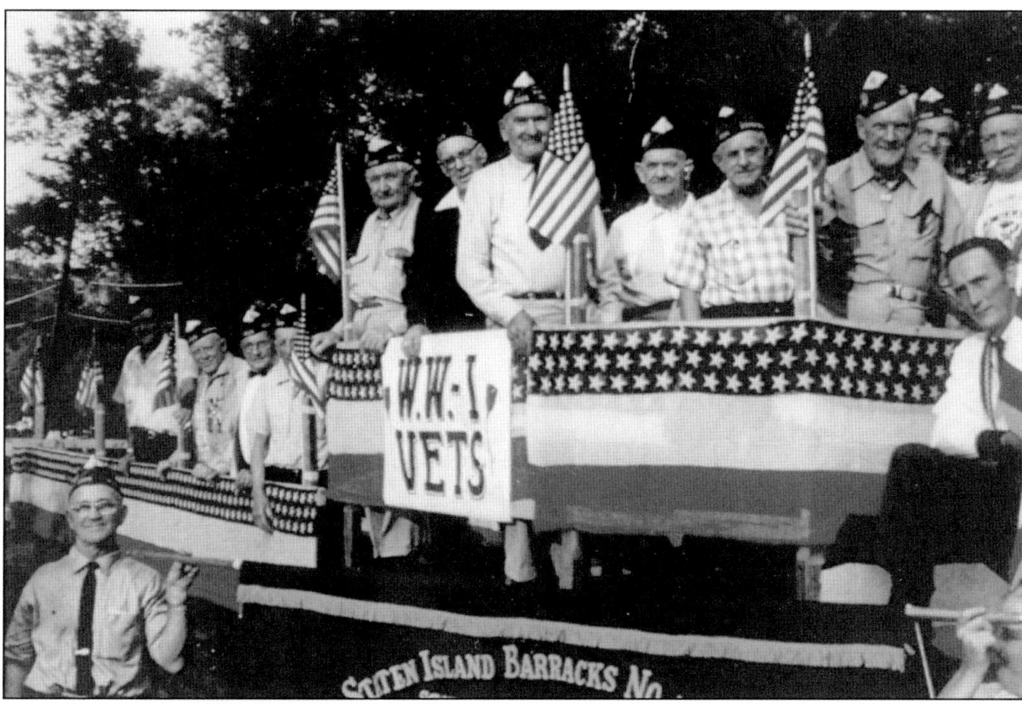

Veterans of World War I stand proud during the 1964 Flag Day Parade. Those identified on the upper float include Alfred Augustine (third from left), George Parsons (third from right), and "Foxy" Jarret (far right). William Burgess, bottom right, donated the decorated truck and float. (Courtesy of the Muriel Burgess Collection.)

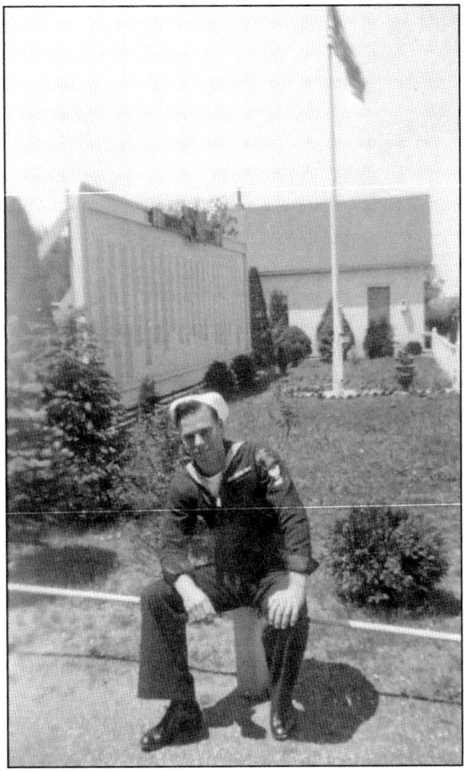

During World War II, many towns across America erected billboard-sized wooden memorials to honor local servicemen and women. Navy man Frederick Cutler is pictured alongside the Honor Roll Plaque that was erected on Main Street in 1942. The 100 Club–Tottenville was instrumental in the plaque's design, construction, and installation. Julius DelGrosso and John Youngberg can be credited with hand painting the names of all servicemen. (Courtesy of the Cutler family.)

John Youngberg, a resident of Perth Amboy, New Jersey, displays his oil painting of the World War II Honor Roll plaque. (Courtesy of the Gloria Stuart Collection.)

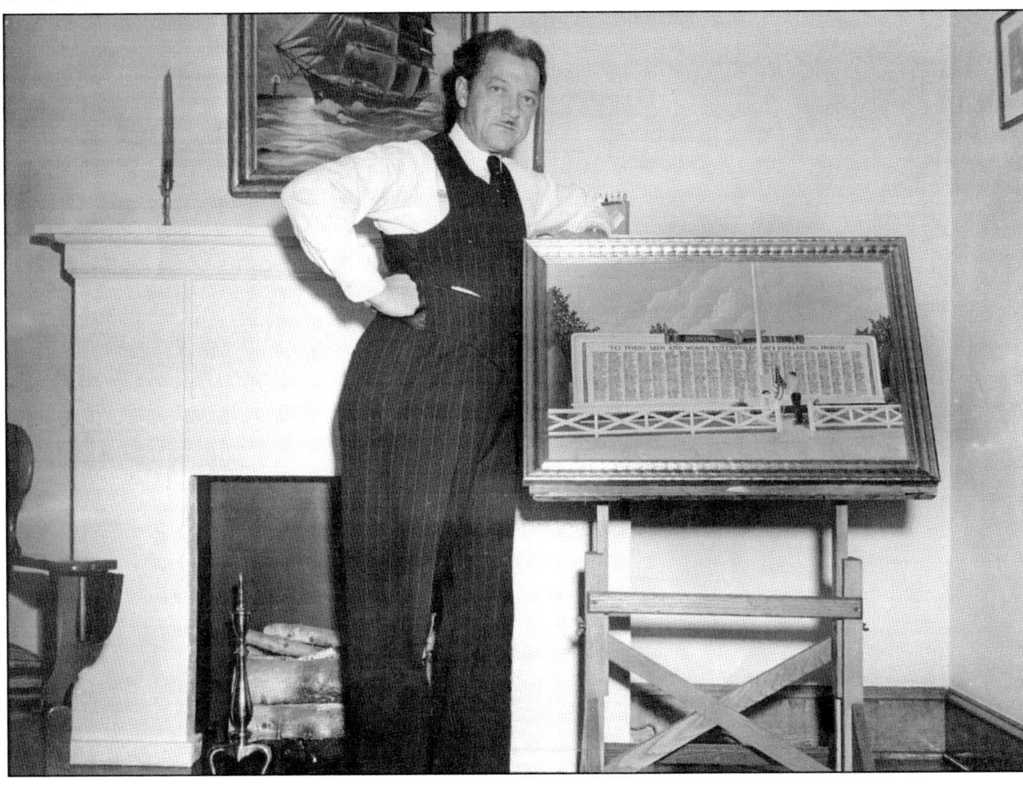

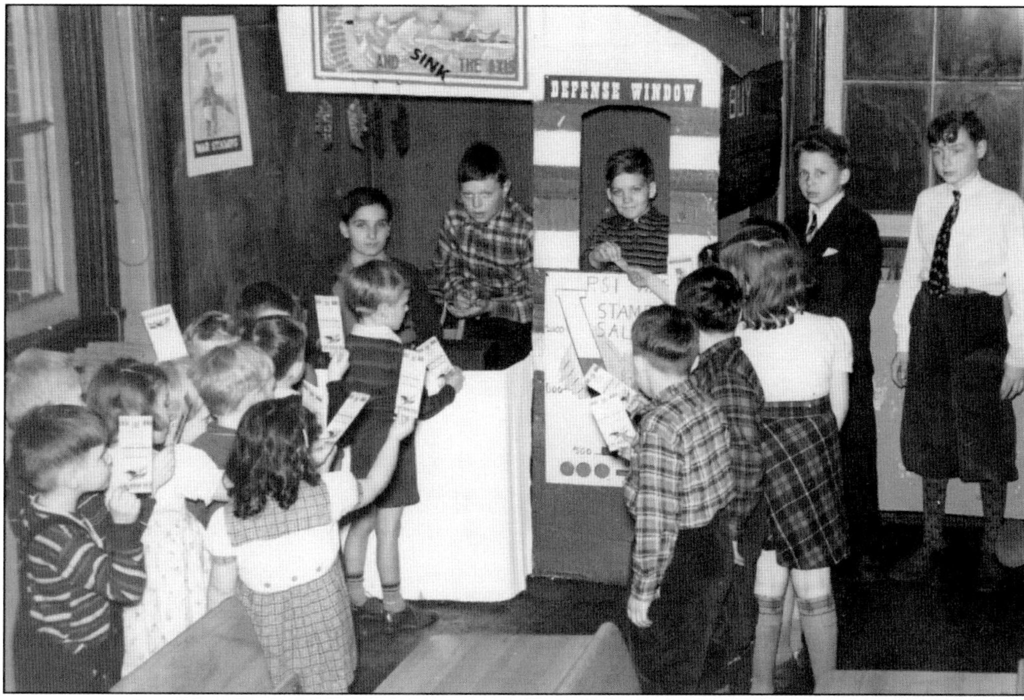

During World War II, P.S. 1 enlisted in the Schools at War Program, organized by the U.S. Treasury Department and the Office of Education. To raise funds for the war effort, school children sold war stamps and bonds. From September 1942 through January 1943, the cash value of stamps and bonds sold by P.S. 1 was an impressive $4,967.75.

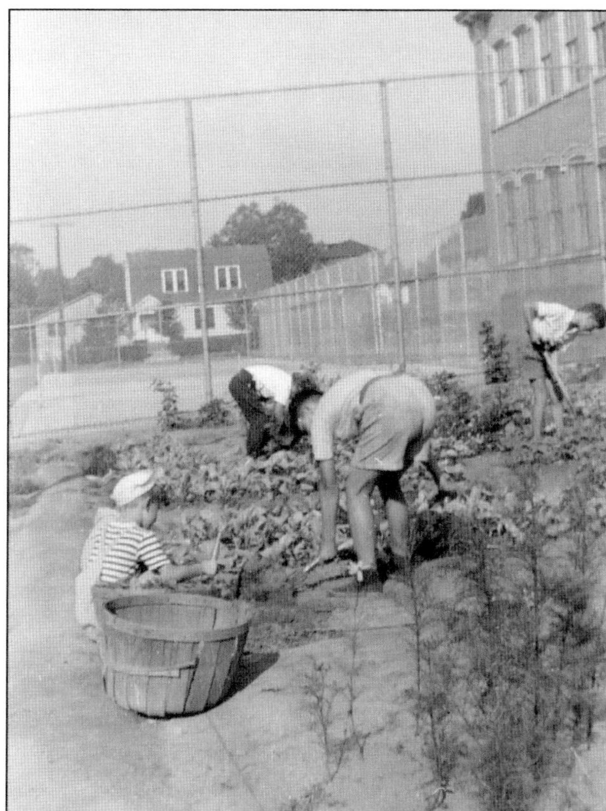

World War II victory gardens were planted on both private and public land by corporations, individuals, and regional governments. School children at P.S. 1 are tending to their victory garden on school grounds in this 1943 photograph.

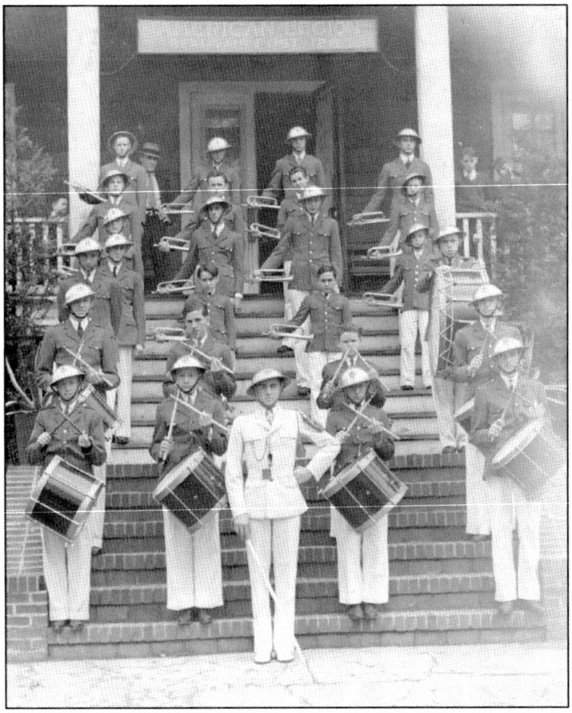

The American Legion Beauvais Post No. 126 Drum and Bugle Corps was organized in 1927. The group is pictured on the front steps of the Legion building at 291 Main Street in this c. 1931 photograph. Drummer Joseph Bedell is standing in the bottom row at far left. (Courtesy of Evelyn H. Bedell.)

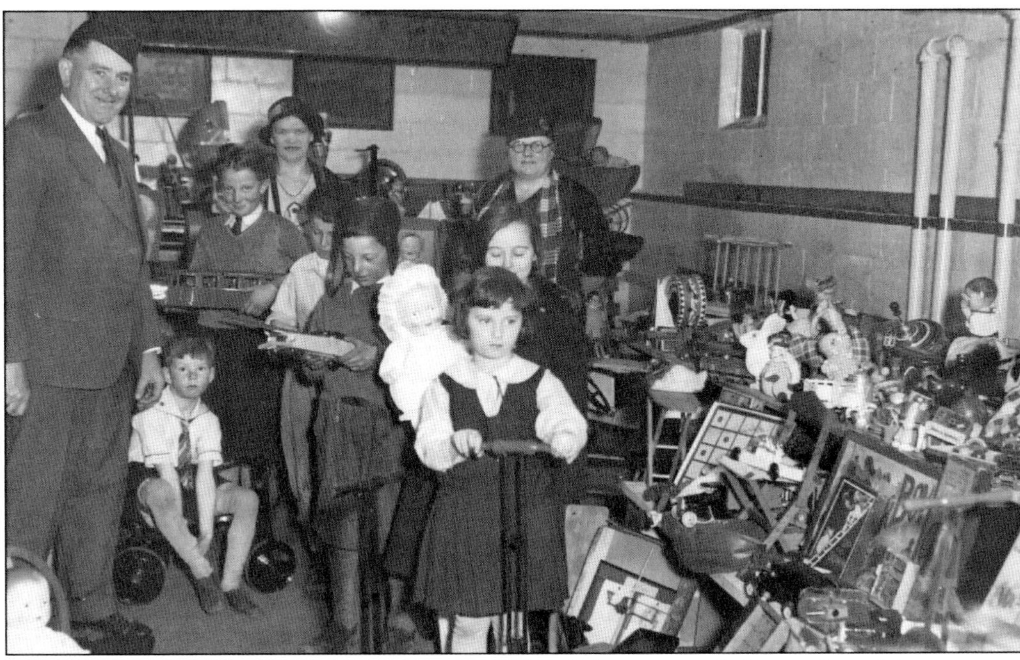

By 1931, the full impact of the Depression was felt by all Americans. In December of that year, and for several consecutive years, members of the Legion Post 126 refurbished toys in the basement of the American Legion building. From left to right, post commander Edward Clinchy, ladies auxiliary president Mildred Andersen, and Mary Radell, county auxiliary president, are pictured in this 1932 photograph distributing toys to children in the community. (Courtesy of the Beauvais-Hudson Post No. 126, American Legion.)

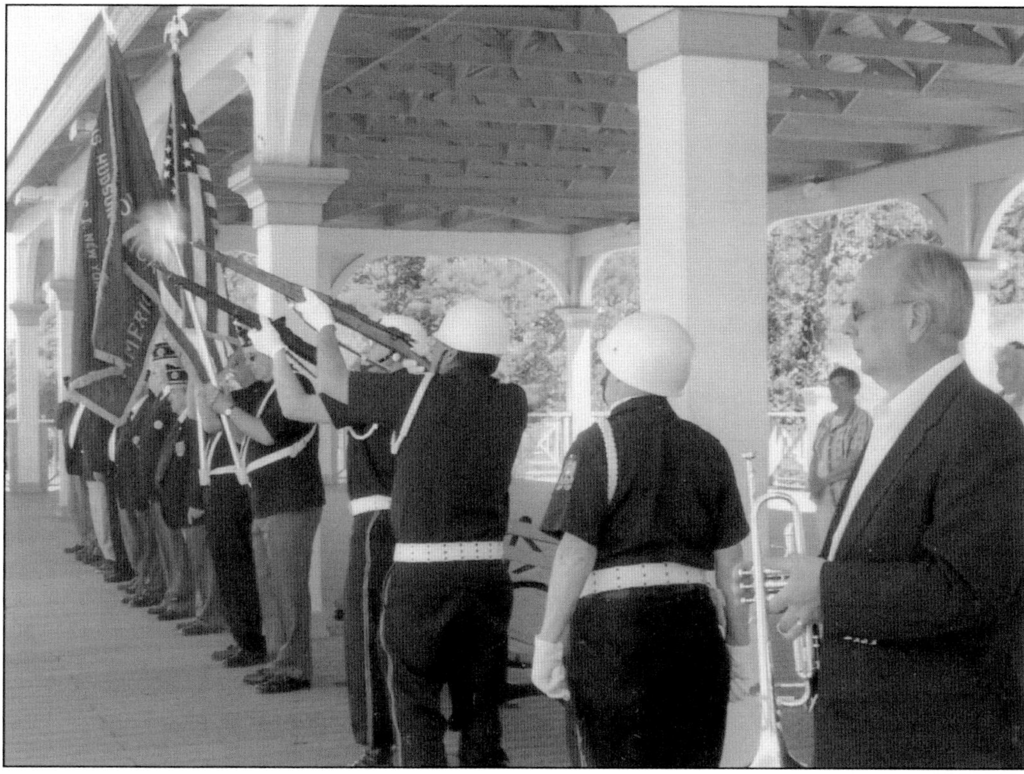

According to Legion Post 126 records, the foot of Hylan Boulevard "in the shadow of the historical Old Billopp House [now Conference House] was designated for the annual services to the sailor dead" in 1927. Today, members of the post continue to honor their fallen comrades during Memorial Day and Veterans Day ceremonies at the same site. An honor guard fires three rounds during Memorial Day services on the Almer G. Russell Pavilion in this 2009 photograph.

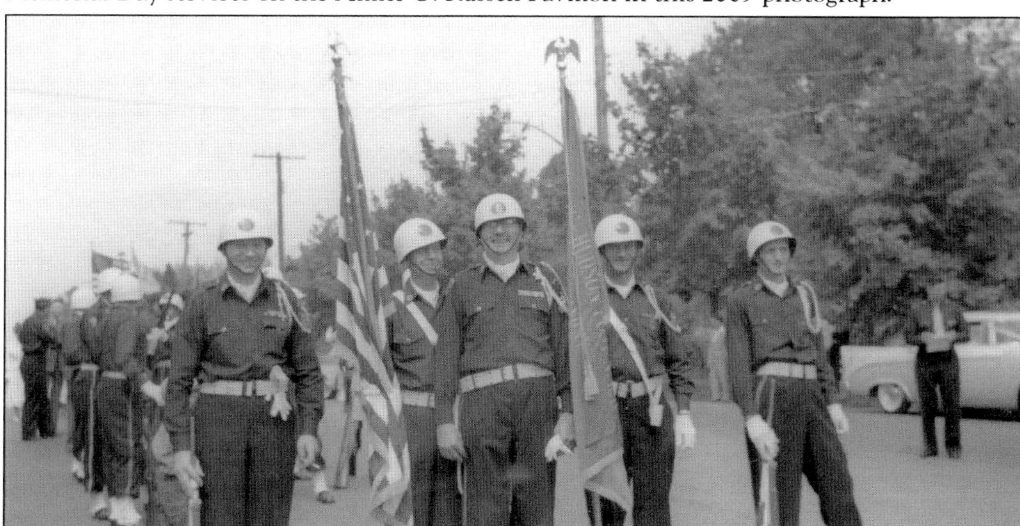

The American Legion Honor Guard shares a few relaxing moments before stepping off in the 1956 Memorial Day Parade. Warren Wuethrich, a World War II veteran, is pictured on the right. (Courtesy of the Wuethrich family.)

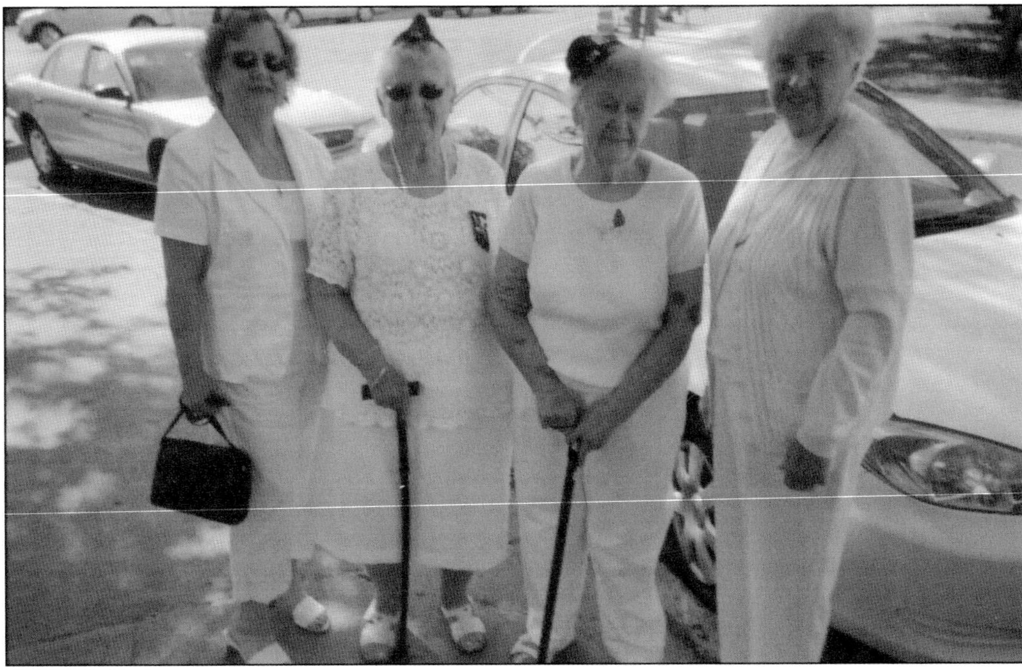

The American Legion Post No. 126 was organized in 1919 and became active not only in veterans affairs but also in community activities and civic issues. Shortly after, on April 19, 1921, the ladies auxiliary was organized. Since then, the auxiliary and the post have worked together organizing commemorative events and supporting veteran activities, including visitations, fund-raising, parades, and ceremonies. Ladies auxiliary members pictured here include, from left to right, Mercedes Pace, Margaret Goller, Mildred Ekstrand, and Irene Wuethrich. (Courtesy of the Wuethrich family.)

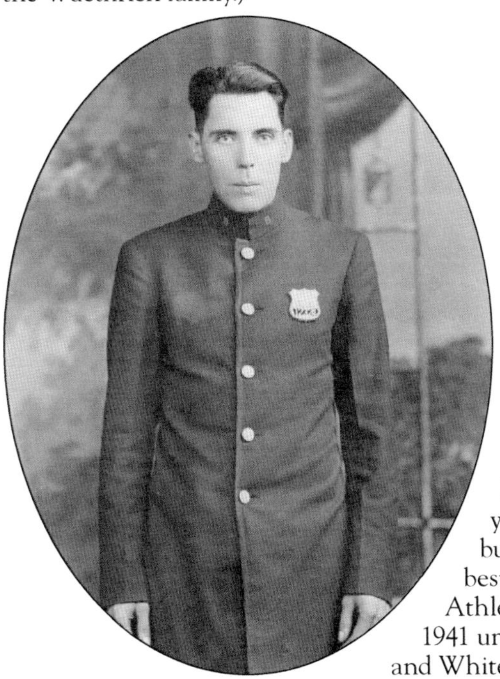

Patrolman William J. White joined the New York City police force in 1928, and spent most of his career in Tottenville's 123rd Police Precinct. Patrolman White served as precinct youth coordinator, organizing several drum and bugle corps on Staten Island's South Shore. He is best known for working with the Tottenville Police Athletic League (P.A.L.) Drum and Bugle Corps from 1941 until his retirement in 1956. (Courtesy of the Leyes and White families.)

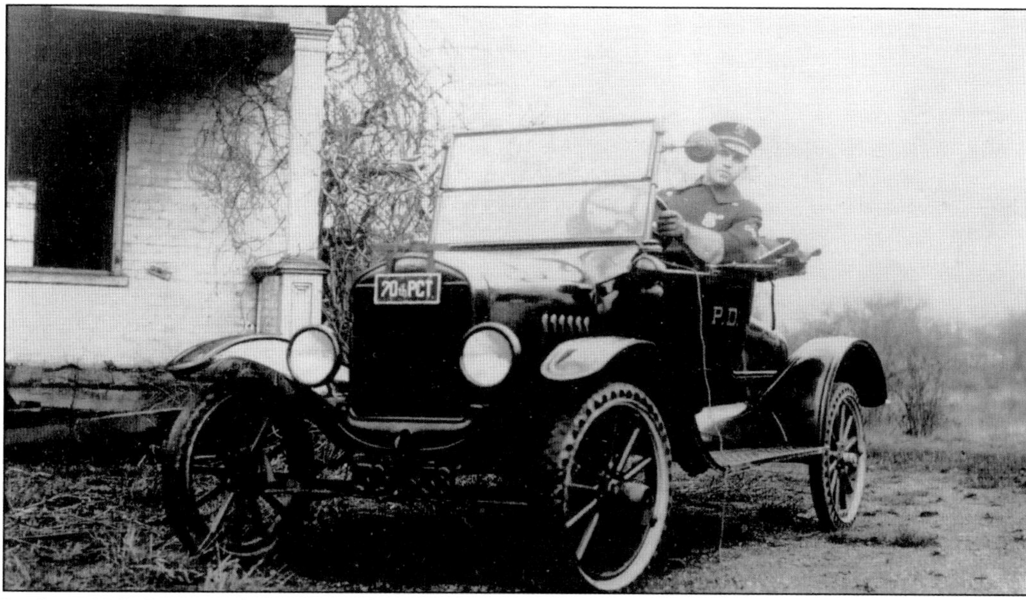

In this 1925 photograph, Sgt. Stanley Jiroudek of the 70th Police Precinct in Tottenville (renamed the 123rd Precinct) is driving one of the area's earliest patrol cars. Jiroudek later served as captain of the Tottenville precinct from 1940 to 1948. He retired in 1952 from the New Dorp stationhouse after 45 years of service. (Courtesy of Daphne Brooks; Louise Thompson Collection.)

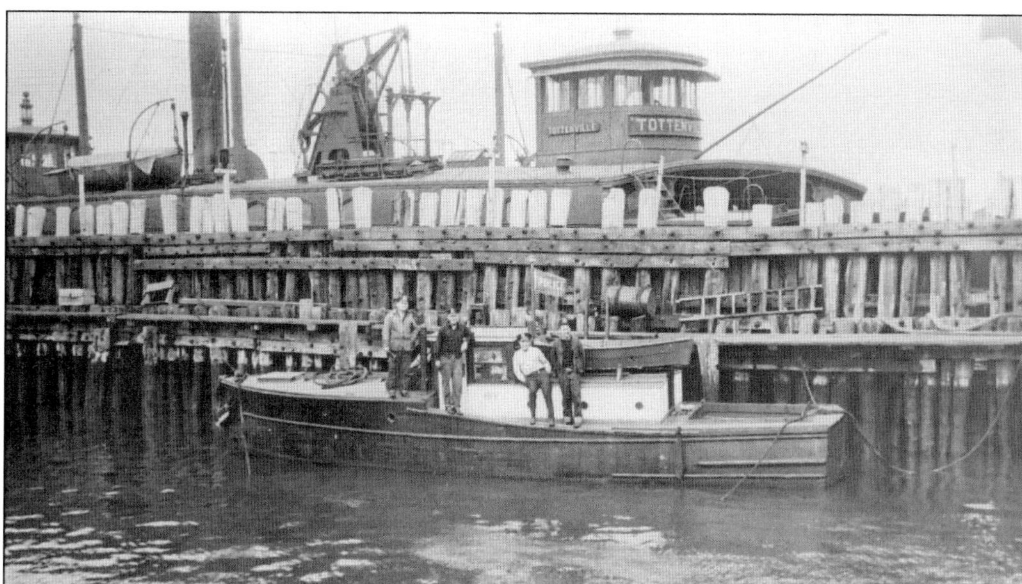

One of the oldest branches of the New York City Police Department is the Harbor Precinct. Pictured in this 1930 photograph are, from left to right, harbor patrolmen William H. Gruenberg, ? Fehring, ? Coates, and Timothy J. Ryan. The launch is docked adjacent to the Tottenville–Perth Amboy ferry slip. The ferry *Tottenville* is seen in the background. (Courtesy of the Nancy Ryan Williams Collection.)

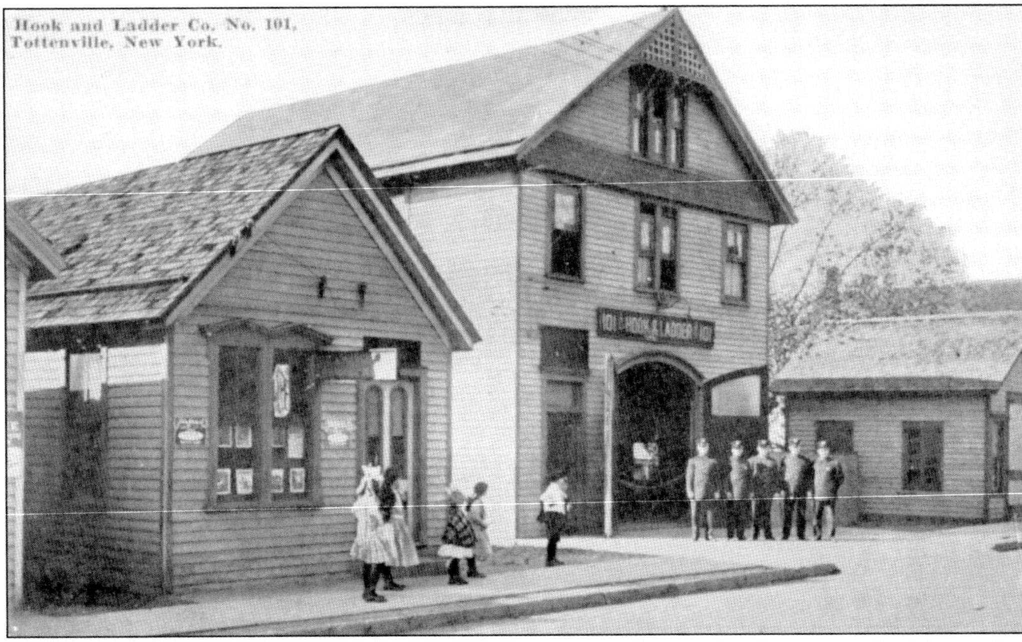

In the community's early years, when many streets were dirt roads often topped with crushed oyster shells, the first volunteer fire company, the Protection Hook and Ladder Company No. 21, was housed in a two-story frame building. Organized in 1886, the firehouse was located on Broadway, now called Arthur Kill Road. In 1905, it became Hook and Ladder Company No. 101. The firehouse, the center building in this 1910 image, was demolished in the 1930s. (Courtesy of the Harwayne family.)

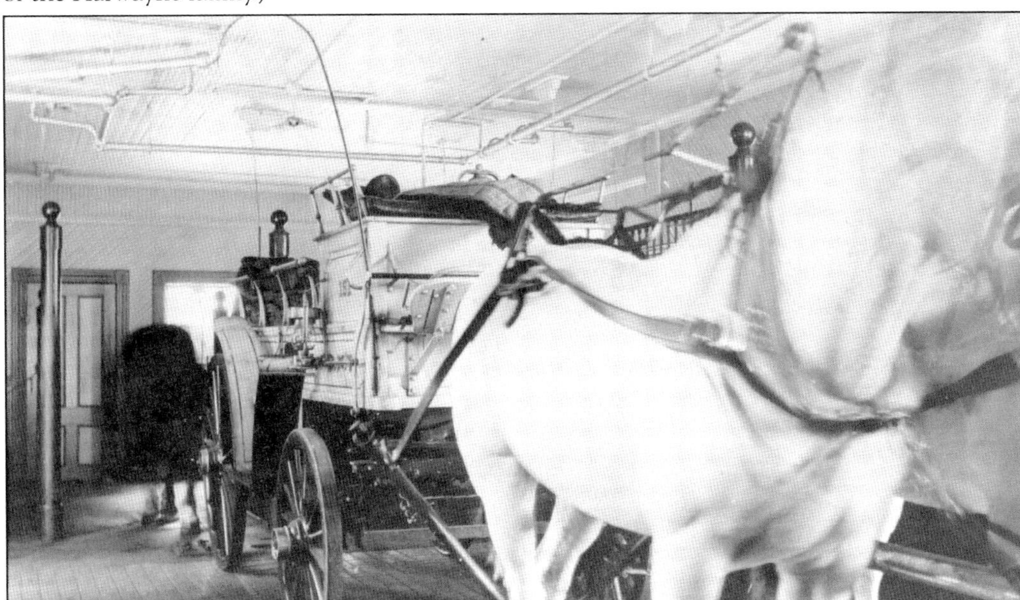

A second volunteer unit organized in 1888, the Eureka Engine Company No. 201, was located at the corner of Butler Avenue and Craig Avenue (formerly Eureka Place). Its wagon and steam engine were pulled by Arabian horses, as shown in this rare image. (Courtesy of the Lenahan and Wood families.)

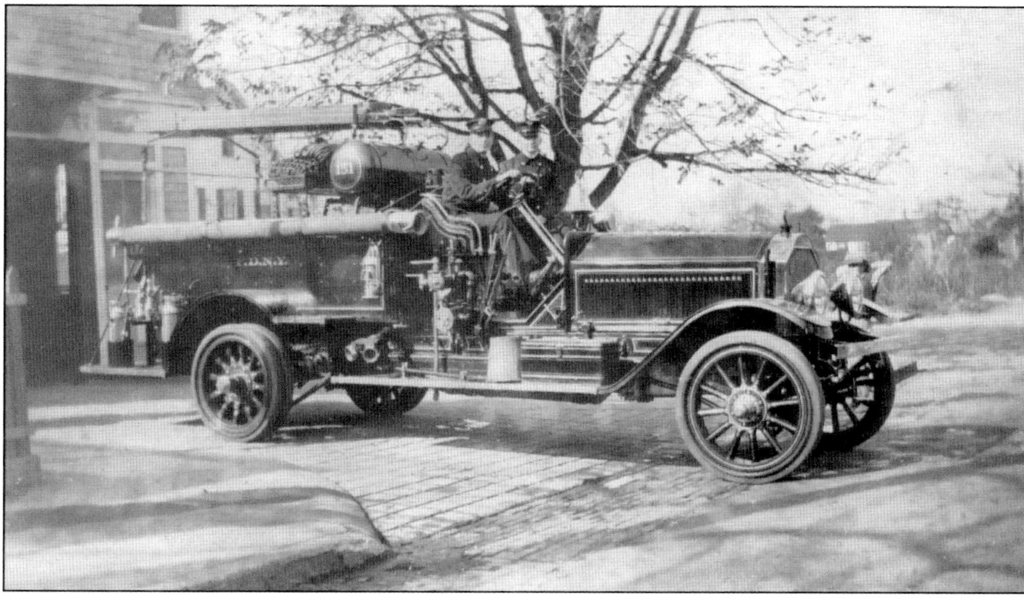

By 1905, following the consolidation of the five boroughs into New York City, most firehouses were absorbed into the city's paid fire department (FDNY). At that time, Engine Company 151 replaced the Eureka Company and the horse-drawn fire wagon. The new motorized fire truck, labeled FDNY 151, is seen in this *c.* 1905 photograph. (Courtesy of the Lenahan and Wood families.)

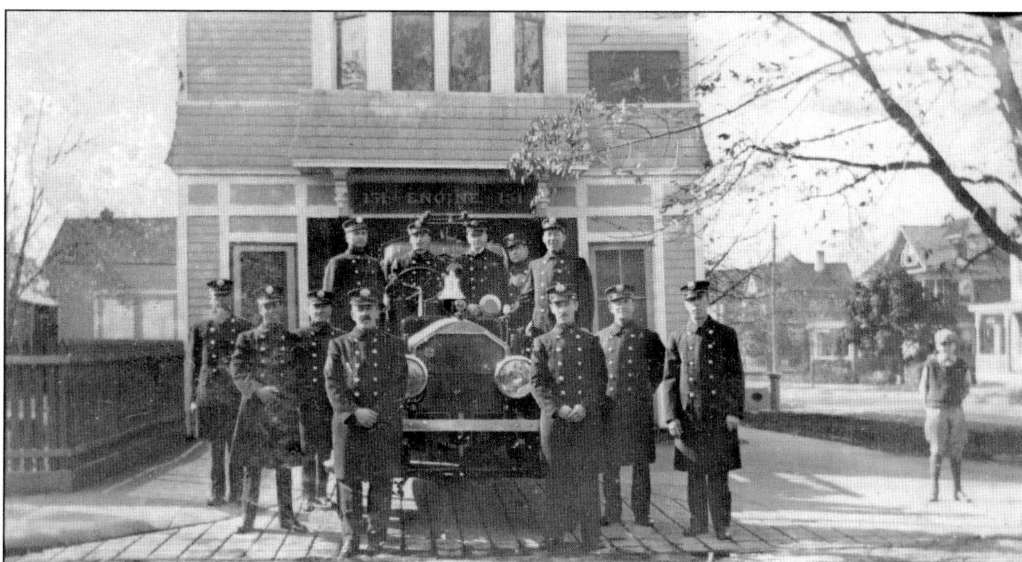

Aldolphus Wood is pictured among the members of FDNY Company 151, who pose in dress uniform at the former Eureka Engine Company. In 1929, a larger brick firehouse was built at 7219 Amboy Road to accommodate Engine Company 151 as well as Hook and Ladder Company 76. (Courtesy of the Lenahan and Wood families.)

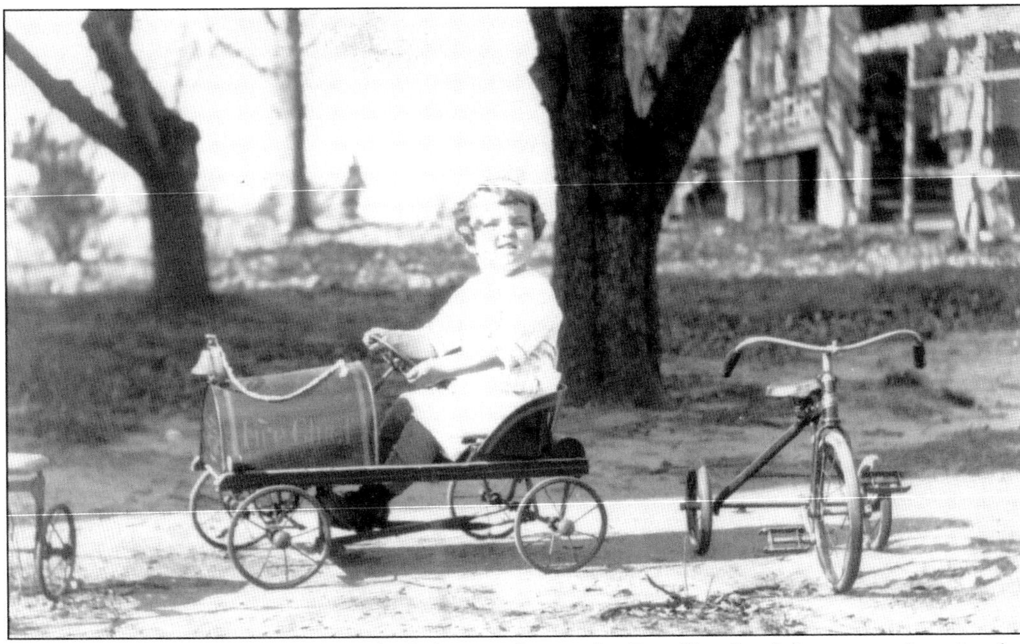

It must have been fate that led this little boy to choose the Fire Chief pedal car over the tricycles. John Bieser, just three years old in this 1925 photograph, would later join the New York City Fire Department and retire as a lieutenant from Ladder Company 76 after more than 30 years of service. (Courtesy of the John Bieser Estate.)

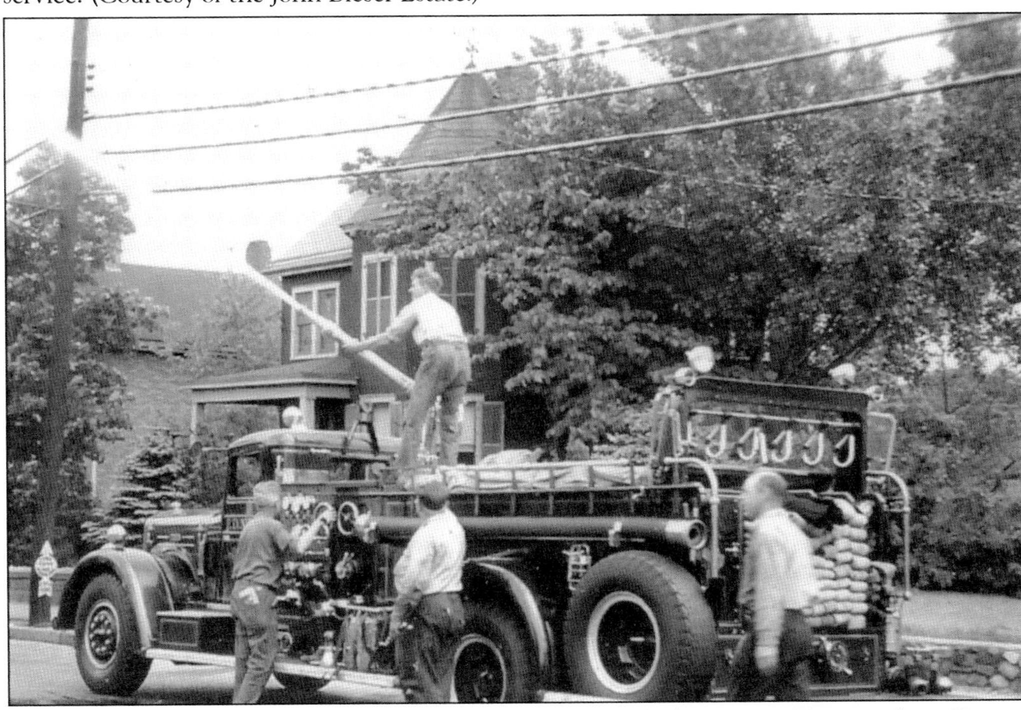

Regular equipment inspections are part of a firefighter's daily routine. Firemen from Engine Company 151 are testing a high-pressure nozzle in front of 7208 Amboy Road during a drill in this 1947 photograph. (Courtesy of the John Bieser Estate.)

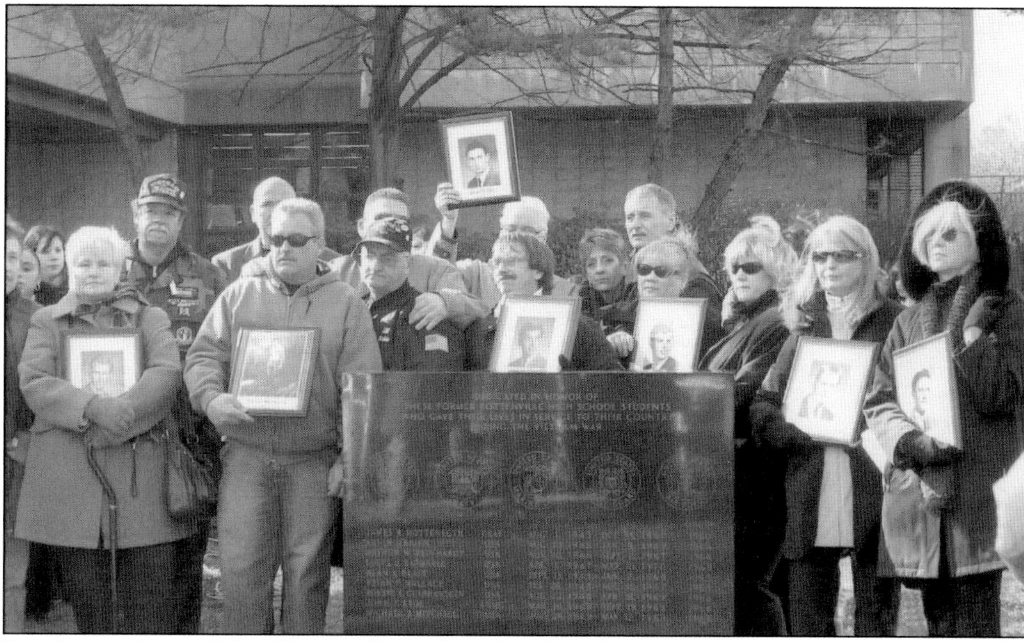

Family members of the Tottenville High School graduates killed in Vietnam, each holding a photograph of their loved one, gather during a monument unveiling ceremony on school grounds in 2008.

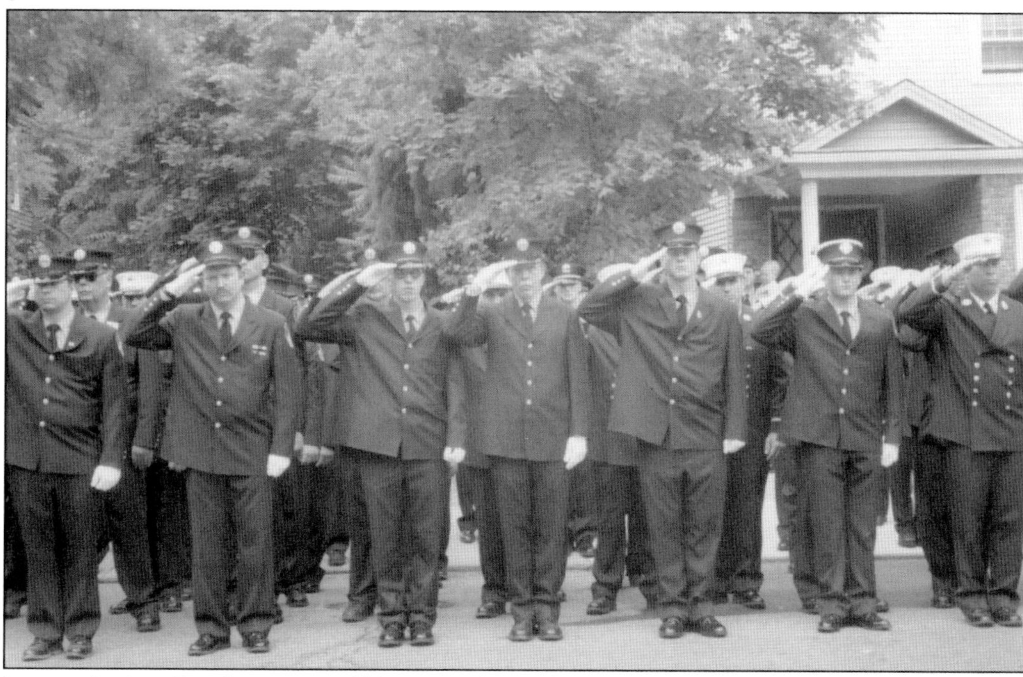

Lining Amboy Road in a sea of blue, members of New York City's bravest salute their fallen comrade at a funeral for one of Tottenville's firefighters who perished in the September 11 attack on the World Trade Center. Tottenville resident Fred Schaming (center) is flanked by his firefighter sons Steven (on his right) and Eric (on his left) in this 2002 photograph. (Courtesy of the Schaming family.)